THE FLOATING ISLAND

PACIFIC BASIN BOOKS

Edited by Kaori O'Connor

THE FLOATING ISLAND

JULES VERNE

Introduction by Kaori O'Connor

Kegan Paul International

LONDON AND NEW YORK

First published in French in 1895
First published in English in 1896
This edition published in 1990 by Kegan Paul International Limited
PO Box 256, London WC1B 3SW, England

Distributed by
John Wiley & Sons Ltd
Southern Cross Trading Estate
1 Oldlands Way, Bognor Regis,
West Sussex, PO22 9SA, England

Routledge, Chapman and Hall Inc
29 West 35th Street
New York, NY 10001, USA

The Canterbury Press Pty Ltd
Unit 2, 71 Rushdale Street
Scoresby, Victoria 3179, Australia

© *This edition Kegan Paul International 1990*

Printed in Great Britain by T.J. Press Ltd

ISBN 0 7103 0292 4

British Library Cataloguing in Publication Data
Verne, Jules, 1828–1905
The floating island. – (Pacific Basin books)
I. Title
843.8

ISBN 0–7103–0292–4

US Library of Congress Cataloging in Publication Data
Applied for

INTRODUCTION

To know Jules Verne only through such of his books as *Journey to the Centre of the Earth* (1864), *From the Earth to the Moon* (1865), *Twenty Thousand Leagues under the Sea* (1870), and *Around the World in Eighty Days* (1873) is to know but a small part of the work of this extraordinary man who left his stamp upon his century and our own.

The books for which Verne is best known today are early works imbued with the spirit of the first part of the nineteenth century – an era of unparalleled excitement, expansion and experiment when the popular imagination could barely keep pace with the scientific developments that promised to change the human condition forever. The mood of the times was one of optimism and an unquestioning belief in science and progress, and no one captured this spirit more perfectly than Jules Verne. As soon as they were written, the books that comprise the first part of his series *Extraordinary Voyages: Known and Unknown Worlds* – which aimed, in the words of his publisher, to 'summarize all geographical, geological, physical and astronomical knowledge amassed by modern science' – were translated into every European language, and were read as avidly by adults as by the young. In them, Verne bridged the gap between science and romance, founded the genre of modern science fiction, and inspired generations of future scientists, explorers, inventors and adventurers. Radar, teleprinters, audiovisual telephones, lasers, synthetic diamonds and air conditioning were only a few of the inventions that first appeared in the pages of a Verne book; polar exploration, long-range submarine navigation and space travel were exploits of Verne heroes long before they were enacted in real life. He envisaged the modern world with a remarkable clarity that was far from accidental, for all his literary inventions were based solidly on established scientific principles, and he prided himself on being a realist rather than a fantasist. As he put it in his book *The Carpathian Castle*;

This story is not fantastic, it is only romantic. It would be a mistake to conclude from its improbability that it cannot be a true story. We are living in days when anything can happen – one may say that everything has happened. If our tale seems improbable today, it need not do so tomorrow, thanks to the resources science will make available in the future, and nobody will then think of calling it fanciful.

Yet as the nineteenth century drew to a close, Verne had grave doubts about the course the new world he had envisaged was taking, and he began to reflect on what the social and political consequences of technological progress would be. What he foresaw overshadowed the later years of his life and changed the course of his writing. He had begun as an innovative writer who invested scientific fact with romance, adventure, melodrama and idealism – he developed into a savage social satirist who has been compared to Montesquieu, Swift and Voltaire. In recent years, the works of Jules Verne have been subject to a critical re-evaluation in France and elsewhere, and it is largely on the basis of his satirical novels that Verne is now seen as one of the most significant writers and social commentators of modern times. *The Floating Island* (1895) – an account of a sea-going city of American millionaires cruising about the Pacific – is the finest of Verne's satirical novels, a masterpiece whose theme is as timely now as when it was written.

Jules Verne was born in Nantes, France on February 8, 1828, the first of four children of Sophie Allotte de la Fuye, who came from a family long established in the West Indies mercantile trade and Pierre Verne, a solicitor whose father and grandfather had been judges. Pierre Verne, who exerted a considerable influence over his son's life and work, was remembered by a member of his family as 'highly intelligent . . . a passionate music lover . . . a very erudite scholar, a gifted and witty poet, but also very interested in science and the latest discoveries'[1] – a description that would in many respects serve for Jules in later years. Extremely pious, he was an ardent Jansenistic Christian who ensured that his children acquired a clear moral sense. Although the law was not his consuming interest in life, Pierre Verne had a deep respect for his profession and a prudent appreciation of the fact that it provided the means for him to keep his family in moderate comfort and the time to engage in scholarly studies. Although his eldest son displayed a taste for literature and the arts from childhood, Pierre Verne expected Jules to follow him into his solicitor's practice, and to pursue his other interests privately, as he himself had done.

The young Jules was a dilatory student during his schooldays, filling his notebooks with drawings of ships and strange machines, and spending as much time as he could at the Nantes docks. At eleven he made an unsuccessful attempt to run away as a cabin boy on a ship bound for the West Indies; thereafter he was obliged to restrict himself to sailing a small skiff on the Nantes estuary, and to voyages of the imagination in which he fantasised that the island suburb where his family lived would float out to sea, and on to faraway lands. The effort he might have expended on school compositions was lavished instead on poetry and dramatic sketches, and he was bitterly disappointed when his works received little encouragement from his family or his cousin Caroline, whom he hoped to marry. After passing his baccalaureate, Jules entered his father's practice and began to prepare for his law examinations, becoming increasingly restive after his cousin announced her engagement to a rival. Jules passed his preliminary law examinations with little difficulty, but was plunged into depression by his cousin's marriage. Aware that their son had little interest in the law at the best of times, Jules's parents reluctantly agreed to allow him to complete his legal studies in Paris, and he arrived in the capital in November, 1848 on the day that the Premier, Lamartine, inaugurated the new regime that had deposed Louis Phillipe from the throne.

In Paris, Pierre Verne kept Jules on a stringent allowance intended to encourage diligence by making all distractions except eating unaffordable. He deluged his son with letters commending the law, and warning against the literary and artistic temptations that were sure to come his way. Although Jules replied with fulsome reassurances, his true interests began to assert themselves. Too much the dutiful son to abandon his law books, he spent an equal amount of time reading novels, poetry and plays, going without sleep to accommodate both fields of study. The theatres had been closed in the early months of the 1848 revolution, but there was plenty to interest a young man determined to make the most of what the capital had to offer. Relations of his mother who had settled in Paris introduced Jules to literary salons that he attended as often as his resources would permit. Above all, he hoped to meet the author and playright Alexandre Dumas the elder, whom he described as 'that demigod'.[2] The longed-for introduction was effected and the hospitable Dumas took Jules under his wing, encouraging his interest in literature and the theatre. Within weeks of arriving in Paris, Jules was writing to his father of 'the new and marvellous pleasure to be in *immediate contact* with literature'[3] – sentiments that produced a flurry of anxious letters from Nantes that Jules soon learned to parry deftly. Inspired by Dumas, he began to concentrate on dramatic writing, and in the course of 1849 managed to complete a five-act tragedy, a two-act farce and a one-act comedy called *Broken Straw*, in addition to pursuing his legal and literary studies. The Paris theatres reopened the same year and in 1850 Dumas, who was director of the Théâtre Historique, edited and produced Jules's *Broken Straw*; it ran for twelve performances and attracted reviews that were kind, if not over-enthusiastic.

Jules spent two years in frantic activity, studying, writing, journeying to Nantes in the holidays to reassure his father, then returning to Paris to experiment with dramatic sketches and libretti. On passing his final law examinations, Jules refused the summons to return to Nantes, writing to his father – 'I may become a good writer, but I shall never be anything but a poor lawyer . . . The only career for which I am really suited is the one I am already pursuing: literature.'[4] Sustained by a small parental allowance, Jules stayed on in Paris and plunged into a punishing daily regime that began at five in the morning with a writing session, followed by research and study in the Bibliothèque Nationale, and ended with more writing late into the night. A meeting with the explorer and writer Jacques Arago had prompted Jules to add science to the list of his interests and he followed the latest discoveries in many fields assiduously, noting the results of his research on meticulous data cards that ultimately numbered over 20,000. He experimented feverishly with different forms of writing and in 1851 dashed off two short but promising works of prose fiction that were published in the journal *Musée des Familles*, but his obsession with the theatre led him to concentrate on writing comedies, dramas and libretti, very few of which were ever published or performed.

In 1852, Jules became secretary of Paris's Théâtre Lyrique, a position that entailed the demanding responsibilities of dealing with artistes, producing posters and seeing to all the details of stage management for little or no pay, but with the possibility of making contacts that would enable him to get his plays produced – a hope in which he was to be disappointed. Despite his dedication to the dramatic arts and his capacity for hard work, his temperament and talents were not ideally suited to the milieu he longed to enter or the theatrical pieces he struggled to write. Although he was witty and his gift for clever repartee was much admired among the circle of young artists and writers who surrounded Alexandre Dumas, Jules lacked the *bonhomie* that makes for success in theatrical circles. He did not make friends easily, had no time for conventional social pleasantries, and his manner struck many as curt and abrupt. As one of his friends put it, 'he is a mixture of coldness and sensibility, of dryness and gentleness . . . like tempered steel he bends for those who are his friends, and remains stiff before those who are strangers', while another observed 'when one has the key one can see into him, but nothing will ever make him expansive about himself'.[5] The key to Jules's character lay largely in the prudent provincial values and stern moral principles that he seemed, at this stage in his life, to be trying to slough off like an unwanted skin. He had a seriousness of character that was utterly at odds with the frivolity of the theatrical farces then in vogue, and he had a deep dislike of emotional display that prevented him from writing convincingly excessive melodramas. Above all, he had a literal mind that always took precedence over his imagination. He could not abandon himself to flights of fancy unless he was convinced of the soundness of the premises on which the actions were predicated, and this more than anything explains his inability to produce convincing comedies of manners and emotional tragedies in which the characters and values were so different to his own.

Pierre Verne considered Jules's association with the Théâtre Lyrique 'bizarre';[6] resigned to the fact that his son would never

be a lawyer, he had come to believe that Jules could become a
good writer if his talents were directed into the right channels. In
the same year that he joined the theatre, Jules wrote a third
novella for the *Musée* called *Martin Paz*, based largely on Jacques
Arago's adventures in South America. Albeit in rudimentary
form, this work displayed many of the elements that would
typify Jules's later books – the combination of imagination and
solid fact, a visual approach to narrative and a concern with
social issues – in this case the predicament of peoples of mixed
race in Peru. On reading *Martin Paz*, Pierre Verne decided that
Jules's true forte was the novel, and tried to divert him from the
theatre without success. The impasse continued until 1855 when
Jules left the Théâtre Lyrique having failed to make his mark as a
dramatist or impresario, but having overworked himself to the
extent that he acqured a facial tic that would recur throughout his
life in times of stress. He returned to the solitary life of a writer,
and immersed himself in work. His passion for science now
nearly equalled that for the stage, and he applied himself to
trying to develop a new style of scientific writing in which
technical phrases could be integrated into ordinary language, thus
making science accessible and avoiding cumbersome academic
periphrases. In his approach to science he represented the
viewpoint of the intelligent and well-informed layman interested
less in pure theory than in its practical application, and he most
admired engineers, explorers and other men of action whose
exploits and invention put theory into practice. While not a
scientist himself, he numbered many eminent scientists among
his acquaintances, and would often meet with them to discuss the
latest scientific theories and technological innovations. But the
theatre continued to distract him and he carried on writing
unsuccessful comedies and plays.

   Pierre Verne continued to provide encouragement and financial
assistance, but his confidence in his son's future received a heavy
blow in 1856 when Jules fell in love with Honorine Morel, a
widow with two children, and announced that he wished to
marry and to go into stockbroking in partnership with
Honorine's brother. 'One more illusion gone – my son, instead
of being a writer, is to become a stock-jobber'[7] lamented Pierre
Verne, but he bought Jules a share in a stockbroking business and

Jules married Honorine in 1857. Marriage made little difference to Jules's regime. He continued to rise at five to write before he went off to the Stock Exchange, where he proved to be better at banter than broking, and Honorine complained to her mother-in-law 'There are manuscripts everywhere – nothing but manuscripts! Let's hope they don't finish up under the cooking-pot!'[8] Jules continued to pursue success doggedly. The pieces of scientific reportage he wrote for the *Musee* and other journals were always well received, but he persisted in writing undistin-guished comedies and plays which drew a steady stream of rejections from publishers and producers. Jules had dreamed of being a success by the age of thirty-five; at thirty-four he had failed to make a mark in any field. Finally, even Jules's confidence began to flag. As he wrote to his father;

> It's as if, the moment I get an idea or launch on any literary project, the idea or the project at once goes wrong. If I write a play for a particular theatre director, he moves elsewhere; if I think of a good title, three days later I see it on the billboards announcing someone else's play; if I write an article, another appears on the same subject, etc. Even if I discovered a new planet, I believe it would at once explode, just to prove me wrong.[9]

In 1862, Jules submitted a manuscript on hot-air ballooning to the innovative Parisian publisher Pierre-Jules Hetzel. In its first draft, the manuscript was an uneven combination of narrative and scientific reportage – Hetzel advised Jules to rewrite the work and 'make a real novel of it'.[10] Two weeks later Jules returned to Hetzel with the rewritten manuscript for *Five Weeks in a Balloon* which Hetzel accepted for immediate publication, offering Jules a long-term contract for three books a year into the bargain. Jules accepted with alacrity, and took his leave of the Stock Exchange with a formal speech to his friends;

> I have an idea, the sort of idea that . . . ought to come to a man once a day, but which has come to me only once in my life, the sort of idea that should make a man's fortune. I have just written a novel in a new form, one that's entirely my

own. If it succeeds, I shall have stumbled upon a gold mine. In that case, I shall go on writing and writing without pause, while you others will go on buying shares the day before they drop and selling them the day before they rise. I am leaving the Exchange.[11]

Jules's confidence was not misplaced. *Five Weeks in a Balloon* was an instant best-seller among readers of all ages, who recognized that a new literary genre had been created – that of the scientific novel. The response was overwhelming and sensational, as befit a unique work so ideally suited to the times. As Jules's publisher Hetzel put it;

> The novels of M. Jules Verne have come just at the right time. When an eager public can be seen flocking to attend lectures given at a thousand different places in France, and when our newspapers carry reports of the proceedings of the Academy of Sciences alongside articles dealing with the arts and theatre, it is surely time for us to realize that the idea of art for art's sake no longer meets the needs of the time we live in, and that the day has come when science must take its rightful place in literature. To M. Jules Verne goes the merit of being the first to tread this new ground . . .[12]

All Jules's interests – previously seemingly irreconcilable – now come together. The years he had spent developing a new and simple scientific prose style made the theoretical passages of his writing accessible to all; the enthusiasm with which he outlined his theories made them fascinating. The pace and flow that had eluded him in his plays now came easily, giving excitement to the narrative and drama to the action. The wit and humour that he had been unable to convey in his comedies now came to the fore, and the moral sense that had kept him from devising convincing characters for the stage now found expression in the lofty moral idealism of his heroes.

He was a writer of genius who had finally found his true medium and over the next forty-two years he devoted himself to writing what he planned as 'a long, imposing procession of works'[13] – ultimately sixty-four in number – in which the reader was led through different fields of human knowledge through the device of having the plots, the action and often the denouement turn on the proof or disproof of various scientific theories, on inventions that were extension of known scientific principles, or on confrontation with natural phenomena. All his early works were imbued with a belief in the virtue of progress and in the potential of science to improve the human condition by enabling man to master the forces of nature and harness them to his will for the general good of all, in the idealistic and humanitarian tradition of Saint-Simon. In the new world Jules envisaged, the exploitation of man by man would be replaced by the exploitation of nature by man; machines were designed to serve man and enhance the conditions in which he lived by offering new possibilities in travel, communication and comfort, and the true responsibility of science was not to engage in endless theoretical speculations or to serve special interest groups, but to put their theories into practice for the benefit of mankind.

At the time he met Jules, Hetzel had been planning to start a monthly magazine for young people called the *Magazin d'Education et Recreation*. Many of Jules's books were serialized in the magazine before they were published in book form, but it would be a mistake to think of Jules as a children's author for he was read as avidly by adults as by the young, and the French writer Raymond Roussel reflects current literary opinion when he argues that Jules's writings have so many hidden depths of meaning that

> It is just as monstrous to give them to children to read as it is to give them the Fables of La Fontaine, which are so profound that few adults are capable of appreciating them.[14]

In 1886, when Jules's fame and fortune were at their apex, he suffered a series of personal tragedies – the deaths of his mother and his publisher Hetzel, who had been his closest confidant since the death of Pierre Verne in 1871, and a physical attack by his deranged nephew who shot him in the leg, inflicting injuries from which he never completely recovered. Always something of a misanthrope, he now became reclusive and melancholic, a change that coincided with a growing conviction that his earlier

faith in progress had been misplaced. He had once believed that
science and human character were sufficient to change the destiny
of mankind; he now began to believe that science would only
progress as quickly as society and, on the evidence of the last
twenty-five years society had, if anything, regressed. In describing
his grandfather's state of mind at this time, Jean Jules-Verne
recalled

> He lost his blind faith in unlimited progress. The conquest of
> nature was dependent on the conquest of wisdom – and
> mankind had no wisdom. Men's pride made them forget the
> ephemerality of their existence and the worldly possessions
> they were so eager to acquire. In order to gain a momentary
> possession of a fragile fragment of a precarious world, pride
> made them continue to indulge in the absurd and cruel strife
> from which they were the first to suffer.[15]

The French writer Jean Chesneaux has traced Jules's disillu-
sionment with science to the socioeconomic and political
developments of the late nineteenth century – the development of
large-scale industry had increased human misery instead of
alleviating it, and the rise of industry had enabled the development of large-scale finance capitalist enterprise in Europe.
Colonial rivalries increased as the great powers raced to expand
their colonial empires, the armaments race reflected the growth
of war technology, the possibilities of science had become
increasingly subordinated to the power of money, much of
Europe was in economic crisis and governments had become
more repressive in character. Faced with these hard social
realities, Jules's orientation began to change, and he extended his
interest beyond scientific forecasts to include the problems of
social organization, social conditions and the responsibility of
science towards society.[16] He now embarked on a series of
satirical novels that pass judgement on an age whose legacy is
still very much with us.

For Jules, the greatest disappointment of the previous quarter
century had been America, which had held a special place in his
affections. America had once seemed to him to be a near-perfect
embodiment of the new world he envisaged, and he set twenty-

three of his books there. The demographic, economic and technological development of America was unparalleled; industrial
enterprise was carried out on a grand scale, innovation and
initiative were actively encouraged, new inventions were seized
upon with alacrity and the population of America enjoyed the
highest modern standard of living in the world. It was a country
where it seemed that all things were possible – as Jules put it in
From the Earth to the Moon, 'Nothing can astonish an American
. . . In America everything is simple, everything is easy, and as
for mechanical difficulties, they are resolved before they arise.'
The passage of time had shown Jules another face of America,
and he became alarmed as the 'expansionist trends of the "big
stick" policy took shape . . . as the power of the dollar grew
stronger and as a materialist technology increased its hold over
mankind'.[17] For Jules, America had been a symbol and a model
for the future – now America seemed to constitute a threat which
he countered by writing *The Floating Island* – a satire on the
American way of life.

Set in an indefinite future, it envisages a time when the flag of
the United States has sixty-seven stars, America having annexed
Canada, Mexico and the countries of Central America down to
the Panama Canal. The floating island itself is the ultimate
achievement of materialist technology – every comfort has been
provided, effort has been eliminated, and the millionaire
residents have nothing more demanding to do than to enjoy an
endless luxury cruise as the island voyages about the Pacific in
search of splendid climes and picturesque atolls. As always, Jules
constructed his innovative vehicle on sound mechanical grounds
– to the extent of working out the draught, displacement and
horsepower of his propeller-driven island. But the alleviation of
all material cares and the technological refinement of the island
cannot make up for the flaws in human nature, and the rivalries
of the inhabitants ultimately tear the island apart in what
Chesneaux has called a parable of capitalist society destroying
itself. Of all his works, *The Floating Island* is considered to be the
one that best expresses Jules's mature social credo. A great classic
of science fiction and a sophisticated social satire, it was never
intended by its author to be taken as a fantasy. As he wrote to his
brother Paul when he was preparing the work, 'It will be related

to *existing customs and facts*, but I am a novelist first and foremost, and my books will always have the *appearance* of being fiction.'[18] Stripped of its obvious period references, the text of *The Floating Island* and the implicit warning it contains are as timely now as when it was written.

Jules Verne died in Amiens, France on 24 March, 1905. He had fulfilled his dream of becoming a world-famous author, he had created a new literary genre and the *Extraordinary Voyages* had amply achieved his objective of portraying the earth in all its aspects yet he died a disappointed man, still disillusioned at the betrayal of science by society. The uncanny predictive quality of his work is unquestioned, and scores of the inventions scattered across his pages are now a part of everyday life. Inexorably, the doubts he raises in his later satirical works are now becoming apparent. As Jean Chesneaux puts it

> If Jules Verne and his *Voyages Extraordinaires* are still alive for us if is because they – and with them the whole of that fascinating nineteenth century – were already posing the problems which the twentieth century has not been, and will not be, able to avoid.[19]

KAORI O'CONNOR

NOTES

1 Jules-Verne, Jean *Jules Verne, A Biography*, translated and adapted by Roger Greaves, Macdonald and Jane's, London, 1976; p 2.
2 Allotte de la Fuye, Marguerite *Jules Verne*, translated by Erik De Mauny, Stapes Press Ltd, London, 1954; p 39.
3 ibid; p 39.
4 ibid; pps 46–7.
5 ibid; p 85.
6 ibid; p 51.
7 ibid; p 78.
8 ibid; p 94.
9 ibid; p 94.
10 ibid; p 96.
11 ibid; p 98.

12 Chesneaux, Jean *The Political and Social Ideas of Jules Verne*, translated by Thomas Wikeley, Thames and Hudson, London, 1972; p 23.
13 Allotte de la Fuye, ibid; p 97.
14 Chesneaux, ibid; p 20.
15 Jules-Verne, ibid; p 225.
16 see Chesneaux, ibid; p 181.
17 ibid; p 158.
18 ibid; p 198, my italics.
19 ibid; p 208.

FLOATING ISLAND

Part I.

CHAPTER I.

WHEN a journey begins badly it rarely ends well. At least that ought to have been the opinion of the four instrumentalists whose instruments lay on the ground, the carriage in which they were riding having suddenly upset against a mound by the side of the road.

"Anybody hurt?" asked the first, actively springing to his feet.

"I have got off with a scratch," replied the second, wiping his cheek, striped by a piece of glass.

"And I with a graze," replied the third, whose calf was bleeding.

There was nothing serious as yet.

"And my violoncello?" said the fourth. "It is to be hoped nothing has happened to my violoncello."

Fortunately the cases were untouched.

Neither the violoncello, nor the two violins, nor the alto had suffered from the shock, and it was hardly necessary to put them in tune. They were high-class instruments, of course.

"Confound that railway which left us in distress when we had only gone half-way," said one.

"Confound that carriage which has thrown us out in the open country," retorted another.

"Just at the moment night was beginning," added a third.

"Fortunately our concert is announced for the day after to-morrow," observed the fourth.

Then a few ridiculous repartees were exchanged between the artistes who took their adventure so gaily. One of them, according to his inveterate habit, gave his nonsense a musical twist.

"There is our carriage with the *mi* on the *do*."

"Pinchinat!" exclaimed one of his companions.

"And my opinion is," continued Pinchinat, "that there are rather too many accidents in this key."

"Will you be quiet?"

"And that we shall have to transpose our pieces in another carriage!" added Pinchinat.

Yes! rather too many accidents, as the reader will not be slow to learn.

The driver had suffered most, having been pitched off his seat as the front axle broke. The damage was restricted to a few contusions more painful than serious; but he could not walk on account of a sprain. Hence the necessity of finding some means of transport to the nearest village.

It was a miracle, indeed, that somebody had not been killed. The road winds across a mountainous country, skirting high precipices, bordered in many places with deep tumultuous torrents and crossed by fords only passable with difficulty. If the axle had broken a moment sooner the vehicle would have rolled deep down the rocks, and no one could have survived the catastrophe.

Anyhow, the carriage was useless. One of the two horses, whose head had struck against a sharp stone, was gasping on the ground. The other was severely wounded on the quarter; so that there were no horses and no carriage.

In short, ill-fortune had not spared these four artistes, in these regions of Lower California. At this period San Francisco, the capital of the State, was in direct railway

communication with San Diego, situated almost on the
frontier of the old Californian province. The four
travellers were on their way to this important town, where
on the next day but one they were to give a concert much
advertised and long expected. The night before they had
left San Francisco, but when they were within fifty miles
of San Francisco the first contretemps had occurred.
Yes, contretemps, as the most jovial of the troupe
remarked, and the expression might be tolerated on
the part of an old master of solfeggio.

The train was stopped at Paschal owing to the line
having been swept away by a flood for three or four miles.
The accident had occurred but a few hours before, and the
communication with the other end had not been organized.
The passengers must either wait until the road was
repaired, or obtain in the nearest village a vehicle of some
sort for San Diego.

And this it was that the quartette decided to do. In a
neighbouring village they discovered an old landau,
rickety, noisy, and moth-eaten, but not uncomfortable.
They hired it from the owner, promised the driver a handsome present, and started with their instruments, but
without their luggage, about two o'clock in the afternoon ;
and up to seven o'clock in the evening the journey was
accomplished without much difficulty or fatigue. But
here a second contretemps occurred, the upsetting of the
carriage, and that with such damage that it was impossible
for the said carriage to continue the journey.

And the quartette were a good twenty miles from San
Diego.

But why had four musicians, French by nationality,
and Parisians by birth, ventured across these out-of-the-
way regions of Lower California ?

Why? We will tell you in twenty lines, with a few
explanatory notes regarding the four virtuosos which
chance, that fantastic distributor of parts, was about to
introduce among the personages of this extraordinary
story.

At this same time a feeling for art had developed among the Americans; and if their productions were of limited number in the domain of the beautiful—if their national genius was still somewhat refractory in painting, sculpture, and music—the taste for good work was, at least, widely spread among them. By purchasing, for their weight in gold, the pictures of old and modern masters for public or private galleries; by engaging, at enormous prices, lyrical and dramatic artistes of renown, instrumentalists of the highest talent, they had infused among themselves that sense of beautiful and noble things which they had been in want of so long.

As regards music, it was by listening to Meyerbeer, Halévy, Gounod, Berlioz, Wagner, Verdi, Massé, Saint-Saëns, Reyer, Massenet, Delibes, the famous composers of the second half of the nineteenth century, that the dilettanti of the New Continent first awoke to enthusiasm. Then gradually they advanced to the comprehension of the profounder work of Mozart, Haydn, Beethoven; mounting back to the sources of the sublime art which expanded to full flood in the course of the eighteenth century. After the operas, the lyric dramas; after the lyric dramas, the symphonies, sonatas, and orchestral pieces. And, just at the moment we speak of, the sonata was the rage among the different States of the Union. The people would willingly have paid so much a note—twenty dollars a minim, ten dollars a crotchet, five dollars a quaver.

When this infatuation was at its height, four instrumentalists of ability conceived the idea of tempting success and fortune in the United States of America. Four excellent fellows, old pupils of the Conservatoire, well known in Paris, much appreciated by the audiences of what is known as " chamber music," which was then little known in North America. With what rare perfection, what marvellous time, what profound feeling, they interpreted the works of Mozart, of Beethoven, of Mendelssohn, of Haydn, of Chopin, written for four-stringed instruments, a first and second violin, alto, and violoncello. Nothing noisy, nothing showy, but what consummate execution, what incomparable virtuosity! The success of the quartette was all the more intelligible, as at the time people were beginning to tire of formidable harmonic and symphonic orchestras. That music is only an artistic combination of sonorous waves may be true, but there is no reason why these waves should be let loose in deafening tempests.

In short, our four instrumentalists had decided to introduce the Americans to the gentle and ineffable delights of chamber music. They set out together for the New World, and for two years the dilettanti Yankees had spared them neither cheers nor dollars. Their matinées and soirées were well attended. The Quartette Party, as they called themselves, were hardly able to accept their invitations from the wealthy. Without them there was no festival, no meeting, no rout, no five o'clock teas, no garden parties worth talking about. This infatuation had put a good deal of money in the pockets of the fortunate four, and if they had placed it in the Bank of New York it must have constituted a fairly large capital. But why should we not confess it? They had spent their money freely, had these Americanized Parisians! They never thought of saving, did these princes of the bow, these kings of the four strings! They enjoyed to the full this life of adventure, sure of meeting everywhere and always with a good welcome and a profitable engagement. They had travelled from New York to San Francisco, from Quebec to New Orleans, from Nova Scotia to Texas, living rather a Bohemian life—that Bohemia of the young which is the most ancient, the most charming, the most enviable, the most loved province of our old France! We are much mistaken if the moment has not come to introduce them individually to those of our readers who never had, and never will have, the pleasure of listening to them.

Yvernès—first violin—thirty-two years old, above the

medium height, slight in build, fair, curly hair, smooth face, large black eyes, long hands, made to stretch to any extent over his Guarnerius, of elegant bearing, wearing a flowing cloak of some dark colour, and a high silk hat, somewhat of an attitudinizer perhaps, the most careless of the four, the least troubled about matters of interest, in all respects the artiste, an enthusiastic admirer of beautiful things, a virtuoso of great talent and great promise.

Frascolin—second violin—thirty years old, short, with a tendency to stoutness—which he by no means liked—brown in hair and brown in beard, big in the head, black eyes, and a long nose, marked at the side with red by the pinch of his gold eyeglasses—which he could not do without—a good fellow, good natured in every way, acting as the banker of the quartette, preaching economy, and never listened to, not at all envious of the success of his comrade, having no ambition of being promoted as solo violin, excellent musician nevertheless—and then wearing but a simple dust coat over his travelling suit.

Pinchinat—alto, commonly addressed as "his highn'ess" —twenty-seven years of age, the youngest of the troupe, the most frolicsome too, one of those incorrigibles who are boys all their life, a fine head, intelligent eyes, always wideawake, hair approaching to red, pointed moustache, teeth white and sharp, tongue never still, never tired of puns and nonsense, and alert for repartee, invariably good-humoured, for ever making light of the discomforts that fell to his comrades, and therefore continually being reprimanded and taken up short by the chief of the Quartette Party.

For it had a chief, the violoncellist, Sebastien Zorn, chief by his talent, chief by his age, for he was fifty, short, rotund, hair abundant, and curled on the temples, moustache bristling, and losing itself in the whiskers which ended in points, complexion brick red, eyes gleaming through the glasses of his spectacles, which he doubled by means of an eyeglass when he read music, hands plump, the right accustomed to the undulatory movements of the bow, ornamented with large rings on the second and little finger.

This slight sketch is probably sufficient description for the man and the artiste, but one cannot with impunity for forty years hold a sonorous box between one's knees. It affects one's whole life, and the character is influenced. Most violoncellists are talkative and quick tempered, impetuous and domineering, and such was Sebastien Zorn, to whom Yvernès, Frascolin, and Pinchinat had willingly abandoned the management of their musical tour. They let him say what he liked, and do what he liked, for they understood him. Accustomed to his imperious manners, they laughed when he "outran the measure"—which is regrettable in the case of an executant, as was remarked by the irrepressible Pinchinat. The composition of the programmes, the direction of the routes, the correspondence with the managers, devolved on him, and permitted his aggressive temperament to manifest itself under a thousand circumstances. Where he did not interfere was with regard to the receipts and the management of the purse, which formed the particular duty of the second violin and chief accountant, the exact and careful Frascolin.

The quartette are now introduced as if they were before you on a platform. We know the types, if not very original, at least very distinct, of which it was composed. As the reader allows the incidents of this strange history to unroll themselves he will see to what adventures were destined these four Parisians, who, after receiving so many bravos throughout the States of the American Confederation, were to be transported.

But let us not anticipate, "not hurry the movement," as "his highness" would exclaim, and let us have patience.

The four Parisians then, at eight o'clock this evening, were on a deserted road in Lower California, near the ruins of their overturned carriage. The chief of the quartette was violently angry. Why not? Yvernès pretended that he was descended from Ajax and Achilles, those two illustrious angry heroes of antiquity.

Let it not be forgotten that though Zorn might be bilious, Yvernès phlegmatic, Frascolin quiet, and Pinchinat of superabundant joviality, all were excellent comrades, and felt for each other like brothers. They were united by a bond which no dispute or self-love could break, by a community of taste originating from the same source. Their hearts, like well-made instruments, always kept in tune.

While Zorn fretted and fumed, and patted the case of his violoncello to make sure that it was safe and sound, Frascolin went up to the driver.

"Well, my friend," he said; "what are we to do now, if you please?"

"What you can do when you have neither a carriage nor a horse, and that is to wait."

"Wait for what comes," said Pinchinat.

"And if nothing comes?"

"We must look for it," said Frascolin, whose practical mind never failed him.

"Where?" roared Zorn, in a great state of agitation.

"Where it is," replied the driver.

"Is that the way you ought to answer?" said the 'cellist, in a voice that gradually mounted towards the high notes. "What! A clumsy fellow who pitches us out, smashes his carriage, lames his horses, and then contents himself with saying, 'Get out of it as you like!'"

Carried away by his natural loquacity, Zorn began to launch forth into an interminable series of objurgations, all of them of no use, when Frascolin interrupted him,—

"Allow me, my old Zorn."

And then, addressing himself to the driver, he asked,—

"Where are we, my friend?"

"Five miles from Freschal."

"A railway station?"

"No, a village near the coast."

"Where can we find a carriage?"

"A carriage, nowhere—perhaps a cart."

"A bullock cart, as in Merovingian times!" exclaimed Pinchinat.

"What does it matter?" said Frascolin.

"Eh!" resumed Zorn. "Ask him if there is a hotel in this hole of a Freschal. I have had enough for to-night."

"My friend," asked Frascolin, "is there any hotel in Freschal?"

"Yes, the one where we were to change horses."

"And to get there we have only to keep on the main road?"

"Straight on."

"Let us be off!" said the 'cellist.

"But," said Pinchinat, "this poor fellow. It will be cruel to leave him here in distress. Look here, my friend, could you not come along if we were to help you?"

"Impossible!" replied the driver. "Besides, I prefer to remain here with my carriage. When daylight comes I shall see how to get out of this."

"When we get to Freschal," said Frascolin, "we can send you help."

"Yes, the hotel-keeper knows me, and will not let me remain here in this state."

"Shall we go?" asked the 'cellist, picking up the case of his instrument.

"In a moment," replied Pinchinat. "Just lend a hand to lift the driver to the side of the road."

Pinchinat and Frascolin lifted him up, and placed him against the roots of a large tree, the lower branches of which formed a cradle of verdure as they fell.

"Shall we go?" roared Zorn for the third time, having hoisted his case on to his back by means of a double strap arranged for the purpose.

"We have done now," said Frascolin, who then addressed the man, saying,—

"It is understood that the hotel-keeper at Freschal will send you help. Till then you want nothing, is that so?"

"Yes," said the driver, "unless you happen to have a drink with you."

Pinchinat's flask happened to be full, and "his high-ness" willingly made the sacrifice.

"With that, my good man," said he, "you will never catch cold to-night—inside you."

A final objurgation from the 'cellist decided his companions to make a start. Fortunately their luggage was in the train, instead of with them in the carriage. It might be delayed in getting to San Diego, but they would not have the trouble of carrying it to Freschal. They had enough to do to carry the violin cases, and perhaps rather too much with the 'cello case. True, an instrumentalist worthy of the name never separates from his instrument any more than a soldier does from his arms, or a snail from its shell.

CHAPTER II.

To journey at night along an unknown road, amid an almost deserted country, where there are usually more malefactors than travellers, was enough to make them rather anxious. Such was the fate of the quartette. Frenchmen are brave, of course, and these were as brave as any. But between bravery and temerity there is a limit which no healthy mind will overstep. After all, if the railway had not run into a flooded plain, if the carriage had not upset five miles from Freschal, our instrumentalists would not have had to venture by night along this suspicious road. It was to be hoped that no harm would happen to them.

It was about eight o'clock when Sebastien Zorn and his companions started towards the coast, as directed by the driver. As they had only their leather violin cases, light and handy, the violinists had little reason to grumble. Neither the wise Frascolin, nor the cheery Pinchinat, nor the idealist Yvernès, had a word of complaint. But the 'cellist with his case—a cupboard as it were on his back! Knowing his character, we can understand that he found every opportunity of working himself into a rage. Hence groans and grunts exhaling under the onomatopœic forms of "ahs," and "ohs," and "oufs."

The darkness was already profound. Thick clouds chased each other across the sky, drifting apart into narrow rifts, from which occasionally peeped a fitful moon, almost in its first quarter. Somehow, why we know not, unless it were that he was peevish and irritable, the pale Phœbe did not please Sebastien Zorn. He pointed his finger at her, exclaiming,—

"What are you doing there with your stupid face? I know nothing more imbecile than that slice of unripe melon up there!"

"It would be better if the moon were to look us in the face," said Frascolin.

"And for what reason?" asked Pinchinat.

"Because we could see it more clearly."

"O chaste Diana!" declaimed Yvernès. "O messenger of the peaceful night! O pale satellite of the earth! O adored idol of the adorable Endymion!—"

"Have you finished your ballad?" asked the 'cellist. "When the first violins take to flourishing on the fourth string—"

"Take longer strides," said Frascolin, "or we shall have to sleep under the stars."

"If there are any," observed Pinchinat. "And lose our concert at San Diego."

"A fine idea, my word!" exclaimed Zorn, shaking his box, which gave forth a plaintive sound.

"But this idea, my old friend, was yours," said Pinchinat.

"Mine?"

"Undoubtedly! That we did not remain at San Francisco, when we had quite a collection of Californian ears to charm."

"Once more," asked the 'cellist, "why did we start?"

"Because you wished it!"

"Well, I must admit that it was a deplorable inspiration, and if—"

"Ah, my friends!" said Yvernès, pointing towards a point in the sky where a narrow moon-ray fell on the whitish edges of a cloud.

"What is the matter, Yvernès?"

"Look at that cloud turning into the shape of a dragon, its wings open, a peacock's tail eyed as with the hundred eyes of Argus."

Perhaps Sebastien Zorn did not possess that power of hundredfold vision which distinguished the guardian of the son of Machus, for he did not notice a deep rut into which he trod. Consequently he fell on his face, with his box on his back, and looked like some huge beetle creeping over the ground.

Violent rage of the instrumentalist—and he had cause to be angry—and then objurgations on account of the first violin's admiration of the aerial monster.

"It is the fault of Yvernès!" said Sebastien Zorn. "If I had not been looking at that confounded dragon—"

"It is no longer a dragon, it is an amphora! with the gift of imagination but feebly developed you can see it in the hands of Hebe who is pouring out the nectar—"

"Take care that there is not too much water in that nectar," exclaimed Pinchinat, "and that your charming goddess of youth does not give us an overdose of it."

Here was another trouble in store; rain was apparently coming. Prudence required that they should make haste so as to get into shelter at Freschal.

They picked up the 'cellist, as angry as he could be. They put him on his legs, growling all the time. Frascolin good-naturedly offered to carry the case, but this Zorn refused. Separate himself from his instrument! one of Gand and Bernardel's, almost a part of himself? But he had to give in, and this precious half passed on to the back of the useful Frascolin, who entrusted his light violin case to Zorn.

The route was resumed. They walked at a good pace for two miles. No incident worth mentioning; the night getting blacker and blacker with every promise of rain. A few drops fell, very large ones, a proof that they came from clouds high in the air and stormy. But Hebe's amphora did not overflow, and our four travellers hoped to reach Freschal perfectly dry.

Careful precautions were constantly necessary against falls on the dark road, deeply cut into by ravines, turning suddenly, bordered by high crags, skirting gloomy precipices with the roar of the torrents beneath.

Yvernès thought the position was poetical; Frascolin that it was alarming. There was the fear of certain meetings which make the safety of travellers on the roads of Lower California rather problematical. The only weapons possessed by the quartette were the bows of the violins and the 'cello, and these would appear to be insufficient in a country where Colt's revolvers were invented. If Sebastien Zorn and his comrades had been Americans, they would have been furnished with one of those engines of warfare, kept in a special pocket of the trousers. Even for a trip from San Francisco to San Diego a real Yankee would never have started without carrying a six-shot viaticum. But Frenchmen had not thought it necessary. We may add that they had not thought about it, and perhaps would repent it. Pinchinat marched at the head, peering right and left as he walked. Practical joker as he was, "his highness" could not help playing off a few pleasantries on his comrades. Pulling up short, for instance, every now and then, and muttering in a voice tremulous with fear,—

"Ah! There! What is that I see before me? Be ready to fire."

But when the road plunged through a thick forest, amid mammoth trees, sequoias a hundred and fifty feet high, vegetable giants of these Californian regions, his joking humour disappeared. Ten men might hide behind one of these enormous trunks. A bright flash, followed by a report, the swift whistling of a bullet, might they not see it, might they not hear it? In such places so suitable for a nocturnal attack, an ambush was plainly suggested. If luckily they did not meet with bandits, it was because these estimable people had totally disappeared from Western America, or were then engaged in financial operations on the borders of the old and new continent. What an end for the great great grand-children of the Karl Moors and Jean Sbogars. To whom could these reflections come but to Yvernès? Decidedly, he thought, the play is not worthy of the stage.

Suddenly Pinchinat stopped still. Frascolin, who was behind him, also stopped.

Zorn and Yvernès were up with them immediately.

"What is it?" asked the second violin.

"I thought I saw something," said the alto.

And this was no joke on his part. Really there was a form moving amid the trees.

"Human or animal?" asked Frascolin.

"I do not know."

Which was the more formidable no one would have ventured to say. They crowded together, without retreating, without uttering a word.

Through a rift in the clouds the rays of the moon lighted the dome of this gloomy forest, and flittered to the ground through the branches of the sequoias. For a hundred yards or so the surroundings were visible.

Pinchinat had not been the dupe of an illusion. Too large for a man, the mass could only be a big quadruped. What quadruped? A wild beast? A wild beast certainly. But what wild beast?

"A plantigrade," said Yvernès.

"Oh! bother the animal!" muttered Zorn, in a low impatient tone, "and by animal, I mean you, Yvernès. Why cannot you talk like other people? What do you mean by a plantigrade?"

"An animal that walks on its plants!" explained Pinchinat.

"A bear!" replied Frascolin.

It was a bear, and a large bear too. Lions, tigers, leopards are not met with in these forests of Lower California. Bears are, however, constantly found there, and encounters with them are generally disagreeable.

No surprise will be felt at the Parisians, with one accord, resolving to get out of the way of this plantigrade. Besides, was he not at home? And so the group closed up and retreated backwards, facing the bear, but moving slowly and deliberately, without seeming to be running away.

The bear followed at a slow pace, shaking his fore paws like the arms of a semaphore, and balancing himself on

his haunches. Gradually he approached, and his demonstrations became hostile—gruff growls and a snapping of
the jaws, which were rather alarming.

"Suppose we run each on his own account?" proposed
"his highness."

"Do nothing of the sort," replied Frascolin. "One of
us would be sure to be caught, and who would pay for the
others?"

The imprudence was not committed; it was evident
that its consequences might be disastrous.

The quartette thus arrived huddled together on the
edge of the clearing where the darkness was not so great.
The bear had approached within a dozen yards. Did
the spot appear to him convenient for an attack? Probably, for his growls redoubled, and he hastened his
advance.

Precipitate retreat of the group, and earnest appeals
from the second violin, "Be cool! be cool, my friends!"

The clearing was crossed and they found the shelter of
the trees. But there the peril was as great. By running
from one tree to another, the animal could leap on them
without its being possible to foresee his attack, and he was
about to act in this way, when his terrible growlings
ceased, he began to halt—

The deep gloom was filled with a penetrating musical
sound, an expressive *largo*, in which the soul of an artiste
was fully revealed.

It was Yvernès, who had drawn his violin from its case
and made it vibrate under the powerful caress of the bow.
An idea of genius! Why should not the musicians owe
their safety to music? Had not the stones moved by the
strains of Amphion ranged themselves round Thebes?
Had not the wild beasts, thrilled by his lyrical inspirations,
run to the knees of Orpheus? It seemed as though this
Californian bear, under atavistic influence, was as artisti-
cally gifted as his congeners in the fable, for his fierceness
disappeared, his instincts of melomania took possession of
him, and as the quartette retreated in good order, he fol-

lowed them uttering little cries of approval. It would not
have taken much to make him say "Bravo!"

A quarter of an hour later Zorn and his companions
were at the edge of the wood. They crossed it, Yvernès
fiddling all the time.

The animal stopped. It looked as though he had no
intention of going further. He patted his big paws against
each other.

And then Pinchinat also seized his instrument, and
shouted,—

"The dancing bear. Come on!"

And while the first violin ploughed away steadily at the
well-known tune in the major, the alto assisted with a base
shrill and false in the mediant minor.

The bear began to dance, lifting the right foot, lifting
the left foot, turning and twisting, while the four men
went further and further away.

"Well," said Pinchinat, "he is only a circus bear."

"It does not matter," replied Frascolin, "Yvernès had a
capital idea."

"Let us run for it, *allegretto*," said the 'cellist, "and
don't look behind."

It was about nine o'clock when the four disciples of
Apollo arrived at Freschal. They had come along splen-
didly during the latter half of their journey, although the
plantigrade was not on their traces.

Some forty wooden houses around a square planted
with beeches, that was Freschal, a village isolated in the
country and about two miles from the coast.

Our artistes glided between a few houses shaded with
large trees, came out on the square, looked up at the
humble spire of a little church, stopped, formed in a circle
as if they were about to give an appropriate performance,
and began to talk.

"Is this a village?" asked Pinchinat.

"Did you expect to find a city like Philadelphia or New
York?" asked Frascolin.

"But your village is asleep!" replied Sebastien Zorn.

"Awake not a village that sleeps," sighed **Yvernès,** melodiously.

"On the contrary," said Pinchinat, "wake it up well."

And unless they were to spend the night in the open air they would have to do so.

Yet the place was quite deserted, the silence complete. Not a shutter was open, not a light was at a window.

"And where is the hotel?" asked Frascolin.

Yes, the hotel which the driver had mentioned, where travellers in distress would receive good welcome and treatment. And the hotel-keeper who would send help to the unfortunate coachman. Had the poor man dreamt of these things? Or—another suggestion—had Zorn and his companions gone astray? Was this really Freschal?

These questions required an immediate reply. The villagers must be applied to for information, and the door of one of the houses must be knocked at; that of the hotel if possible, if by a lucky chance they could find which it was.

The four musicians began to reconnoitre round the place, prowling along the front of the houses, trying to find a sign hanging overhead. But there was nothing to show them which was the hotel.

As they could not find the hotel, perhaps there was some private house that would give them shelter. What native of Freschal would refuse a couple of dollars for a supper and a bed?

"Let us knock," said Frascolin.

"And in time," said Pinchinat, "in six-eight time."

They knocked three or four times with the same result. Not a door, not a window opened.

"We are deceived," said Yvernès, "it is not a village, it is a cemetery, where if they sleep their sleep is eternal. *Vox clamantis in deserto.*"

"*Amen!*" replied "his highness" in a deep voice, as if chanting in a cathedral.

What was to be done as the silence remained unbroken? Continue the journey towards San Diego? They were **dying**—that is the word—of hunger and fatigue. And

then what road were they to follow without a guide through
this dark night ? Try to reach another village ? Which
one ? According to the coachman there was no other
village on this part of the coast. The best thing they
could do was to wait for daylight. But to spend six hours
without shelter beneath a sky overcast with heavy clouds
threatening rain every instant— that was not to be thought
of, even by artistes.

Pinchinat had an idea. His ideas were not always
excellent, but they abounded in his brain. This one,
however, obtained the approval of the wise Frascolin.

"My friends," said he, " why should not what succeeded
with a bear succeed with a Californian village? We
tamed the plantigrade with a little music ; let us wake
up these rustics with a vigorous concert, in which we will
not spare either the *forte* or the *allegro*."

"We might try that," replied Frascolin.

Zorn did not wait for Pinchinat to finish. His case
was opened, his 'cello upright on its steel point, for he
had no seat, his bow in hand, ready to extract all the
human voices stored up in the sonorous carcase.

Almost immediately his comrades were ready to follow
him to the utmost limits of their art.

"'Onslow's quartette,' in B flat," said he. "Come."

Onslow's Quartette they knew by heart, and good instrumentalists did not want to see clearly to use their
skilful fingers on the 'cello, the violins, and the alto.

Behold them given up to their inspiration. Never perhaps have they played with more talent and more soul in
the concert halls and theatres of the American Union.
Space is filled with sublime harmony, and unless they
were deaf how could human beings resist it ? Had it
been a cemetery, as Yvernès pretended, the tombs would
have opened at the music's charm, the dead would have
risen, and the skeletons clapped hands.

But none of the houses opened ; the sleepers did not
awake. The piece ended in its powerful *finale*, yet
Freschal gave no sign of life.

"Ah!" exclaimed Zorn, in a fury. "Is it like that? They want a serenade like their bears for their savage ears? Be it so! Let us have it over again ; but you, Yvernès, play in D ; you, Frascolin, in E ; you, Pinchinat, in G. I will keep to B flat ! and now then, with all your might."

What cacophony! What ear-torture! It was as bad as the improvised orchestra directed by the Prince de Joinville in an unknown village in Brazil. It seemed as though they were playing Wagner backwards on " vinai-griuses."

Pinchinat's idea was excellent. What admirable execution could not obtain this absurdity did. Freschal began to awake. Lights appeared. Windows opened here and there. The natives of the village were not dead, for they gave signs of life. They were not deaf, for they heard and listened.

"They are going to throw apples at us," said Pinchinat, during a pause, for the time throughout had been scrupulously kept.

"So much the better," said the practical Frascolin, "we will eat them."

And at Zorn's command the players suddenly shifted into their proper key, and ended with a perfect chord of four different notes.

No! They were not apples that came from the twenty or thirty open windows, but plaudits and cheers. Never had the Freschalian ears been filled with such musical delights! And there could be no doubt that every house was ready to receive with hospitality such incomparable virtuosos.

But while they were engaged in their performance, a spectator had approached them within a few yards without being seen. This personage had descended from a sort of electrical tram-car at one angle of the square. He was a man of tall stature, and somewhat corpulent, so far as could be judged in the darkness.

While our Parisians were asking if, after the windows

the doors of the houses were going to open to receive them—which appeared at least to be rather uncertain—the new arrival approached, and said, in an amiable tone,—

"I am a dilettante, gentlemen, and I have the very great pleasure of applauding you."

"For our last piece?" replied Pinchinat, ironically.

"No, gentlemen, for the first. I have seldom heard Onslow's Quartette given with more talent."

The personage was evidently a connoisseur.

"Sir," said Sebastien Zorn, in the name of his companions, "we are much pleased by your compliments. If our second piece tortured your ears, it is—"

"Sir," replied the unknown, interrupting a phrase that might have been a long one, "I have never heard a thing played out of tune with so much precision. But I understand why you did it. It was to wake up the natives of Freschal, who have already gone to sleep again. Well, gentlemen, what you endeavoured to obtain from them by this desperate means permit me to offer you."

"Hospitality?" demanded Frascolin.

"Yes, hospitality. Unless I am mistaken I have before me the Quartette Party renowned throughout our superb America, which is never stingy in its enthusiasm."

"Sir," said Frascolin, "we are indeed flattered. And —this hospitality, where can we find it, thanks to you?"

"Two miles from here."

"In another village?"

"No, in a town."

"A town of importance?"

"Certainly."

"Allow me," observed Pinchinat. "We were told that there were no towns until we got to San Diego."

"It is a mistake—which I cannot explain."

"A mistake?" repeated Frascolin.

"Yes, gentlemen, and if you will accompany me I promise you a welcome such as artistes of your class are entitled to."

"I am of opinion that we should accept it," said Yvernès.

" And I share that opinion," said Pinchinat.

" One moment !" said Zorn, " do not go faster than the leader of the orchestra."

" Which means ? " asked the American.

" That we are expected at San Diego," replied Frascolin.

" At San Diego," added the 'cellist, " where the city has engaged us for a series of musical matinées, the first of which is to take place on Sunday afternoon."

" Ah ! " replied the personage, in a tone that betrayed extreme annoyance.

Then he continued,—

" That does not matter.   In a day you will have time to visit a city which is well worth the trouble, and I will see that you are taken to the nearest station, so that you can be at San Diego at the appointed time."

The offer was attractive and welcome.   The quartette were assured of finding a good room in a good hotel—to say nothing of the attention promised by this obliging personage.

" Gentlemen, do you accept ? "

" We accept," replied Zorn, whom hunger and fatigue disposed to welcome such an invitation.

" Agreed," replied the American.   " We start at once. In twenty minutes we shall be there, and you will thank me, I am sure."

We need scarcely say that after the cheers provoked by the burlesque serenade the windows of the houses were shut.   With its lights extinguished, the village of Freschal was again plunged in sleep.

The American and the four artistes went to the car, put down their instruments, and placed themselves behind them, while the American installed himself forward next to the engineer.   A lever was touched, the electric accumulators worked, the vehicle trembled, and began to get up a rapid rate of speed, travelling westward.

A quarter of an hour afterwards an immense whitish
light appeared, as if it were a dazzling diffusion of lunar
rays. This was the town, the existence of which none
of the Parisians had suspected.

The car stopped, and Frascolin said,—

" Here we are on the shore."

" The shore—no," replied the American, " but a watercourse we have to cross."

" And how ? " asked Pinchinat.

" By means of this boat in which the car is carried."

It was one of the ferry boats, so numerous in the
United States, and on it the car was placed with its
passengers. Probably the ferry boat was worked by
electricity, for there was no steam, and in two minutes
they were on the other side of the watercourse, alongside
a quay. The car resumed its course along some country
roads, and entered a park over which aerial appliances
poured an intense light. The gate of the park gave access
to a wide and long road paved with sonorous flags. Five
minutes later the artistes descended at the steps of a comfortable hotel, where they were received with a welcome
that augured well, thanks to a word from the American.
They were immediately placed before a well-served table,
and supped with good appetite, as may be believed.

The repast over, the major-domo led them to a spacious
chamber lighted by incandescent lamps, to which shades
were fitted, so as to shut out nearly all the light at will.
Then, postponing to the morrow the explanation of all
these marvels, they slept in the four beds placed in the four
angles of the room, and snored with that extraordinary
simultaneity which had given the Quartette Party its
renown.

CHAPTER III.

NEXT morning at seven o'clock, these words, or rather these cries, resounded in the room after a startling imitation of a trumpet-call—something like the reveillée.

"Now then! Whoop! On your feet; and in two-time!" vociferated Pinchinat.

Yvernès, the most careless of the four, would have preferred three-time, and even four-time, to disengage himself from the warm coverings of his bed. But he had to follow the example of his comrades, and leave the horizontal for the vertical.

"We have not a minute to lose—not one!" observed "his highness."

"Yes," replied Zorn, "for to-morrow we must be at San Diego."

"Good," replied Yvernès; "half-a-day will suffice for us to visit the town of this amiable American."

"What astonishes me," added Frascolin, "is that there is an important city in the neighbourhood of Freschal. How could our driver have forgotten to tell us about it?"

"The point is that we should be here, my old G key," said Pinchinat. "And here we are."

Through the large windows the light was pouring into the room, and the view extended for a mile down a superb road planted with trees.

The four friends proceeded to their toilette in a comfortable cabinet—a quick and easy task, for it was fitted with all the latest inventions, taps graduated thermometrically for hot water and cold water, basins emptying automatically, hot baths, hot irons, sprays of perfumes, ventilators worked by voltaic currents, brushes moved mechanically, some for the head, some for the clothes, some for the boots, either to clean the dust off them, or to black them. And then there were the buttons of the bells and telephones communicating with every part of the establishment. And not only could Sebastien Zorn and his companions obtain communication with every part of the hotel, but with the different quarters of the town, and perhaps—such was Pinchinat's opinion—with every town in the United States of America.

"Or even in the two worlds," added Yvernès. But before they had an opportunity of trying the experiment, a message was telephoned to them at forty-seven minutes past seven, as follows :—

"Calistus Munbar presents his morning civilities to each of the honourable members of the Quartette Party, and begs them to descend as soon as they are ready to the dining-room of the Excelsior Hotel, where their first breakfast awaits them."

"Excelsior Hotel!" said Yvernès. "The name of this caravanserai is superb."

"Calistus Munbar, that is our obliging American," remarked Pinchinat. "And the name is splendid."

"My friends," said the 'cellist, whose stomach was as imperious as its proprietor ; "as breakfast is on the table, let us breakfast, and then—"

"And then take a run through the town," added Frascolin. "But what is this town ?"

Our Parisians were dressed or nearly so. Pinchinat replied telephonically that in less than five minutes they would do honour to the invitation of Mr. Calistus Munbar. And when their toilette was finished, they walked to a lift which deposited them in the large hall of the hotel, at the end of which was the door of the dining-room, an immense saloon gleaming with gilding.

"I am yours, gentlemen, always yours."

It was the man of the night before who had just uttered

this phrase of six words. He belonged to that type of
personages who may be said to introduce themselves. It
seems as though we had known them always.

Calistus Munbar was between fifty and sixty years of
age, but he did not look more than forty-five. He was
above the usual height, rather stout, his limbs long and
strong, and every movement vigorous and healthy.

Zorn and his friends had many times met with people
of this type, which is not rare in the United States.
Calistus Munbar's head was enormous, round, with hair
still fair and curly, shaking like leaves in a breeze ; his
features were highly coloured, his beard long, yellow,
divided into points ; moustache shaven ; mouth, with the
corners raised, smiling, satirical perhaps ; teeth white as
ivory; nose rather large at the end, with quivering
nostrils, marked at the base of the forehead with two
vertical folds supporting an eyeglass fastened to a thread
of silver as fine and supple as a thread of silk. Behind
the glasses gleamed an eye always in movement, with a
greenish iris and a pupil glowing like fire.

Calistus Munbar wore a very ample loose jacket of
brown diagonal stuff. From the side pocket peeped a
handkerchief with a pattern on it. His waistcoat was
white, very open, and fastened with three gold buttons.
From one pocket to the other a massive chain was
festooned, with a chronometer at one end of it and a
pedometer at the other, to say nothing of the charms
which jingled in the centre. His jewellery was completed
by a series of rings which ornamented his fat, pink hands.
His shirt was of immaculate whiteness, stiff with starch,
dotted with three diamonds, surmounted by a wide, open
collar, beneath the fold of which lay an almost imperceptible cravat of reddish brown cord. The trousers were
striped and very full, and at the feet showed the laced
boots with aluminium fastenings.

The Yankee's physiognomy was in the highest degree
expressive—the face of a man who suspected nobody, and
could only see good in others. This was a man who

could get out of difficulties, certainly, and he was also
energetic, as was shown by the tonacity of his muscles, the
apparent contraction of his superciliary and his masseter.
He laughed noisily, but his laugh was nasal rather than
oral, a sort of giggle, the *hennitus* of the physiologists.

Such was Calistus Munbar. He raised his big hat at
the entrance of the Quartette Party. He shook hands with
the four artistes. He led them to a table where the tea-
urn was steaming and the traditional toast was smoking.
He spoke all the time, giving them no opportunity to ask
a single question—perhaps with the object of avoiding
having to reply—boasting of the splendours of his town,
the extraordinary creation of this city, keeping up the
monologue without interruption, and when the breakfast
was over, ending his monologue with these words,—

"Come, gentlemen, and follow me. But one piece of
advice."

"What?" asked Frascolin.

"It is expressly forbidden to spit in the streets."

"We are not accustomed to," protested Yvernès.

"Good! That will save you a fine."

"Not spit—in America!" murmured Pinchinat, in a tone
in which surprise was mingled with incredulity.

It would have been difficult to have obtained a guide
and cicerone more complete than Calistus Munbar. This
town he knew thoroughly. There was not a hotel of
which he did not know the owner's name, not a house that
he did not know who lived there, not a man in the street
by whom he was not saluted with sympathetic familiarity.

The city was built on a regular plan. The avenues and
roads, provided with verandahs above the footways,
crossed each other at right angles, forming a sort of chess-
board. There was no want of variety about the houses; in
their style and interior arrangements they were according
to no other rule than the fancy of their architects. Except
along a few commercial streets, these houses had a look of
the palace about them, with their courtyards flanked by
elegant wings, the architectural arrangement of their front,

the luxury of the furniture of their rooms, the gardens, not to say parks, in their rear. It was remarkable that the trees, of recent planting, no doubt, were none of them fully grown. So it was with the squares at the intersection of the chief arteries of the city, carpeted with lawns of a freshness quite English, in which the clumps of trees of both temperate and torrid species had not drawn from the soil its full vegetative· power. This peculiarity presented a striking contrast with the portion of Western America, where forest giants abound in the vicinity of the great Californian cities.

The quartette walked in front of him, observing this part of the town, each according to his manner—Yvernès attracted by what did not attract Frascolin; Zorn interested in what did not interest Pinchinat—all of them curious as to the mystery which enveloped this unknown city. From this diversity of views arose a fairly complete assemblage of remarks. But Calistus Munbar was there, and he had an answer for everything. An answer? He did not wait to be asked; he talked and talked, and never left off talking. His windmill of words turned and turned at the slightest wind.

Twenty minutes after leaving the Excelsior Hotel, Calistus Munbar said,—

"Here we are in Third Avenue, and there are thirty in the town. This is the most business one, it is our Broadway, our Regent Street, our Boulevard des Italiens. In this stores and bazaars you find the superfluous and the necessary, all that can be asked for by the requirements of modern comfort."

"I see the shops," observed Pinchinat, "but I don't see the customers."

"Perhaps it is too early in the morning?" added Yvernès.

"It is due," said Calistus Munbar, "to most of the orders being given telephonically, or rather telautographically."

"What does that mean?" asked Frascolin.

"It means that we commonly use the telautograph, an instrument which sends the written as the telephone sends the spoken word, without forgetting the kinetograph, which registers the movements; being for the eye what the phonograph is for the ear, and the telephote, which reproduces the images. The telautograph gives a better guarantee than the mere message, which the first to come is free to make bad use of. We sign our orders and deeds by electricity."

"Even the marriage registers?" asked Pinchinat, ironically.

"Doubtless, Mr. Alto. Why should you not marry by the telegraphic wire?"

"And divorce?"

"And divorce; that is the very thing that keeps the wires busiest."

And he laughed a long laugh that made all the jewellery on his waistcoat jingle.

"You are merry, Mr. Munbar," said Pinchinat, joining in the American's hilarity.

"Yes, as a flock of finches on a sunshiny day."

At this point a transverse artery was reached. This was Nineteenth Avenue, from which all trade was banished. Tram lines ran down it as down the others, swift cars passed along without raising a grain of dust, for the roadway, laid with an imputrescible pavement of Australian karry or jarrah, was as clean as if it had been polished. Frascolin, always observant of physical phenomena, noticed that the footway sounded under his feet like a plate of metal.

"These are splendid workers in iron," he said, "they make their footways of sheet iron."

And he stepped up to Calistus Munbar to hear what he had to say.

"Gentlemen," said Munbar, "look at that mansion."

And he pointed to a vast construction of monumental aspect, the courtyard of which had along its front a railing of aluminium.

"This mansion—I might say this palace—is inhabited by the family of one of the principal notables of the town, that is Jem Tankerdon, the owner of inexhaustible mines of petroleum in Illinois, the richest, perhaps, and consequently the most honourable and most honoured of our citizens."

"Millions?" asked Zorn.

"Phew!" said Calistus Munbar. "The million is for us but the current dollar, and here we count them by hundreds! Only the richest men are in this city. That explains why the shopkeepers make fortunes in a few years. I mean retail shopkeepers, for wholesale traders there are none in this unique microcosm of the world."

"And manufacturers?" asked Pinchinat.

"There are no manufacturers."

"And shipowners?" asked Frascolin.

"There are none."

"People living on their investments?" asked Zorn.

"Only those and merchants on the way to be like them."

"What about the workmen?" observed Yvernès.

"When we want workmen we get them from somewhere else, and when their work is over we return them—with a good sum in wages."

"Look here, Mr. Munbar," said Frascolin, "you have a few poor in the town, just to keep the race from becoming extinct?"

"Poor! Mr. Second Violin! We have not got a single poor man in the town."

"Then mendicity is forbidden?"

"There is no necessity to forbid it, as the town is not accessible to beggars. That is all very well for the cities of the Union, with their depôts, their asylums, their workhouses, and the houses of correction."

"Do you mean to say you have no prisons?"

"No more than we have prisoners."

"But criminals?"

"They remain in the old and new Continent, where they

can exercise their vocation under moie advantageous conditions."

"Really, Mr. Munbar," said Sebastien Zorn; "one would think to listen to you that we were no longer in America."

"You were yesterday," replied this astonishing cicerone.

"Yesterday!" exclaimed Frascolin, wondering what could be the meaning of this strange expression.

"Doubtless. To-day you are in an independent city, over which the Union has no claim, which belongs only to itself."

"And its name?" asked Sebastien Zorn, whose natural irritability began to peep out.

"Its name?" replied Calistus Munbar. "Allow me to be silent a little longer."

"And when shall we know?"

"When you have finished the visit by which it is so much honoured."

This reserve was at least peculiar. But it was of no consequence. Before noon the Quartette would have finished their curious walk, and to learn the city's name as they were leaving it would be quite enough. The only puzzle about it was this: How could so considerable a city occupy one of the points on the Californian coast without belonging to the United States, and how was it that the driver of the carriage had never mentioned it? The main thing after all was that in twenty-four hours the Quartette would be at San Diego, where they would learn the word of this enigma if Calistus Munbar decided not to reveal it to them.

This strange personage had again given himself over to the indulgence of his descriptive faculty, not without letting it be seen that he did not wish to explain himself more categorically.

"Gentlemen," said he, "we are at the beginning of Thirty-Seventh Avenue. Behold the admirable perspective. In this quarter there are no shops, no bazaars, none of that movement in the streets which denotes a business existence. Nothing but hotels and private houses, but the fortunes are inferior to those of Nineteenth Avenue. Incomes of from ten to twelve millions."

" Mere beggars ! " observed Pinchinat, with a significant grimace.

" Eh, Mr. Alto ! " replied Calistus Munbar, "it is always possible to be a beggar in comparison with someone else ! A millionaire is rich in comparison with a man who possesses only a hundred thousand, but not in comparison with him who has a hundred millions."

Many times already our artistes had noticed that of all the words used by their cicerone it was "million" which recurred most frequently. And a fascinating word it was, pronounced as he pronounced it with metallic sonorousness.

The quartette continued their walk through the extraordinary town, the name of which was unknown to them. The people in the streets were all comfortably dressed ; nowhere could the rags of a beggar be seen. Everywhere were trams, drays, trucks, moved by electricity. A few of the larger streets were provided with moving pavements, worked by an endless chain, and on which people walked as if on a travelling train sharing in its own motion. Electric carriages rolled along the roads with the smoothness of a ball on a billiard-table. Equipages in the true sense of the word, that is to say, vehicles drawn by horses. were only met with in the wealthy quarters.

" Ah ! there is a church," said Frascolin, and he pointed to an edifice of heavy design, without architectural style, rising from the green lawns of a square.

" That is the Protestant temple," said Calistus Munbar, stopping in front of the building.

" Are there any Catholic churches in your town ? " asked Yvernès.

" Yes, sir, and I would like you to observe that although there are about a thousand different religions on our globe, we here confine ourselves to Catholicism and Protestantism. It is not here as in the United States disunited by religion, if not by politics, in which there are as many sects as families—Methodists, Anglicans, Presbyterians, Baptists, Wesleyans, &c. Here there are only Protestants faithful to the Calvinistic doctrine or Roman Catholics."

" And what language do they speak?"

" English and French are both used."

"We congratulate you," said Pinchinat.

" The town," continued Calistus Munbar, " is divided into two sections, which are almost equal. Here we are in the section— "

" West, I think?" said Frascolin, looking up at the sun.

" West, if you like."

" What, if I like?" replied the Second Violin, much surprised at the reply. " Do the cardinal points of this city vary as somebody pleases?"

" Yes and no," said Calistus Munbar, " I will explain that later on. Let us return to this section, west if you please, which is only inhabited by Protestants; it is here that the practical people live, while the Catholics, who are more intellectual and refined, occupy the east section. That tells you that this temple is the Protestant temple."

" It looks like it," observed Yvernès. " With its heavy architecture, prayer would not be an elevating towards the sky, but a crushing towards the ground."

" Well expressed!" said Pinchinat. " Mr. Munbar, in a town so up-to-date in its inventions I suppose you listen to the sermon or the mass by telephone?"

" Quite so."

" And confession?"

" Just as you can get married by telautograph; you must admit that it is practicable enough— "

" Not to be believed," replied Pinchinat, " not to be believed."

CHAPTER IV.

At eleven o'clock, after so long a walk, it was permissible to be hungry. And our artistes took advantage of this permission; and they agreed that at any price they must have some luncheon. This was also the opinion of Calistus Munbar.

Should they return to the Excelsior Hotel? Yes, for there did not seem to be many restaurants in this town, where the people probably preferred to have their meals at home, and tourists were apparently rather rare.

In a few minutes a tramcar took the hungry men to their hotel, where they took their places before a well-served table. It afforded a striking contrast with the ordinary American style, in which the multiplicity of the dishes is not at all in proportion to the quantity they contain. Excellent was the beef and mutton; tender and tasty was the poultry; of tempting freshness was the fish. And instead of the iced water of the restaurants of the Union, there were several kinds of beer and wines which the sun of France had distilled ten years before on the hill sides of Medoc and Burgundy.

Pinchinat and Frascolin did honour to this repast, as did also Zorn and Yvernès. Calistus Munbar had invited them, and it would have been bad taste not to have accepted his hospitality.

Besides, this Yankee, whose conversational powers were inexhaustible, displayed quite a charming humour. He told them all about the town except the one thing his guests wished to know, namely, what was this independent city, the name of which he hesitated to reveal? " A little patience," he would say ; "wait till the exploration is finished." Was his idea to make the quartette tipsy, with the object of letting them miss the train to San Diego ? No, but they drank well after having eaten well, and the dessert was being finished with tea, coffee and liqueurs, when an explosion shook the glasses in the hotel.

"What is that ?" asked Yvernès, with a start.

"Do not be uneasy, gentlemen," replied Calistus Munbar, "that is the gun at the observatory."

"If it only means noon," said Frascolin, looking at his watch, "I beg to state that it is late."

"No, Mr. Alto, no ! The sun is no later here than elsewhere."

A singular smile played on the American's lips, his eyes sparkled behind his spectacles, and he rubbed his hands. He seemed to be congratulating himself on having perpetrated some excellent joke.

Frascolin, less excited than the others by the good cheer, looked at him suspiciously without knowing what to make of it.

"Come, my friends," added the American, in his most amiable manner, "allow me to remind you that there is the second part of the town for us to visit, and I shall die of despair if a single detail escapes you. We have no time to lose."

"At what time does the train start for San Diego?" asked Zorn, always anxious not to fail in his engagements by arriving late.

"Yes, at what time ?" repeated Frascolin.

"Oh, in the evening," replied Calistus Munbar, with a wink of his left eye. "Come, my guests, come. You will not repent of having had me as a guide."

How could they disobey such an obliging personage ? The four artistes left the Excelsior Hotel and strolled along the road. It really seemed as though they had drunk rather freely of the wine, for a kind of thrill seemed to run through their legs, although they had not taken their places on one of the moving footways.

"Eh! eh! Support us, Chatillon!" exclaimed "his highness."

"I think we have had a little to drink," said Yvernès, wiping his forehead.

"All right," observed the American, "once is not always! We had to water your welcome."

"And we have emptied the watering-pot," replied Pinchinat, who had never felt in a better humour.

Calistus Munbar took them down one of the roads leading to the second half of the town. In this district there was more animation than in the other. It was as though they had been suddenly transported from the northern to the southern States of the Union; from Chicago to New Orleans, from Illinois to Louisiana. The shops were better filled, the houses of more elegant architecture, the family mansions more comfortable, the hotels as magnificent as those in the Protestant section but of more cheerful aspect. The people were different in bearing and character. The city was apparently double, like certain stars, only the sections did not revolve round one another.

When they had nearly reached the centre of the district, the group stopped about the middle of Fifteenth Avenue, and Yvernès exclaimed,—

"Upon my word, that is a palace!"

"The palace of the Coverley family," replied Calistus Munbar, "Nat Coverley, the equal of Jem Tankerdon."

"Richer than he is?" asked Pinchinat.

"Quite as rich," said the American. "An ex-banker of New Orleans, who has more hundreds of millions than he has fingers on both hands."

"A nice pair of gloves, Mr. Munbar!"

"Just so."

"And these two notables, Jem Tankerdon and Nat Coverley, are enemies, naturally?"

"Rivals, at least! each striving for preponderance in the city's affairs, jealous of one another."

"Will they end by eating one another?" asked Zorn.

" Perhaps, and if one devours the other—"

" What an attack of indigestion will follow ! "

And Calistus Munbar absolutely shook with laughter, so much was he amused at the reply.

The Catholic church rises in a vast open space so as to give a good view of its fine proportions. It is in the Gothic style, the style that can be admired close to, for the vertical lines which constitute its beauty lose their character when seen from a distance. St. Mary's Church merits admiration for the slenderness of its pinnacles, the delicacy of its rose work, the elegance of its flamboyant pointed arches, the gracefulness of its windows.

" A fine specimen of Anglo-Saxon Gothic," said Yvernès, who was a good judge of architecture. "You are right, Mr. Munbar, the two sections of your town have no more resemblance between them than the temple of the one and the cathedral of the other ! "

" And yet, Monsieur Yvernès, these two sections are born of the same mother—"

" But not of the same father, probably ? " said Pinchinat.

" Yes, of the same father, my excellent friends. Only they have been built in a different way. They were designed for the convenience of those in search of an existence, tranquil, happy, free from all care, an existence offered by no other city of the old or new world."

" By Apollo, Mr. Munbar," replied Yvernès, "take care not to excite our curiosity too much. It is as if you were singing one of those musical phrases which make you long for the key-note."

" And the result is that they tire your ear," added Zorn. " Has the moment come when you will consent to tell us the name of this extraordinary town ? "

" Not yet, my dear guests," replied the American, adjusting his gold eyeglasses on his nasal appendage. "Wait until we have finished our walk—let us go on now."

" Before going on," said Frascolin, who felt a sort of vague uneasiness mingling with his curiosity, "I have a proposition to make."

" And what is that ? "

" Why not ascend the spire of St. Mary's church ? From there we could see—"

" Oh, no," said Munbar, shaking his bushy head, " not now, later on."

" And when ? " asked the violoncellist, getting provoked at so many evasions.

" At the end of our excursion, Monsieur Zorn."

" Then we shall return to this church ? "

" No, my friends, our walk will end with a visit to the observatory, the tower of which is a third higher than the spire of St. Mary's church."

" But why not take advantage of this opportunity ? " asked Frascolin.

" Because it would spoil the effect I have in view."

And there was no means of extracting any further reply from this enigmatic personage.

The best thing being to submit, the various avenues of this part of the town were conscientiously explored. A visit was paid to the commercial quarters, those of the tailors, boot-makers, hatters, butchers, grocers, bakers, fruiterers, &c. Calistus Munbar, saluted by most of the people he met, returned the salutes with vainglorious satisfaction. He talked incessantly, this exhibitor of wonders, and the rattle of his tongue was like the ringing of a bell on a feast day.

In about two hours the quartette had arrived at the boundary of the town, which was marked by a superb iron railing, adorned with flowers and climbing plants. Beyond was the country, the circular line of which blended with the horizon of the sky.

And here Frascolin noticed something which he did not think it his duty to communicate to his comrades. Everything would doubtless be explained from the summit of the observatory tower. What he noticed was that the sun, instead of being in the south-west at two o'clock, was in the south-east.

This was something to astonish a mind as reflective as

that of Frascolin, and he had begun to rack his brains
when Calistus Munbar changed the course of his ideas by
exclaiming,—

"Gentlemen, the tram starts in a few minutes. Let us
be off to the harbour."

"The harbour?" asked Zorn.

"Yes, it is only about a mile—and that will enable you
to admire our park?"

The harbour, if it existed, ought to be a little below
or a little above this town on the coast of Lower California. In truth, where could it be if it were not on some
point of the coast?

The artistes, rather perplexed, sat down on the seats
of an elegant car, in which were several other passengers,
all of whom shook hands with Munbar, who seemed to
know everybody, and then the dynamos of the train began
to drive them along. That which Munbar called a park was
the country extending round the city. There were paths
running out of sight, and verdant lawns, and painted
barriers, straight and zigzagged, known as fences, around
preserves, and clumps of trees—oaks, maples, ashes, chest-
nuts, nettle-trees, elms, cedars—all of them young, but the
haunts of a world of birds of a thousand species. It was
a regular English garden, with leaping fountains, baskets
of flowers then in all the abundance of spring, masses of
shrubs of the most diversified species, giant geraniums like
those of Monte Carlo, orange trees, lemon trees, olive
trees, oleanders, lentisks, aloes, camellias, dahlias, roses of
Alexandria with their white flowers, hortensias, white and
pink lotuses, South American passion-flowers, rich collections of fuchsias, salvias, begonias, hyacinths, tulips,
crocuses, narcissi, anemones, Persian ranunculi, bearded
irises, cyclamens, orchids, calceolarias, tree ferns, and also
species characteristic of the tropics, such as cannas, palms,
date trees, fig trees, eucalypti, mimosas, banana trees,
guava trees, calabash trees, cocoanut trees; in a word, all
that a connoisseur could ask for in the richest botanic
garden.

With his propensity for evoking the memories of ancient poetry, Yvernès thought he was transported to the bucolic landscapes of the romance of Astrea. It is true if sheep were not wanting in these fresh pastures, if ruddy cows grazed between the fences, if deer and other elegant quadrupeds of the forest fauna bounded among the trees, it was the absence of the shepherds of D'Urfé and their charming shepherdesses which they had to regret. As to the Lignon, it was represented by a serpentine river, whose vivifying waters followed the valleys of the land-scape.

But at the same time it all seemed artificial.

This provoked the ironical Pinchinat to exclaim,—

"Ah ! is that all you have in the shape of a river ?"

And Calistus Munbar to reply,—

"Rivers ? What is the good of them ?"

"To have water, of course."

"Water ! That is to say, a substance generally un-healthy, microbian, and typhoic ?"

"Yes, but it can be purified."

"And why give yourself that trouble when it is easy to make a water pure, hygienic, free from all impurity, and even gaseous or ferruginous, if you please."

"You manufacture this water ?" asked Frascolin.

"Certainly, and we distribute it hot or cold to the houses as we distribute light, sound, the time, heat, cold, power, the antiseptic agents, electrization by auto-conduc-tion."

"Allow me," said Yvernès, "to believe that you also make the rain for watering your lawns and flowers."

"And so we do, sir," said the American, making the jewels on his fingers sparkle across the flowing masses of his hand.

"Do you have your rain on tap?" exclaimed Sebastien Zorn.

"Yes, my dear friends, rain which the conduits arranged underground distribute in a way that is regular, con-trollable, opportune, and practical. Is not that better

than waiting for nature's good pleasure, and submitting
to the climate's caprices, better than complaining against
excesses without the power of remedying them, sometimes a too persistent humidity, sometimes too long a
drought?"

"I have you there, Mr. Munbar," declared Frascolin.
"That you can produce your rain at will may be all very
well, but how do you prevent it falling from the sky?"

"The sky? What has that got to do with it?"

"The sky, or, if you prefer it, the clouds which break,
the atmospheric currents with their accompaniment of
cyclones, tornadoes, storms, squalls, hurricanes. During
the bad season, for example."

"The bad season?" repeated Calistus Munbar.

"Yes; the winter."

"The winter? What do you mean by that?"

"We said winter—hail, snow, ice!" exclaimed Zorn,
enraged at the Yankee's ironical replies.

"We know them not!" was Munbar's tranquil reply.

The four Parisians looked at one another. Were they in
the presence of a madman or a mystificator? In the first
case he ought to be shut up; in the second he ought to
be taken down.

Meanwhile the tramcar continued its somewhat leisurely
journey through these enchanting gardens. To Zorn and
his companions it seemed as though beyond the limits of
this immense park were pieces of ground, methodically
cultivated, displaying their different colours like the
patterns of cloth formerly shown at tailors' doors. These
were, no doubt, fields of vegetables, potatoes, cabbages,
carrots, turnips, leeks, in fact, everything required for the
composition of a perfect *pot-au-feu*. At the same time,
they would have been glad to get out into the open
country to discover what this singular region produced in
corn, oats, maize, barley, rye, buckwheat, and other
cereals.

But here a factory appeared, its iron chimneys rising
from its low, rough glass roofs. These chimneys,

strengthened by iron stays, resembled those of a steamer under way, of a *Great Eastern* whose hundred thousand horses were driving her powerful screws, with this difference, that instead of black smoke they were only emitting mere threads which in no way injured the atmosphere.

This factory covered about ten thousand square yards. It was the first industrial establishment the quartette had seen since they had started on their excursion, under the American's guidance.

"And what is that establishment?" asked Pinchinat.

"It is a factory worked with petroleum," replied Munbar, looking as though his eyes would perforate his glasses.

"And what does this factory manufacture?"

"Electrical energy, which is distributed through the town, the park, the country, in producing motive force and light. At the same time, it keeps going our telegraphs, telautographs, telephones, telephotes, bells, cooking stoves, machinery, arc lights, incandescent lights, aluminium moons, and submarine cables."

"Your submarine cables?" observed Frascolin, sharply.

"Yes, those that connect the town with the different points of the American coast."

"And is it necessary to have a factory of such size for that purpose?"

"I think so, considering what we do with our electrical energy, and also our mental energy!" replied Munbar. "Believe me, gentlemen, it required a pretty strong dose to found this incomparable city without a rival in the world!"

They could hear the dull rumbling of the huge factory, the vigorous belchings of the steam, the clanking of the machines, the thuds on the ground, bearing witness to a mechanical effort greater than any in modern industry. Who could have imagined that such power was necessary to move dynamos or charge accumulators?

The tram passed, and a quarter of a mile further on stopped at the harbour.

The travellers alighted, and their guide, still profuse in his praises of everything, took them along the quays by the warehouses and docks. The harbour was oval in form, and large enough to hold some twenty ships. It was more of a wet dock than a harbour terminated by jetties; two piers, supported on iron piles, and lighted by two lamps, facilitating the entry of vessels from the sea.

On that day the wet dock contained only half a dozen steamers, some destined for the transport of petroleum, others for the transport of the goods needed for daily consumption, and a few barques fitted with electrical apparatus employed in sea fishing.

Frascolin noticed that the entrance of the harbour faced the north, and concluded that it must be on the north shore of one of those points which jut out from Lower California into the Pacific. He also noticed that there was a current in the sea running eastward at an appreciable speed, as it ran against the pierheads like the water along the side of a ship when under way—an effect due doubtless to the action of the rising tide, although the tide does not run very strong on the western coast of America.

"Where is the river we crossed yesterday in the ferry boat?" asked Frascolin.

"That is at the back of us," the Yankee was content to reply.

But it would not do to delay if they wished to return to the town in time to take the evening train to San Diego.

Zorn mentioned this to Munbar, who answered,—

"Never fear, my dear friends. We have plenty of time. A tram will take us back to the town after we have followed the shore a little. You wished to have a bird's-eye view of the place, and in less than an hour you will get that from the top of the observatory."

"You guarantee that?" said Zorn.

"I guarantee that at sunrise to-morrow you will no longer be where you are now."

This enigmatic reply had to be accepted; although Frascolin's curiosity, which was much greater than that of his comrades, was excited to the utmost. He was impatient to find himself at the summit of this tower, from which the American affirmed that the view extended to a horizon of at least a hundred miles in circumference. After that, if he could not fix the geographical position of this extraordinary city, he would have to give up the problem for ever.

At the head of the dock was a second tram line running along the coast. There was a train of cars, six in number, in which a number of passengers had already taken their seats. These cars were drawn by an electric locomotive, with a capacity of two hundred ampères-ohms, and their speed was from nine to twelve miles an hour.

Calistus Munbar invited the quartette to take their places in the tram, and it seemed as though it had only been waiting for our Parisians. The country appeared to differ very little from the park which lay between the town and the harbour. The same flat soil, and as carefully looked after. Green fields and meadows instead of lawns, that was all, fields of vegetables, not of cereals. At this moment artificial rain, projected from subterranean conduits, was falling in a beneficent shower on the long rectangles traced by line and square. The sky could not have distributed it more mathematically or more opportunely.

The tram road skirted the coast, with the sea on one side, the fields on the other. The cars ran along in this way for about four miles. Then they stopped before a battery of twelve guns of heavy calibre, the entrance to which bore the inscription " Prow Battery."

" Cannons which load but do not discharge by the breech, like so many of those in Old Europe," said Calistus Munbar.

Hereabouts the coast was deeply indented. A sort of cape ran out, very long and narrow, like the prow of a ship, or the ram of a man-of-war, on which the waves divided, sprinkling it with their white foam. The effect of the current probably, for the sea in the offing was reduced to long undulations, which were getting smaller and smaller with the setting of the sun.

From this point another line of rails went off towards the centre, while the other continued to follow the curve of the coast ; and Calistus Munbar made his friends change cars, announcing that they would return direct towards the city.

The excursion had lasted long enough.

Calistus Munbar drew out his watch, a masterpiece of Sivan, of Geneva—a talking watch, a phonographic watch —of which he pressed the button, and which distinctly spoke, " Thirteen minutes past four."

" You will not forget the ascent of the observatory ? " Frascolin reminded him.

" Forget it, my dear, and I may say my old, friends ! I would sooner forget my own name, which enjoys a certain celebrity, I believe. In another four miles we shall be in front of the magnificent edifice, built at the end of First Avenue, that which divides the two sections of our town."

The tram started. Beyond were the fields, on which fell the afternoon rain, as the American called it ; here again was the enclosed park with its fences, its lawns, its beds and its shrubberies.

Half-past four then chimed. Two hands indicated the hour on a gigantic dial, like that of the Houses of Parliament at Westminster, on the face of a quadrangular tower.

At the foot of this tower were the buildings of the observatory, devoted to different duties, some of which, with round metal roofs and glass windows, allowed the astronomers to follow the circuit of the stars. There were arranged round a central court, from the midst of which rose the tower for a hundred and fifty feet. From its upper gallery the view around would extend over a radius of sixteen miles, if the horizon were not bounded by any high ground or mountains.

Calistus Munbar, preceding his guests, entered a door which was opened to him by a porter in superb livery.

At the end of the hall the lift cage was waiting, which was worked by electricity. The quartette took their places in it with their guide. The cage ascended slowly and quietly. Forty-five seconds after they stopped at the level of the upper platform of the tower. From this platform rose the staff of a gigantic flag, of which the bunting floated out in the northerly breeze.

Of what nationality was this flag? None of our Parisians could recognize it. It was like the American ensign, with its lateral stripes of white and red, but the upper canton, instead of the sixty-seven stars which twinkled in the Confederation at this epoch, bore only one, a star or rather a sun of gold on a blue ground, which seemed to rival in brilliancy the star of day.

"Our flag, gentlemen," said Calistus Munbar, taking off his hat as a mark of respect.

Sebastien Zorn and his comrades could not do otherwise than follow his example. Then they advanced to the parapet and looked over.

What a shriek—at first of surprise and then of anger—escaped them!

The country lay extended beneath them. The country was a perfect oval, surrounded by a horizon of sea, and as far as the eye could carry no land was in sight. And yet the night before, after leaving the village of Freschal in the American's company, Zorn, Frascolin, Yvernès, Pinchinat had travelled for two miles on the land. They had then crossed the river in the ferry boat and again reached land. In fact, if they had left the Californian shore for any sea voyage they would certainly have noticed it.

Frascolin turned towards Calistus Munbar.

"We are on an island?" he asked.

"As you see!" said the Yankee, with the most amiable of smiles.

"And what is this island?"

"Floating Island."

"And this town?"

"Milliard City."

CHAPTER V.

AT this period the world was still waiting for the audacious statistical geographer who could give the exact number of the islands scattered over the face of the globe. The number, we may make bold to say, would amount to many thousands. Among all these islands was there not one that answered the requirements of the founders of Floating Island, and the wants of its future inhabitants? No, not one. Hence this peculiarly American notion of making an island which would be the latest and greatest thing in modern construction.

Floating Island was an island worked by screws. Milliard City was its capital. Why this name? Evidently because the capital was the town of the millionaires, a Gouldian, Vanderbiltian, Rothschildian City.

An artificial island; there was nothing extraordinary in the idea. With a sufficient mass of materials submerged in a river, a lake, a sea, it was not beyond the power of men to make it. But that was not sufficient. Having regard to its destination, to the requirements it had to satisfy, it was necessary that this island could be moved from place to place, and consequently that it should float. There was the difficulty, which was not too great for iron-workers and engineers to overcome.

Already, at the end of the nineteenth century, with their instinct for the "big," their admiration for the "enormous," the Americans had conceived the project of forming a large raft some miles out at sea, and their mooring it with anchors. If this was not a city, it was at least a station in the Atlantic with restaurants, hotels, clubs, theatres, &c., where tourists could find all the conveniences of the watering places then most in vogue. This project was realized and completed. And then, instead of a stationary raft, they made a movable island.

Six years before the opening of this story an American company, under the title of *Floating Island Company, Limited*, had been formed with a capital of five hundred million dollars, divided into five hundred shares, for the construction of an artificial island, affording the nabobs of the United States the various advantages of which the stationary regions of the globe are deprived. The shares were quickly taken up, for immense fortunes were then plentiful in America, gained either by manipulating railways, or banking operations, or oil transactions, or speculations in pickled pork.

Four years were occupied in the construction of this island, of which we may conveniently give the chief dimensions, the internal arrangements, the means of locomotion which enabled it to cruise amongst the most beautiful regions of the immense Pacific Ocean.

There are floating villages in China on the River Yang-tse-Kiang, in Brazil on the Amazon, in Europe on the Danube. But these are only ephemeral constructions, a few small houses built on the top of long rafts of wood. When it reaches its destination the raft is broken up, the houses taken off—the village has lived and died.

But it was quite another affair with regard to this island ; it was to be launched on the sea, it was to last as long as any of the works issued from the hands of man.

And besides, who knows if the earth will not some day be too small for its inhabitants, whose numbers will almost reach six milliards in 2072—as the statisticians following Ravenstein affirm with astonishing precision. And will it not be necessary to build on the sea when the continents are overcrowded ?

Floating Island was an island in steel, and the strength of its hull had been calculated for the weight it had

to bear. It was composed of 270,000 caissons, each of
them eighteen yards high, by ten long and ten wide·
Their horizontal surface represented a square of ten yards
on the side, that is to say, of a hundred square yards.
When the caissons were all bolted and riveted together,
they gave the island an area of about twenty-seven
million square yards. In the oval form which the con-
structors had given it, it measured about four and a half
miles long and three broad, and its circuit in round
numbers was about eleven miles.

Floating Island drew thirty feet of water, and had a
freeboard of twenty feet. In volume it was about
430,000,000 cubic yards, and its displacement, being three-
fifths of its volume, amounted to 258,000,000 cubic yards.

The whole of the caissons below the water line had
been covered with a preparation up to then undiscoverable
—which had made a millionaire of its inventor—which
prevented barnacles and other growths from attaching
themselves to the parts in contact with the sea.

The subsoil of the new island was made safe from
distortion and breakage by cross girders, riveting and
bolting.

Special workshops had had to be erected for the construction of this huge example of naval construction.
These were built by the Floating Island Company, who had
acquired Madeleine Bay and its coast, at the extremity of
the long peninsula of Old California, which is just on the
Tropic of Cancer. It was in this bay that the work was
executed under the direction of the engineers of the
Floating Island Company, the chief being the celebrated
William Tersen, who died a few months after the comple-
tion of the work, as Brunel did after the unfortunate
launch of the *Great Eastern*. And Floating Island was
but a *Great Eastern* modernized—only several thousand
times larger.

It will be understood that there could be no question of
launching the island as a ship is launched. It was built
in sections, in compartments alongside one another on the

waters of Madeleine Bay.   This portion of the American
coast became the station of the moving island, to which it
could return when repairs were necessary.

The carcase of the island, its hull, if you will, was formed
of two hundred and seventy thousand compartments, and
filled in with vegetable soil, all except the site of the city,
where the hull was of extraordinary strength.   The depth
of mould was ample for a vegetation restricted to lawns,
flower beds, shrubberies, clumps of trees and fields of
vegetables.   It had seemed impracticable to require this
artificial soil to produce cereals and feed for cattle, which
could be regularly imported.   But the necessary arrangements had been made, so as not to be dependent on importation for milk and poultry.

The three quarters of the soil of Floating Island
devoted to vegetation amounted to about thirteen square
miles, in which the park lawns afforded permanent
verdure, and the carefully tilled fields abounded in vegetables and fruits, and the artificial prairies served as
grazing ground for the flocks and herds.   Electro-culture
was largely employed, that is to say, the influence of continuous currents, the result being an extraordinary
acceleration of growth and the production of vegetables
of remarkable dimensions, such as radishes eighteen inches
long and carrots weighing seven pounds apiece.   The
flower gardens, vegetable gardens, and orchards could hold
their own with the best in Virginia or Louisiana.   In this
there was nothing astonishing ; expense was no object in
this island so justly called the " Pearl of the Pacific."

Its capital, Milliard City, occupied about a fifth of the
seventeen square miles reserved for it, and was about six
miles in circumference.   Our readers who are willing to
accompany Sebastien Zorn and his comrades on their
excursion will soon know it well enough in every part.
They will find it unlike the American towns which have
the happiness and misfortune to be modern—happiness on
account of the facilities for communication, misfortune on
account of the artistic side, which is absolutely wanting.

Milliard City, as we know, is oval in form, and divided
into two sections divided by a central artery, First Avenue,
which is about two miles long. The observatory is at one
end, and the town hall at the other. Here are centralized
all the public departments, the water supply and high-
ways, the plantations and pleasure grounds, the municipal
police, custom-house, markets, cemeteries, hospitals,
schools, and science and art.

And now what was the population contained within this
circuit of eleven miles?

The earth, it appears, has only twelve towns—of which
four are in China—which have more than a million
inhabitants. Well, Floating Island had but ten thousand,
all of them natives of the United States. It was never
intended that international discussions should arise among
the citizens, who might repose in tranquility on this most
modern of constructions.

It was enough, or rather more than enough, that they
could not be mustered under the same banner with
regard to religion. But it would have been difficult to
reserve the exclusive right of residence on the island to
the Yankees of the North, who were the port watch of
Floating Island, or the Americans of the South, who
formed its starboard watch. The interests of the Floating
Island Company would not have admitted of this.

When the frame of the hull was finished, when the part
reserved for the town was ready for building on, when the
plan of the streets and avenues had been adopted, the
buildings began to rise—superb hotels, less ornate mansions, houses destined for shops, public edifices, churches
and temples, but none of those monstrosities of twenty-
seven floors, those "sky-scrapers" one sees at Chicago.
The materials used were light and strong. The inoxydis-
able metal that prevailed was aluminium, seven times as
light as iron, the metal of the future, as it was called by
Sainte-Claire-Deville, and which is suitable for all the
requirements of solid construction. This was used in
conjunction with artificial stones, cubes of cement which

can be worked with so much ease. Use was also made of
glass bricks—hollow, blown, and moulded like bottles—set
with mortar, transparent bricks with which if desired the
ideal glass house could be realized. But it was really
metal framework which was most employed, as in the
different kinds of naval architecture. And what was
Floating Island but an immense ship?

These various properties all belonged to the Floating
Island Company. Those who lived in them were only
tenants whatever the amount of their fortune might be.
Care had been taken to provide for all the requirements
of comfort demanded by these extraordinarily rich Americans, by the side of whom the sovereigns of Europe and
the nabobs of India cut but a sorry figure.

If the statistics are correct which give the stock of gold
accumulated in the world at eighteen millions and that of
silver at twenty millions, it must be admitted that the
inhabitants of the Pearl of the Pacific had their fair share.

From the outset the financial side of the enterprise had
been kept well in view. The hotels and houses had been
let at fabulous prices. The rents amounted to millions,
and many of the families could without inconvenience
afford this payment for annual lodging. Hence, under
this head alone the Company secured a good revenue.
Evidently the capital of Floating Island justified the
name it bore in geographical nomenclature.

Setting aside these opulent families, there were several
hundreds paying a rental of from four to eight thousand
a year. The surplus of the population comprised the
professors, tradesmen, shopmen, and servants, and the
foreigners, who were not very numerous, and were not
allowed to settle in Milliard City or in the island.
Lawyers were very few, and lawsuits consequently rare ;
doctors were fewer, and the death rate was consequently
absurdly low. Every inhabitant knew his constitution
exactly, his muscular force measured by the dynamometer,
his pulmonary capacity measured by the spirometer, his
power of cardial contraction measured by the sphyg-

mometer, his degree of vital force measured by the magnetometer. In the town there were neither bars nor cafés, nor drinking saloons, nothing to encourage alcoholism. Never was there a case of dipsomania—let us say drunkenness, to be understood by those who do not know Greek. The municipal departments distributed electric energy, light, power, warmth, compressed air, rarefied air, cold air, water under pressure, as well as pneumatic telegrams and telephonic messages. If you died on this Floating Island, regularly withdrawn from intemperate climates and sheltered from every microbic influence, it was because you had to die after the springs of life had been worked to a centenarian old age.

Were there any soldiers in Floating Island? Yes, a body of five hundred men under the orders of Colonel Stewart, for it had to be remembered that some parts of the Pacific are not always safe. In approaching certain groups of islands it is prudent to be prepared against any attack by pirates. That this militia was highly paid, that every man received a salary superior to that of a full general in old Europe, need not occasion surprise. The recruiting of these soldiers, lodged, boarded, and clothed at the expense of the administration, took place under excellent conditions, controlled by chiefs who were as rich as Crœsus ; the candidates were numerous enough to be embarrassing.

Were there any police on Floating Island ? Yes, a few companies, and they sufficed to keep the peace of a town which had no reason to be troubled. To reside there, permission was necessary from the municipal administration. The shores of the island were watched day and night by custom-house officers. You could only land at the ports. How could rascals get in there ? And as to those who went wrong on the island, they were arrested at once, sentenced, and put ashore in the west or east of the Pacific, on any corner of the old or new continent, without the possibility of ever returning to Floating Island.

We said the ports of Floating Island. Were there
many of them, then? There were two, situated at the
extremity of the smaller diameter of the oval. One of
these was called Starboard Harbour, the other Larboard
Harbour. In this way there was no danger of regular
communications being interrupted. If, owing to bad
weather, one of these harbours was unavailable, the other
was open to ships, which could thus reach the island in
all winds. It was through these harbours that the island
was supplied with goods, with petroleum brought by
special steamers, with flour and cereals, wines, beers and
other drinks, tea, coffee, cocoa, groceries, preserves, etc.
At these were landed the cattle, sheep, and pigs from the
best markets of America. Thus was assured a full supply
of fresh meat and everything required by the most exacting gourmet. There were also landed the dress materials,
linen, and fashions required by the most refined dandy or
the most elegant lady. These things were bought from
the tradesmen in the island at prices we dare not name, for
fear of exciting the incredulity of the reader.

It may be asked how a regular service of steamers could
be established between the American coast and an island
which constantly changed its position—one day in one
position, next day twenty miles away. The reply is very
simple. Floating Island did not cruise about at a
venture. Its position was in accordance with a programme drawn up by the adminstration, at the advice of
the meteorologists of the observatory. It was a voyage—
open to modifications, however—across that part of the
Pacific containing the most beautiful archipelagoes,
avoiding as much as possible sudden bursts of cold or
heat, which are the causes of so many pulmonary affections. ¯ It was this which enabled Calistus Munbar to say,
with regard to winter, "we know it not!" Floating
Island only manœuvred between the thirty-fifth parallels
of north and south latitude. Seventy degrees to traverse,
over four thousand sea miles. What a magnificent field
of navigation! Ships always knew where to find the

Pearl of the Pacific, for its movements were arranged in advance among the various groups of these delightful islands, which form the oases in the desert of this mighty ocean.

But, in any case, vessels were not reduced to having to find Floating Island by chance. The company did not care to avail themselves of the twenty-five cables, six thousand miles long, belonging to the Eastern Extension, Australia and China Company. No! Floating Island must not be dependent on anybody! Scattered about the surface of the sea were a few hundred buoys, supporting the ends of electric cables connected with Madeleine Bay. One of these buoys would be picked up, the cable attached to the instruments in the observatory, and the agents in the Bay informed of the present latitude and longitude of Floating Island, the shipping service being consequently conducted with railway regularity.

There is, however, an important question which is worth dealing with at length.

How was enough fresh water procured for the wants of the island?

It was made by distillation in two special establishments, and was brought in pipes to the inhabitants of Milliard City, or led under the fields and country around. In this way it was provided for house and street service, and fell in beneficent rain on the fields and lawns, which were thus independent of the caprices of the sky. And not only was this water fresh, it was distilled, electrolyzed, more hygienic than the purest springs of both continents, of which a drop the size of a pin's head may contain fifteen milliards of microbes.

But we have still to describe how the island was moved. Great speed was unnecessary, as for six months it was not intended to leave the region comprised between the tropics and the hundred and thirtieth and hundred and eightieth meridians. From fifteen to twenty miles a day was all that Floating Island required. This speed it would have been possible to obtain by towage, by having

a cable made of the Indian plant known as bastin, which
is very strong and light, and would float just below the
surface so as not to be damaged by shoals.   This cable
could be passed over pulleys at the extremities of the
island, which could be towed backwards and forwards as
barges are towed up and down certain rivers.   And this
cable would have had to be of enormous size for such a
mass, and it would have been subject to many injuries.
And the freedom would be that of an island in chains,
obliged to follow a definite line ; and such freedom the
citizens of free America revolted at.

At this period electricians had fortunately so far
advanced that they could obtain almost anything from
electricity.   And it was to it they entrusted the locomotion
of their island.   Two establishments were enough to drive
dynamos of enormous power, furnishing electrical energy
by continuous current under a moderate voltage of two
thousand volts.   These dynamos drove a powerful system
by screws, placed near the two ports.   They each developed
five millions of horse-power, by means of their hundreds
of boilers fed with petroleum briquettes, which are less
cumbersome, less dirty than oil, and richer in caloric.
These works were under the direction of the two chief
engineers, Watson and Somwah, assisted by a numerous
staff of engineers and stokers under the supreme command
of Commodore Ethel Simcoe.   From his residence in the
observatory, the commodore was in telephonic communication with the works.   From him came the orders for
advance or retreat, according to the programme.   It was
owing to him that, during the night of the 25th, the order
to start had been given just as Floating Island was in the
vicinity of the Californian coast, at the commencement of
its annual campaign.

The maximum speed to which the island could attain,
when the engines were developing their ten million
horse-power, was eight knots an hour.   The most powerful
waves, when raised by a storm, could have no influence on
it.   Its size rendered it unaffected by the undulations of

the surge. Fear of sea-sickness there could be none. For the first few days just a slight thrill could be perceived, which the rotation of the screws communicated to its subsoil. Terminated by rams extending at each end for some sixty yards, dividing the waters without effort, it passed without shock or jolt over the immense liquid field open to its excursions.

The electrical energy produced at the works was employed for other purposes than the locomotion of Floating Island. It lighted the country, the park, and the city. It gave the luminant for the lighthouse, whose beams signalled from afar the presence of the island and prevented all chance of collision. It furnished the various currents required by the telegraphs, telephotes, telautographs, telephones used in the private houses and business establishments. It fed the artificial moons, of five thousand candle-power, which lighted an area of five hundred square yards.

This extraordinary construction was now on its second voyage across the Pacific. A month before it had left Madeleine Bay and coasted up to the thirty-fifth parallel, so as to be in the latitude of the Sandwich Islands. It was off the coast of Lower California when Calistus Munbar, learning by telephone that the Concert Quartette had left San Francisco, had started for San Diego to secure those eminent artistes. We know the way he effected this, how he brought them on to Floating Island, then moored a few cable lengths off the coast, and how, thanks to this peculiarly smart proceeding, the dilettanti of Floating Island were to be charmed with chamber music.

Such was this new wonder of the world, this masterpiece of human genius, worthy of the twentieth century, of which two violins, an alto, and a 'cello were the guests, and which was bearing them to the west across the Pacific.

CHAPTER VI.

EVEN supposing that Sebastien Zorn, Frascolin, Yvernès, and Pinchinat were men who could be astonished at nothing, it would have been difficult for them to resist a legitimate outburst of anger, and a desire to spring at Calistus Munbar's throat. To have every reason to think that they were in North America, and yet to be really in mid ocean! To believe that they were within twenty miles of San Diego, where they were expected to give a concert next day, and to suddenly learn that they were moving away from it on an artificial island! Really their anger was excusable.

Fortunately for himself, the American had taken care to get out of the way. Profiting by the surprise, or rather the amazement of the quartette, he had left the platform and gone down in the lift, where he was for the moment out of range of the recriminations and exuberances of the four Parisians.

"Rascal!" exclaimed the 'cellist.

"Animal!" exclaimed the alto.

"Suppose that, thanks to him, we are to see wonders!" remarked the solo violin.

"Are you going to make excuses for him, then?" asked the second violin.

"No excuses!" said Pinchinat. "If there is a magistrate on Floating Island, we will have this Yankee hoaxer sent to prison."

"And if there is an executioner," said Zorn, "we will have him hanged."

But to obtain their different results it was first necessary to descend to the level of the inhabitants of Milliard City, the police not acting at a hundred and fifty feet in the air. And that they would have done in a few moments, if descent had been possible. But the cage of the lift had not come up again, and there was nothing like a staircase. At the summit of this tower the quartette found themselves cut off from communication with the rest of humanity.

After their first outburst of vexation and anger, Sebastien Zorn, Pinchinat, and Frascolin left Yvernès to his admirations and remained silent, and finally motionless. Above them rose the flagstaff on which the flag floated.

Zorn experienced a furious desire to cut the halliards, and bring down the flag, as a ship lowers its colours. But as this might lead to trouble, his comrades restrained him at the moment when his hand was brandishing a bowie-knife.

" Do not put us in the wrong," said the wise Frascolin.

" Then—you accept the situation ? " asked Pinchinat.

" No, but do not complicate it."

" And our luggage on the road to San Diego ! " remarked his highness, crossing his arms.

" And our concert to-morrow ! " exclaimed Zorn.

" We will give it by telephone," said the first violin, but the joke had anything but a soothing effect on the excited 'cellist.

The observatory, it will be remembered, occupied the middle of a vast square, on which abutted the First Avenue. At the other end of this principal artery, some two miles long, which separated the two sections of Milliard City, the artistes could perceive a sort of monumental palace, surmounted by a belfry of very light and elegant construction. They said to themselves that this must be the seat of government of the island, the residence of the municipality, supposing that Milliard City had a mayor and etceteras. They were not mistaken. And just then the clock in the belfry gave forth a joyous carillon, the notes of which reached the tower with the last undulations of the breeze.

"Listen !" said Yvernès. "That is in D major."

"And in two-four time," said Pinchinat.

The clock was striking five.

"And dinner," exclaimed Sebastien Zorn, "and bed! Are we, owing to this miserable Munbar, to spend the night on this platform a hundred and fifty feet in the air?"

It was to be feared so, if the lift did not afford the prisoners the means of quitting their prison.

In fact the twilight is short in these low latitudes, and the sun falls like a projectile below the horizon. The four looked away to the furthest limits of the sky, over a deserted sea, without a sail, without even a trace of smoke. Across the country ran the trams away to the shore of the island, and between the two harbours. At this time the park was crowded. From the tower it looked like an immense basket of flowers—azaleas, clematis, jasmine, glycenas, passion-flowers, begonias, salvias, hyacinths, dahlias, camellias, roses of a hundred varieties. The people were crowding in, grown men and young folks, none of those little fops which are the shame of the great cities of Europe, but strong, well-built adults. Women and girls, most of them in pale straw-coloured dresses, the hue preferred in the torrid zone, leading little lap-dogs in silk coats with chains laced with gold. Here and there these people were following the sandy paths, capriciously winding among the lawns. Some were reclining on the cushions of electric cars, others were seated on benches sheltered by the trees. Farther off young gentlemen were playing tennis, and cricket, and golf, and also polo, mounted on spirited ponies. Groups of children—American children of astonishing exuberance, among whom originality is so precocious, particularly in the case of the girls—were playing on the grass.

The commercial quarters of the town were still busy at this time of day.

The moving footways still ran on with their burden of passengers down the principal streets. At the foot of the tower, in the square of the observatory, there was a passing crowd whose attention the four prisoners endeavoured to attract.

Pinchinat and Frascolin yelled again and again to them. They were heard, evidently, for arms were stretched out towards them, and even words reached their ears. But there was no sign of surprise. Nobody seemed astonished at the group on the tower.

The words that came aloft were "good-bye" and "how do you do," and "good-evening," and other formulas of polite greeting. It seemed as though the people had been informed of the arrival of the four Parisians on Floating Island.

"Ah!" said Pinchinat, "they are laughing at us."

"I think they are," remarked Yvernès.

An hour went by—an hour during which their appeals were in vain. The pressing invitations of Frascolin met with no more success than the furious invectives of Zorn. And the dinner-hour was approaching, the park was beginning to empty, the idlers in the streets were clearing off. It was maddening.

"Certainly," said Yvernès, "we resemble the people whom some evil genius attracted within a sacred enclosure, and who were condemned to perish for having seen what their eyes should not have seen."

"And we are to be left to the tortures of hunger," said Pinchinat.

"That shall not be until we have exhausted every means of prolonging our existence," said Zorn.

"If we have to eat each other, we will let Yvernès b number one!" said Pinchinat.

"When you please!" sighed the first violin in a subdued voice, bowing his head to receive the fatal blow.

At this moment a noise was heard in the depths of the tower. The cage of the lift came up and stopped at the platform. The prisoners, expecting to see Calistus Munbar, prepared to give him the welcome he deserved.

The cage was empty.

Be it so. There was plenty of time for that. The hoaxed would not fail to find the hoaxer. The thing to do at once was to descend to his level, and the way to do that was to enter the cage.

That is what they did; and as soon as they were in it began to descend, and in less than a minute they were at the ground level of the tower.

The door opened. The four went out. The interior court was deserted. They crossed it and took one of the paths along the square.

A few people were moving about who appeared to take no notice of the strangers. At a remark from Frascolin, advising him to be cautious, Zorn restrained his tempestuous recriminations. It was of the authorities that they must demand justice. There was no danger in doing that. It was decided to return to the Excelsior Hotel and wait until the morning to claim their rights as free men; and the quartette began to walk along First Avenue.

Did they attract much attention? Yes and no. People looked at them, but not to any great extent—as though, perhaps, they were some of the few tourists occasionally visiting Milliard City. The quartette, under the influence of such extraordinary circumstances, did not feel very comfortable, and thought they were gazed at much more than they really were. On the other hand, it was not astonishing that the people appeared strange to them, these islanders of a moving island, these men voluntarily separated from their kind wandering over the face of the largest ocean of the globe. With a little imagination they might fancy these Floating Islanders belonged to another planet of the solar system. This was the opinion of Yvernès, whose excitable brain was rather attracted by imaginary worlds. As to Pinchinat, he was content to say,—

"These people we are meeting have quite a millionaire look about them, and seem to be fitted with screws behind, like their island."

But they got more and more hungry, and began to hurry towards the hotel. In the morning they would see about getting back to San Diego on one of the Floating Island steamers, after receiving an indemnity which Calistus Munbar would have to pay, as was only just.

But as they were going along First Avenue, Frascolin stopped before a sumptuous edifice, on the front of which, in gold letters, was the inscription "Casino." To the right of the superb arcade which surmounted the principal door a restaurant was visible, and through the arabesqued glass could be seen a series of tables, of which some were occupied by diners, while a numerous staff was busy about them.

"Here people eat!" said the second violin, consulting his famished comrades with a look.

Pinchinat's laconic reply was, " Let us go in."

And they entered the restaurant in single file. No particular notice seemed to be taken of their presence in this establishment, usually patronized by strangers. Five minutes afterwards they were attacking the first course of an excellent dinner, of which Pinchinat had chosen the bill of fare. Fortunately, the quartette's purse was well filled, and if it ran low on Floating Island it would soon be replenished by the takings at San Diego.

The cookery was excellent, being much superior to that of the New York and San Francisco hotels ; the apparatus used was the electric stove, admirably adapted for either a fierce or gentle fire. The preserved oyster soup, fricasseed corn, stewed celery, and rhubarb cakes, which are traditional, were followed by fish of extreme freshness, rump-steaks of incomparable tenderness, game doubtless from the forests and prairies of California, and vegetables grown on the island. As drinks, there was no iced water in American fashion, but various beers and wines which the growers of Burgundy, the Bordelais, and the Rhine had placed in the cellars of Milliard City—at a high price we may be sure.

This bill of fare cheered up the Parisians. Their ideas took another turn. Perhaps they took a less gloomy view of the day's adventures. It is well known that orchestral musicians know how to drink, as is only natural with those who expend their breath in chasing sonorous waves through wind instruments, though less excusable with those who have only to manipulate the strings. It is of no consequence, however. Yvernès, Pinchinat, and Frascolin began to see life in rose colour, and even in the colours of gold, in this city of millionaires. Sebastien Zorn alone refused to follow his comrades' lead, and did not let his anger drown in the vintages of France.

In short, the quartette had become very well satisfied with themselves on the whole, when the time came to ask for their bill. It was handed to Frascolin by the superintendent in a black coat. The second violin cast his eyes on the total, rose from his seat, sat down again, rose again, rubbed his eyes, and looked at the ceiling.

" What is the matter with you ? " asked Yvernès.

" A shudder from head to foot," replied Frascolin.

" Is it dear ? "

" More than dear. We have to pay two hundred francs."

" The four ? "

" No—each."

In fact, the amount was a hundred and sixty dollars. The game cost fifteen dollars, the fish twenty dollars, the rump-steaks twenty-five dollars, the Medoc and Burgundy thirty dollars a bottle, the rest at the same rate.

" Confound it ! " exclaimed his Highness.

" The thieves ! " exclaimed Sebastien Zorn.

These remarks being in French were not understood by the restaurant manager. Nevertheless this personage was quite aware of what was passing. But if a slight smile appeared on his lips, it was a smile of surprise not of disdain. It seemed to him quite natural that a dinner should cost a hundred and sixty dollars. That was the price in Floating Island.

" No scandal ! " said Pinchinat. " France is looking at us. Let us pay."

" And no matter how," replied Frascolin. " On the road

to San Diego, after to-morrow, we shall not have enough
to buy a sandwich with ! "

So saying, he took out his purse and extracted from it
a respectable number of paper dollars, which, fortunately,
were current at Milliard City, and he was about to hand
them over when a voice was heard,—

" These gentlemen have not to pay anything."

It was the voice of Calistus Munbar. The Yankee had
just entered the room, expansive and smiling as usual.

" At last ! " shouted Zorn, feeling inclined to take him
by the throat and clutch him as he clutched the finger-
board of his 'cello in the *forte* passages.

" Be calm, my dear Zorn," said the American. " Let
us go into the room where coffee is waiting for us. There
we can talk at our ease, and when our conversation is
over—"

" I will strangle you ! " replied Sebastien Zorn.

" No, you will kiss my hands."

" I shall not kiss you at all," said the 'cellist, by turns
red and white with anger.

A minute afterwards, Calistus Munbar's guests were
lounging on soft couches while he was balancing himself
in a rocking-chair.

And this is what he said by way of introduction :—

" Calistus Munbar, of New York, fifty years of age,
great-grand-nephew of the celebrated Barnum, at the
moment Superintendent of the Fine Arts of Floating
Island, entrusted with all that concerns painting, sculpture,
music, and the pleasures generally of Milliard City. And
now that you know me, gentlemen—"

" Is it by chance," said Zorn, " that you are not also an
agent of the police, entrusted with the enticing of people
into traps and keeping them prisoners, whether they like
it or not ? "

" Do not be too hasty, irritable 'cellist," replied the
American, " and wait for the end."

" We will wait," said Frascolin, gravely, " and we are
listening."

"Gentlemen," continued Calistus Munbar, graciously, "all I wish to touch on in this interview is the question of music as it exists in our island. Lyrical theatres, Milliard City does not as yet possess any, but if you wish it, they will rise from the soil as by enchantment. Up to the present our fellow-citizens have satisfied their musical tendencies by keeping themselves acquainted with the masterpieces of lyric art by means of the most approved apparatus. The ancient and modern masters, the great artistes of the day, the most sought after of instrumentalists, have been heard by us by means of the phonograph—"

"A mere bird-organ, your phonograph!" exclaimed Yvernès, disdainfully.

"Not quite so much as you may think," said the superintendent. "We are the possessors of instruments which have enabled us to listen to you when you were at Boston or Philadelphia; and if you please, you can applaud yourself with your own hands."

At this period the inventions of the illustrious Edison had attained their final degree of perfection. The phonograph was no longer the mere musical-box which it resembled so closely to begin with. Thanks to its admirable inventor, the ephemeral talent of singers or instrumentalists had been preserved for the admiration of future races with as much precision as the works of statuaries and painters. An echo, if you will, but an echo faithful as a photograph reproduction, the shades and delicacies of singing or playing in all their unalterable purity.

Calistus Munbar said this so warmly that his hearers were impressed. He spoke of Saint-Saëns, Reyer, Ambroise Thomas, Gounod, Massenet, Verdi, of the imperishable masterpieces of Berlioz, Meyerbeer, Halévy, Rossini, Beethoven, Haydn, Mozart, like one who knew them thoroughly, who appreciated them, who, to make them better known, had devoted his already long life as an impresario, and it was pleasant to listen to him. At the same time he did not seem to have been attacked by the Wagnerian epidemic which, at this period, was subsiding.

When he stopped to take breath, Pinchinat, profiting by the calm, remarked,—

" All that is very well, but your Milliard City, I see, has only heard music in a box, melodic preserves sent to it like tinned sardines or salt beef."

" Pardon me, Mr. Alto."

" I will pardon you, but I insist on this point, that your phonographs only preserve the past, and that you have probably never heard an artiste in Milliard City when he is playing."

" You must pardon me once more."

" Our friend, Pinchinat, will pardon you as much as you like, Mr. Munbar," said Frascolin. " His pockets are full of pardons, but his remark is just. Still, if you could put yourselves in communication with the theatres of America or Europe—"

" And do you think that would be impossible, my dear Frascolin ? " exclaimed the superintendent, stopping in his see-saw.

" What do you mean ? "

" I say that it is only a question of price, and our city is rich enough to satisfy all its fancies, all its aspirations as regards lyric art, and it has done so."

" And how ? "

" By means of the theatrophones installed in the concert room of this casino. The company possesses a number of submarine cables immersed in the waters of the Pacific, one end of which is at Madeleine Bay, and the other held in suspension by powerful buoys. When our fellow-citizens wish to hear one of the singers of the Old or New World, we fix on to one of these cables, and send a telephonic order to our agents at Madeleine Bay. These agents put us in communication with America or with Europe. The cables are connected with such and such a theatre, such and such a concert-room, and our dilettanti seated in this casino really assist at these distant performances and applaud."

"But the people over there cannot hear their applause!" exclaimed Yvernès.

"I beg your pardon, they do—by return wire!"

And then Calistus Munbar launched forth into transcendental considerations on music, considered not only as one of the manifestations of art, but as a therapeutic agent. According to the system of J. Harford, of Westminster Abbey, the good folks of Milliard City had experienced extraordinary results regarding this utilization of the lyric art. The system kept them in perfect health. Music exercising a reflex action on the nervous centres, the harmonic vibrations had the effect of dilating the arterial vessels, influencing the circulation and increasing or diminishing it as required. It provoked an acceleration of the heart's pulsations and respiratory movements by reason of the tonality and intensity of the sounds, and aided the nutrition of the tissues. Consequently, musical energy stations were working at Milliard City, and transmitting sound waves to the houses by means of the telephones, etc., etc.

The quartette listened with open mouths. Never had they heard their art discussed from a medical point of view, and probably they were not particularly pleased. Nevertheless, Yvernès the whimsical, ready to adopt these theories, which are as old as King Saul, according to the practice of the celebrated harpist, David, excitedly exclaimed,—

"Yes, yes. It is clear enough. You must choose your tune according to the diagnosis. Take Wagner or Berlioz, for instance, for the anæmic."

"And Mendelssohn and Mozart for the sanguine instead of bromide of strontium!" replied Calistus Munbar.

Sebastien Zorn here interposed, and hurled his discordant note into this high-flighted conversation.

"We have nothing to do with all this," he said; "why have you brought us here?"

"Because stringed instruments have the most powerful effect."

" Indeed, sir ; and was it to soothe your neurotics that you interrupted our journey, and hindered our reaching San Diego, where we are engaged to give a concert to-morrow ? "

" That was the reason, my excellent friends."

" And all you saw in us was a kind of musical sawbones, or lyrical apothecaries ? " asked Pinchinat.

" No, gentlemen," answered Calistus Munbar rising, " I saw in you only artistes of great talent and great reputation. The cheers which greeted the Quartette Party on its American tour have reached our island. The Floating Island Company thought that the time had come to replace their phonographs and theatrophones by living artistes in flesh and blood, and give the inhabitants of Milliard City the inexpressible pleasure of a direct execution of the masterpieces of art. It wished to begin with chamber music before organizing operatic orchestras. It thought of you, the accredited representatives of that music. It gave me instructions to secure you at any price, to carry you off if need be. You are the first artistes that have had access to Floating Island, and I leave you to imagine the welcome that awaits you ! "

Yvernès and Pinchinat were much affected by these enthusiastic periods of the superintendent. That it might be a hoax did not occur to them. Frascolin, a man of reflection, asked himself if he were to take this adventure seriously. After all, in such an extraordinary island would not things appear under an extraordinary aspect ! As to Sebastien Zorn, he had resolved not to give in.

" No, sir," he said, " men are not to be carried off without their consent ! We will begin an action against you."

" An action ! When you ought to overwhelm me with thanks, ungrateful that you are ! " replied the superintendent.

" And we will obtain damages, sir."

" Damages ! When I offer you a hundred times more than you could hope to get."

"How much?" said the practical Frascolin.

Calistus Munbar took out his pocket-book and produced a sheet of paper bearing the arms of Floating Island. Presenting it to the four artistes, he said,—

"Your four signatures at the end of this agreement, and the matter is done."

"Sign it before we have read it?" said the second violin. "That we will never do."

"You will never have cause to regret it," said Calistus Munbar, indulging in an outburst of hilarity that shook his whole body. "But let us proceed in proper form. It is an engagement which the company proposes to you, an engagement for twelve months from this date, for the execution of chamber music such as you have been giving in your programmes in America. In twelve months Floating Island will have returned to Madeleine Bay, where you will arrive in time—"

"For our concert at San Diego, I suppose?" exclaimed Sebastien Zorn, "San Diego, where we shall be greeted with hisses."

"No, gentlemen, with cheers. Artistes such as you, the dilettanti are always too honoured and too happy to hear, even if a year behind time."

How could they be angry with such a man?

Frascolin took the paper and read it attentively.

"What guarantee have we?"

"The guarantee of the Floating Island Company under the signature of Mr. Cyrus Bikerstaff, our governor."

"And the terms are these I see set forth in this agreement?"

"Exactly. One million francs—"

"For the four?" asked Pinchinat.

"For each," said Calistus Munbar with a smile, "and yet that amount is not in accordance with your merit, which no one can reward at its proper value."

It would, it must be admitted, have been difficult to

have been more pleasant. And yet Sebastien Zorn protested. He would not accept at any price. He would go to San Diego, and it was not without difficulty that Frascolin succeeded in calming his indignation.

Yet there could not help being some mistrust regarding the superintendent's proposition. An engagement for a year at the rate of a million francs apiece, could it be serious? Quite serious, as Frascolin discovered when he asked,—

"When is the money payable?"

"Quarterly," replied the superintendent, "and here is the first payment, in advance."

Of the roll of notes which bulged his pocket-book Calistus Munbar made four bundles of fifty thousand dollars, that is two hundred and fifty thousand francs, which he handed to Frascolin and his comrades.

That is the way to manage matters in American fashion.

Sebastien Zorn could not help being shaken. But his ill-humour never lost its rights, and he could not help remarking,—

"After all, at the prices that prevail in your island, if you pay twenty-five francs for a partridge, you probably pay a hundred francs for a pair of gloves, and five hundred francs for a pair of boots?"

"Oh, Monsieur Zorn," exclaimed Calistus Munbar, "the company does not stand at such trifles, and it desires that the Quartette Party will have all their expenses paid for them during their sojourn on the island."

To these generous offers what other response could there be but to sign the engagement?

This was what Frascolin, Pinchinat, and Yvernès did. Zorn muttered that it was all absurd. To embark on a Floating Island was ridiculous. They would see how it would end. At last he decided to sign.

And this formality accomplished, if Frascolin, Pinchinat, and Yvernès did not kiss Calistus Munbar's hand, they at least shook it warmly. Four shakes of the hand at a million each !

And that is how the Quartette Party were launched on this extraordinary adventure, and it was under such circumstances that its members became the guests of Floating Island.

CHAPTER VII.

FLOATING ISLAND glided gently over the waters of this Pacific Ocean, which justifies its name at this season of the year. Accustomed for twenty-four hours now to this tranquil motion, Sebastien Zorn and his comrades no longer noticed that they were being carried over the sea. So powerful were its hundreds of screws, driven by their ten million horse-power, that the thrill of the steel hull was barely perceptible. There was no sign of the oscillations of the waves, to which even the most powerful ironclads have to yield. In the houses there were no rolling tables or swing lamps. Why should there be? The houses of Paris, London, and New York were not more securely fixed on their foundations.

After a few weeks' stay at Madeleine Bay, the assembly of notables of Floating Island, called together by the president of the administrative council of the company, had determined on the programme of their annual tour. The island would visit the chief archipelagoes of the Eastern Pacific, voyaging through that hygienic atmosphere, so rich in ozone, in condensed electrized oxygen, gifted with active peculiarities not possessed by oxygen in its ordinary state. As the apparatus was free to move anywhere, advantage was taken of this power to go either east or west, to the American or Asiatic shore, as might be desired. Floating Island went where it pleased, so as to experience the distractions of a varied voyage. And even if it were desired to abandon the Pacific for the Indian Ocean or the Atlantic, to round Cape Horn or the Cape of Good Hope, it could proceed in the direction wished for, and rest assured that neither currents nor tempests would prevent its attaining its object.

But there was no question of its visiting these distant seas, in which it would not find what the Pacific offers among its innumerable archipelagoes. That ocean was a theatre quite large enough for its many voyages. Floating Island could move about from one archipelago to another If it was not endowed with that special instinct of animals —that sixth sense of orientation which guides them where their wants call them—it was directed in safety according to a programme discussed at length and unanimously approved. Up to then there had never been any disagreement between the Starboardites and Larboardites. And the present intention was a westerly voyage to the Sandwich Islands. The distance of about twelve hundred leagues which separates this group from the place where the quartette came on board would take about a month to accomplish at moderate speed, and Floating Island could remain in the archipelago until it was found convenient to start again for another group in the southern hemisphere.

On the morrow of this memorable day the quartette left the Excelsior Hotel and took up their quarters in some rooms in the casino which were put at their disposal—a comfortable suite, richly furnished as may be supposed. First Avenue lay displayed in front of its windows. Sebastien Zorn, Frascolin, Pinchinat, Yvernès, had each his own room communicating with a sitting-room common to all. The central court of the establishment yielded them the shade of its trees in full foliage, and the freshness of its fountains. On one side of this court was the museum of Milliard City; on the other the concert-room where the Parisian artistes were so happily to replace the echoes of the phonographs and the transmissions of the theatrophones. Twice a day, three times a day, as many times a day as they wished, their table was laid in the restaurant, where the manager favoured them with no more of his remarkable efforts in addition.

This morning, when they had all met in the sitting-room before descending for breakfast,—

"Well!" said Pinchinat, "what do you say to what has happened to us?"

"A dream," replied Yvernès, "a dream in which we are engaged at a million a year."

"It is unmistakable reality," replied Frascolin. "Search in your pockets, and you can pull out the first quarter of the said million."

"It remains to see how it is going to end! Very badly, I imagine," said Zorn, bent on discovering a folded rose-leaf in the bed on which he had been laid in spite of himself. "Besides, where is our luggage?"

In fact, the luggage was probably at San Diego, to which they could not go in search of it. Oh! Very rudimentary luggage; a few portmanteaus, linen, toilet utensils, a change of clothes, and also, it is true, the costume of the executants when they appeared before the public.

There was nothing to be uneasy about on this point. In forty-eight hours this rather faded wardrobe would be replaced by another presented to the four artistes without their having to pay fifteen hundred francs for a coat or five hundred francs for a pair of boots.

Besides, Calistus Munbar, enchanted at having so ably conducted this delicate affair, took care that the quartette had nothing to wish for. It was impossible to imagine a more inexhaustibly obliging superintendent. He occupied a suite of rooms in the casino of which he had the chief management, and the company had taken care that the fittings and appointments were worthy of his magnificence and munificence. We would rather not say how much they cost.

The casino included lecture-rooms and recreation-rooms, but baccarat, trente et quarante, roulette, poker, and all other games of chance were strictly prohibited. Here was the smoke room from which was delivered direct to the houses the tobacco smoke prepared by a company recently established. The smoke of the tobacco burnt in the furnaces of this central establishment was purified and cleared of nicotine and distributed by pipes with amber mouthpieces to each subscriber. The subscribers had only to apply their lips and a meter registered the daily expense.

In this casino, where the dilettanti came to listen to the music from afar, to which the concerts of the quartette were now to be added, there were also the public collections of Milliard City. To the lovers of paintings, the gallery, rich in ancient and modern pictures, offered a number of masterpieces bought at extravagant prices, canvases of the Italian, Dutch, German and French schools which would make envious the collections of Paris, London, Munich, Rome and Florence. It had examples of Raffaelle, Da Vinci, Giorgione, Correggio, Domenichino, Ribeira, Murillo, Ruysdael, Rembrandt, Rubens, Cuyp, Frans Hals, Hobbema, Van Dyck, Holbein, etc., and also among the moderns, Fragonard, Ingres, Delacroix, Scheffer, Cabat, Delaroche, Regnaut, Couture, Meissonier, Millet, Rousseaux, Jules Dupré, Brascassat, Mackart, Turner, Troyon, Corot, Daubigny, Baudry, Bonnat, Carolus Duran, Jules Lefebvre, Vollon, Breton, Binet, You, Cabanel, etc. In order to make these pictures last for ever, they were placed in glass cases, from which the air was exhausted. It is worth mentioning that the impressionists, the intensists, the futurists had not yet encumbered this gallery, but doubtless that would occur in time, and Floating Island would not escape an invasion of this decadent pest. The museum also possessed statues of real value, marbles of the great sculptors ancient and modern, placed in the courts of the casino. Thanks to this climate being without rain or fog, groups, statues and busts could resist the attacks of the weather without injury.

That these marvels were often visited, that the nabobs of Milliard City had a very pronounced taste for the productions of art, that the artistic sense was very strongly developed amongst them, it would be hazardous to pretend. But it was noteworthy that the Starboardists included more amateurs than the Larboardists. All were, however, agreed when it was proposed to buy any masterpiece, and then their astonishing offers invariably obtained them from all the Dukes of Aumale, and all the Chauchards of the old and new continents.

The most frequented rooms in the casino were the reading-rooms devoted to the newspapers, and the European and American reviews brought by the regular service of steamers to Floating Island from Madeleine Bay. After being turned over, read and re-read, these reviews were placed on the shelves of the library with many thousand other works, the classification of which required the presence of a librarian at a salary of twenty-five thousand dollars, who had probably less to do than any of the other functionaries of the island. This library also contained a number of phonographic books which gave no trouble to read; all you had to do was to press a button and you heard the voice of some excellent reader aloud. For instance, there was the *Phèdre* of Racine read by M. Legouvé. As to the local journals, they were edited, composed and printed in the workshops of the casino under the direction of two editors-in-chief. One was the *Starboard Chronicle* for the Starboard section; the other the *New Herald* for the Larboard Section. The news consisted of the different events on the island, the arrival of the steamers, marine intelligence, ships sighted, the price lists of interest to the commercial quarters, the daily position of the island, the decision of the council of notables, the orders of the governor, the decrees of the civil power; births, marriages, deaths—the last very seldom; besides, there were never any robberies or murders, the courts only dealing with civil matters, actions between private persons. Never were there any articles on centenarians, longevity being no longer the privilege of the few.

For foreign intelligence the papers were indebted to the

daily telephonic communication with Madeleine Bay, whence started the cables submerged in the depths of the Pacific. The people of Milliard City were thus informed of all that passed all over the world, if there were sufficient interest in it. Let it be added that the *Starboard Chronicle* and the *New Herald* were on excellent terms with each other. Up till then they had existed in harmony, but there was no saying that their exchange of courteous discussions would last for ever. Tolerant and conciliatory in all religious matters, Protestantism and Catholicism worked very well together in Floating Island. It is true that if in the future some odious political matter became mixed up with religion, if questions of private interest and selfishness intervened—

Besides these daily high-priced journals, there were weekly and monthly reviews, reprinting the articles from foreign magazines, the articles of Sarcey, Lemaître, Fouquier, and other critics of eminence ; then there were magazines, illustrated or not, without counting half-a-dozen society papers devoted to current fashionable gossip. Their only object was to afford a little enjoyment to the mind—and to the stomach. Yes, some of these society pages were printed on edible pastry with chocolate ink. After they were read they were inwardly digested at the next breakfast. Some of them were astringent, some of them were gently purgative, and all proved very excellent eating. And we may here say that the quartette found this invention as agreeable as it was practical.

"These are lectures of easy digestion," observed Yvernès judiciously.

"Quite a nourishing literature," replied Pinchinat; "pastry and literature combined, that agrees perfectly with hygienic music ! "

Now it is natural to ask what resources the island possessed for maintaining its population in such conditions of welfare as no other city in the world approached. Its revenues must have amounted to a considerable sum, considering the expenditure under the different headings and the handsome salaries paid to its employed.

The quartette inquired of the superintendent concerning this.

" Here," he replied, " we do not bother about business. We have no Board of Trade, no Exchange, no export trade. The only commerce is that needed by the wants of the island, and we shall never offer strangers the equivalent of the World's Fair at Chicago in 1893, or the Paris Exposition of 1900. No! The mighty religion of business does not exist, and we never raise the cry of ' Go ahead ! ' unless it is for the Pearl of the Pacific to keep in front. It is not to trade we look for the needful revenue of Floating Island, but to the custom-house. Yes! our customs dues yield all we require for the exigencies of our budget."

" And this budget ? " asked Frascolin.

" Its total is twenty million dollars, my excellent friends ! "

" A hundred millions of francs ! " exclaimed the second violin, " and for a town of ten thousand souls."

" That is it, my dear Frascolin; and the amount is entirely provided by the customs dues. We have no octroi, the products of the island being almost insignificant. We have nothing but the dues levied at Starboard Harbour and Larboard Harbour. That explains the dearness of our articles of consumption—dearness which is relative, mind you, for the prices, high as they may appear to you, are in accordance with the means of those who pay them."

And hereupot Calistus Munbar started off again, boasting of his town, boasting of his island—in his eyes a fragment of a superior planet fallen into the Pacific, a floating Eden, in which the wise men had taken refuge, and if true happiness could not be found there, it could be found nowhere. It was a showman's speech! It seemed as though he said, " Walk up, gentlemen; walk up, ladies ! take your tickets, there are only a few places left. Who will take a ticket ? " etc., etc.

It is true that the places were few and the tickets dear. Bah ! The superintendent threw the millions about as if they were but units in this city of millionaires.

It was in the course of this tirade, in which the phrases poured forth in cascades, in which the gestures became accelerated with semaphoric frenzy, that the quartette were informed regarding the different branches of the administration. ,And first, the schools, in which the instruction was gratuitous and obligatory, and of which the professors were paid as if they were ministers. Here were taught the dead and living languages, history, geography, the physical and mathematical sciences, and the accomplishments more thoroughly than in any university or academy in the Old World—according to Calistus Munbar. The truth was that there was no great rush of pupils to these public schools, and if the present generation retained some traces of study in the colleges of the United States, the succeeding generation would have less learning than they had dividends.

Did not the inhabitants of this moving island travel in foreign parts ? Did they never visit the great capitals of Europe ? Did they not see the countries that had given them so many masterpieces of all kinds ? Yes ! There were a few whom a certain feeling of curiosity drove to these distant regions. But they found it fatiguing ; they grew weary of it for the most part ; they found there nothing of the uniformity of existence on Floating Island ; they suffered from heat, they suffered from cold ; in short they caught cold, and people never caught cold in Milliard City. Consequently they, the imprudent adventurers, who had had the unhappy idea to leave it, were only too glad and impatient to return to it. What good did they get from these travels ? None.

As to the foreigners who might be attracted by the fame of Floating Island, this ninth wonder of the world, the Eiffel Tower being at least the eighth, Calistus Munbar thought that they never would be very numerous. Of those who had come during the last year the majority had been Americans ; of other nations there were few or none. There had been a few English, recognizable by their curning their trousers up on the pretext that it was raining in London. Besides, Great Britain had looked with no friendly eye on the building of this artificial island, which provided another obstacle to navigation, and would have rejoiced at its disappearance. The Germans obtained but a very cool welcome, as if they would quickly have made Milliard City a new Chicago, once they had set foot in it. The French were of all foreigners those whom the Company would greet with most sympathy and attention, owing to their not belonging to the invading races of Europe. But had a Frenchman ever appeared on Floating Island ?

" That is not likely," said Pinchinat.

" We are not rich enough," added Frascolin.

" To live here, yes," replied the superintendent, " but not to be an official."

" Is there, then, one of our compatriots in Milliard City ? " asked Yvernès.

" There is one."

" And who is this privileged person ? "

" Monsieur Athanase Dorémus."

" And what is he doing here, this Athanase Dorémus ? " exclaimed Pinchinat.

" He is professor of dancing and deportment, with a handsome salary from the government, to say nothing of his income from private finishing lessons."

" Which a Frenchman is alone capable of giving ! " replied his Highness.

The quartette had thus become fairly well acquainted with the organization of the administrative life of Floating Island. They had now only to abandon themselves to the charm of this voyage which was taking them to the west of the Pacific. If it had not been for the sun rising sometimes over one part of the island and sometimes over another, according to the direction in which the island was moving, Sebastien Zorn and his comrades could have believed they were on firm ground. On two occasions during the fortnight that followed there had been a violent storm and gale, for there are always a few on the Pacific notwithstanding its name. The waves dashed up against the metal hull, and covered it with spray as if it was an ordinary shore. But Floating Island did not even groan under the assaults of the raging sea. The fury of the ocean was impotent against it. The genius of man had conquered nature.

On the 11th of June, a fortnight after their arrival, the quartette gave their first concert, the announcement, in electric letters, being exhibited along the larger avenues. It need hardly be said that the instrumentalists had been previously presented to the governor and the municipal council. Cyrus Bikerstaff had given them a most cordial' welcome. The newspapers had referred to the success of the tours of the Quartette Party in the United States of America, and warmly congratulated the superintendent on having secured their services—in rather an arbitrary manner, as we know. What pleasure there would be in seeing as well as hearing these artistes executing the works of the masters! What a treat for connoisseurs!

Although the four Parisians had been engaged for the casino at Milliard City at fabulous expense, do not let it be supposed that the concerts were to be free to the public. Far from that. The administration intended to make a large profit out of the affair, like the American impresarios whose singers cost them a dollar a bar, and even a dollar a note. It was customary to pay for the theatrophonic and phonographic concerts at the casino, and now the people must pay considerably more. The seats were all at the same price, two hundred dollars each—that is a thousand francs in French money—and the superintendent flattered himself that the room would be full.

He was not deceived. Every seat was taken. The comfortable and elegant room of the casino could only contain a hundred, it is true ; and if the seats had been put up to auction, there is no knowing what amount the receipts would have reached. But that would have been contrary to the usages of Floating Island. Everything with a market value appeared in the price lists the superfluous as well as the necessary. Without this precaution, owing to the enormous fortunes of some of the inhabitants, the whole supply might be bought up by one man, and this it was desirable to avoid. The rich Starboardites might, it is true, go to the concert for the love of the art, while the rich Larboardites might possibly go there because it was the fashion.

When Sebastien Zorn, Pinchinat, Yvernès, and Frascolin appeared before the spectators of New York, Chicago, Philadelphia, and Baltimore, it was no exaggeration on their part to say, "there is an audience worth millions." This evening they would have been within the truth in saying that their audience was worth hundreds of millions. Only think of it! Jem Tankerdon, Nat Coverley, and their families were conspicuous in the front row of seats. In other parts of the room, *passim*, were a number of amateurs, who, though only minor millionaires, had none the less "a heavy bag," as Pinchinat very justly remarked.

" Now then ! " said the chief of the quartette when the time came for them to appear on the platform.

And they took their places, not more excited than usual, nor even so much as if they were appearing before a Parisian public, which might have less money in their pockets but more of the artistic sense in their minds.

It is necessary to say that they had not yet taken lessons of their countryman, the professor of deportment. Sebastien Zorn, Yvernès, Frascolin, and Pinchinat were perfect as to their attire—white cravat at twenty-five francs, pearl-grey gloves at fifty francs, shirt at seventy francs, boots at a hundred and eighty francs, waistcoat at two hundred francs, black trousers at five hundred francs, black coats at fifteen hundred francs—all at the expense of the administration, be it understood. They were welcomed with applause or very warmly by the Starboardite hands, more discreetly by the Larboardite hands—a matter of temperament.

The programme of the concert comprised four items which they had obtained from the casino library, which was well supplied with works by the superintendent's care:

First quartette in E flat; Op. 12, Mendelssohn.
Second quartette in F major; Op. 16, Haydn.
Tenth quartette in E flat; Op. 74, Beethoven.
Fifth quartette in A major; Op. 10, Mozart.

The executants played marvellously in this millionized room of the floating island, on the surface of an abyss more than five thousand metres deep in this portion of the Pacific. They obtained a success that was considerable and deserved, more especially among the dilettanti of the Starboardite section. You should have seen the superintendent during this memorable evening. He exulted. It looked as though it was he who had just been playing on both violins, the alto, and the 'cello. What a fortunate first appearance for the champions of chamber music—and for their impresario!

It should be stated that if the room was full, the vicinity of the casino was crowded. What a number there were who had not been able to obtain a bracket-seat or a stall, to say nothing of those whom the high prices kept away. This outside audience heard the music from afar, as if it came from the box of a phonograph or the mouth of a telephone. But their applause was none the less hearty.

And they applauded uproariously when the concert ended, and Sebastien Zorn, Yvernès, Frascolin, and Pinchinat appeared on the terrace of the left-hand pavilion.

First Avenue was inundated with luminous rays. From the heights of space, the electric moons shed rays of which the pale Selene might well be jealous.

In front of the casino, on the footpath, a little apart from the others, a couple attracted the attention of Yvernès. A man was there, with a woman on his arm.

The man was above the middle height, of distinguished physiognomy, severe, sad even, and perhaps fifty years old. The woman was a few years younger, tall, proud-looking, with grey hair peeping from under her hat.

Yvernès, struck with their reserved attitude, pointed them out to Calistus Munbar.

"Who are those people?" he asked.

"Those people?" replied the superintendent, with a disdainful pout. "Oh! they are raving melomaniacs."

"And why did they not have a seat in the casino room?"

"Probably because it cost too much."

"Their fortune?"

"Hardly two hundred thousand francs a year."

"Pooh!" said Pinchinat. "And who are these poor beggars?"

"The King and Queen of Malecarlie."

CHAPTER VIII.

AFTER the construction of this extraordinary concern, the Floating Island Company had to provide for the requirements of a double organization, maritime on the one hand and administrative on the other.

The former, as we know, had as director, or rather captain, Commodore Ethel Simcoe, of the United States navy. He was a man of about fifty, an experienced navigator, thoroughly acquainted with every part of the Pacific, its currents, its storms, its reefs, its coralline shoals. Consequently he was fully qualified for the safe guidance of the floating island confided to his care, and the valuable lives for whom he was responsible to God and the shareholders of the company.

The second organization, that which comprised the various administrative services, was in the hands of the governor of the island. Mr. Cyrus Bikerstaff was a Yankee of Maine, one of the Federal States which took the least part in the fratricidal strife of the American confederation during the War of Secession. Cyrus Bikerstaff had been happily chosen to maintain a golden mean between the two sections of the island.

The governor, who was on the verge of sixty, was a bachelor. He was a man of much coolness and self-control, very strict, very energetic, notwithstanding his phlegmatic appearance, very English in his reserved attitude, his gentlemanly manners, the diplomatic discretion with which he spoke and acted. In any other country than Floating Island, he would have been a considerable man and consequently made much of. But here he was only the chief servant of the company, and though his salary exceeded the civil list of many a petty sovereign of Europe, he was not rich, and could not make much of a figure in the presence of the nabobs of Milliard City.

Cyrus Bikerstaff was not only governor of the island but mayor of the capital. As such he occupied the mansion at the end of First Avenue, facing the observatory where Commodore Simcoe had his residence. There were the public offices, there were received all the civil registrations, the births, with a mean rate assuring the future, the deaths—the dead were taken to the cemetery at Madeleine Bay—the marriages, which had to be celebrated by the civil authorities before the religious ceremonial, according to the code of Floating Island. There the different branches of the administration had their headquarters, and were worked without any complaint from the administered, a fact that did honour to the mayor and his staff. When Sebastien Zorn, Pinchinat, Yvernès and Frascolin were introduced to him by the superin-tendent, he made a very favourable impression on them, such as is produced by the individuality of a good and just man, of a practical turn of mind, who did not abandon himself to prejudices or chimeras.

" Gentlemen," he said to them, " it is very fortunate for us that we have got you. Perhaps the proceedings of our superintendent were not quite as they should have been. But you have forgiven him, I suppose. Besides, you will not have to complain of the way our municipality treats you. All it asks is two concerts a month, and you are free to accept any private engagements that may be offered you. We welcome you as musicians of great merit, and will never forget that you are the first artistes we have had the honour to welcome."

The quartette were delighted at this reception, and made no attempt to hide their satisfaction from Calistus Munbar.

"Yes! He is a nice man, Mr. Cyrus Bikerstaff,"

replied the superintendent, with a slight shrug of his shoulders. "It is a pity that he does not possess a million or two."

"We cannot be perfect," replied Pinchinat.

The governor-mayor of Milliard City had two assistants, who helped him in the very simple administration of Floating Island. Under their orders, a small number of employed, at suitable wages, were engaged in the different branches. There was no municipal council. What would be the use of it ? In its place was a council of notables— thirty of the men best qualified by their intelligence and their fortune. It met when any important measure was in contemplation—among others the choice of the itinerary which was to be followed in the interests of the general health. As far as our Parisians could see, there was frequently, in this respect, matter for discussion and difficulties to be settled. But thanks to his clever and judicious intervention, Cyrus Bikerstaff had always been able to conciliate opposing interests, and gratify the self-respect of those under his control.

One of his assistants, Barthelemy Ruge, was a Protestant, the other, Hubley Harcourt, was a Catholic, both of them chosen from among the high functionaries of the Floating Island Company, and both seconding Cyrus Bikerstaff with zeal and intelligence.

Thus had existed for eighteen months already, in the plenitude of its independence, free from all diplomatic connections, at liberty on this vast sea of the Pacific, sheltered from all unpleasant weather, beneath the skies of its choice, the island on which the quartette were to reside for a whole year. That they would be exposed to any adventures, that the future had in reserve for them anything unforeseen, it was not possible to imagine or to fear, for, as the 'cellist observed, everything on board was done with order and regularity. And yet, in creating this artificial domain, launched on the surface of the ocean, had not human genius exceeded the limits assigned to man by the Creator ?

The voyage continued towards the West. Every day when the sun passed the meridian the position was fixed by the officers of the observatory under the orders of Commodore Ethel Simcoe. Four dials on the lateral faces of the belfry of the town hall gave the exact position of the island in longitude and latitude, and these indications were reproduced telegraphically at the street corners, in the hotels, in the public buildings, in the private houses, in the same way as the time which changed every day as the island moved from west to east. The inhabitants of Milliard City were thus enabled to know at any moment what place on its itinerary Floating Island occupied.

With the exception of this insensible movement on the surface of the ocean, Milliard City differed in no respect from the capitals of the old and new Continents. The existence was the same. The same routine of public and private life. As they were not very busy, our instrumentalists employed their first leisure in visiting all that was curious in the Pearl of the Pacific. The trams took them towards all points of the island. The two factories of electrical energy evoked their sincere admiration by the simplicity of their machinery, the power of their engines driving a double series of screws, and the admirable discipline of their staff, the one directed by Engineer Watson, the other by Engineer Somwah. At regular intervals Larboard Harbour and Starboard Harbour received in their basins the steamers running to and from Floating Island, according as their position offered the easier access.

If the obstinate Sebastien Zorn refused to admire these marvels, if Frascolin was more reserved in his sentiments, in what a constant state of rapture was the enthusiastic Yvernès! In his opinion the twentieth century would not end before the seas were ploughed by floating towns. This would be the last word of progress and comfort in the future. What a superb spectacle was this moving island going to visit its sisters of Oceania. As to Pinchinat, amid these opulent surroundings, he was almost in-

toxicated at hearing the people talk of nothing but
millions, as they talk elsewhere of pounds. The bank-
notes were of the usual values. It was the custom to
carry two or three thousand dollars in the pocket. And
more than once his highness had said to Frascolin,—

"Old boy, you don't happen to have fifty thousand
francs about you, do you?"

Meanwhile the quartette party made many acquaintances,
being assured of an excellent welcome everywhere.
Besides, on the recommendation of the deafening Munbar,
who would not be eager to treat them well?

In the first place they went to visit their compatriot,
Athanase Dorémus, professor of dancing and deportment.

This good fellow occupied in the Starboard Section a
modest house in Twenty-Fifth Avenue, at three thousand
dollars a year rent. His servant was an old negress, at a
hundred dollars a month. He was enchanted to make the
acquaintance of Frenchmen—Frenchmen who did honour
to France.

He was an old man of seventy; thin, emaciated, short,
with a bright look, and all his teeth still perfect, as was his
abundant frizzly hair, which was white as his beard. He
walked sedately, with a certain rhythmic cadence, his chest
in advance, his stomach curved in, his arms rounded, his
feet a little turned out, and with irreproachable boots. Our
artistes took great pleasure in making him talk, and he was
quite willing, for his graciousness was equal to his
loquacity.

"I am delighted, my dear compatriots, I am delighted,"
he repeated twenty times at their first visit. "I am delighted
to see you! What an excellent idea it was of yours to
come and settle in this town. You will not regret it, for
now I have lived here, I do not know how it would be
possible to live in any other way."

"And how long have you been here, Monsieur Dorémus?" asked Yvernès.

"For eighteen months," replied the professor, bringing
his feet to the second position. "I am one of the first

comers on Floating Island. Thanks to the excellent
references I obtained at New Orleans, where I had established myself, my services were accepted by Mr. Cyrus
Bikerstaff, our adored governor. From that blessed day
the salary assigned me for managing a conservatoire of
dancing and deportment has permitted me to live—"

"Like a millionaire!" exclaimed Pinchinat.

"Oh! Millionaires here—"

"I know—I know—my dear compatriot. But from
what we have heard from the superintendent, the courses
of your conservatoire are not largely attended."

" The only pupils I have are all young men, the young
ladies thinking they are provided at birth with all the
necessary graces. And the young men prefer to take
their lessons in private, and it is in private that I teach
them good French manners!" And he smiled as he
spoke, simpering like an old coquette, and disposing himself in graceful attitudes.

Athanase Dorémus, a Picard of Santerre, had left France
in his early youth, and settled in the United States at New
Orleans. There among the French population of our
regretted Louisiana, opportunities did not fail him for
exercising the talents. Admitted into the principal families,
he achieved success, and had begun to save money, when
one of the most American of enterprises lifted him into
smooth water. This was at the time that the Floating
Island Company launched its project, scattering its pro-
spectuses far and wide, advertising itself lavishly in the
newspapers, appealing to all the ultra-rich who had made
their incalculable fortunes out of railways, petroleum wells,
and the pork trade, salt or otherwise. Athanase Dorémus
conceived the idea of asking for employment of the
governor of the new city in which professors of his kind
were not likely to be found. Favourably known in the
Coverley family, who were natives of New Orleans, he was
recommended by its chief, who was about to become one
of the most prominent notables of the Starboardites of
Milliard City, and thereupon accepted. That is how a

Frenchman, and even a Picard, became one of the function-aries of Floating Island.

It is true that his lessons were only given at his house, and the dancing-room at the casino saw nobody but the professor reflected in its mirrors. But what did that matter so long as the lack of pupils made no decrease in his salary?

In short, he was a good fellow, slightly ridiculous and crazy, perhaps, and infatuated with himself, persuaded that he possessed, with the heritage of the Vestrises and Saint Leons, the traditions of Brummel and Lord Seymour. In the eyes of the quartette he was a compatriot—a quality always appreciated when thousands of leagues from France.

He had to be told the later adventures of the four Parisians, under what circumstances they had arrived in the island, how Calistus Munbar had enticed them on board, and how the island had weighed anchor a few hours after they had embarked.

"I am not at all surprised at that, in our superinten-dent," replied the old professor. "That is quite in his style. He has done it, and will do it again with others. He is a true son of Barnum, and will end by getting the company into trouble. He is a free-and-easy gentleman who would be all the better for a few lessons in deport-ment, I assure you; one of those Yankees who see-saw in a chair with their legs on the window-sill. Not bad at the bottom, but thinking they can do what they like. But do not bear him any ill-will. Except for the unpleasantness of having broken your engagement at San Diego, you will have only to congratulate yourselves on your sojourn at Milliard City. People will have a high opinion of you, as you will find."

"Particularly at the end of each quarter!" replied Frascolin, whose functions as treasurer of the party began to be of exceptional importance.

To the question he was asked on the subject of the rivalry between the two sections of the island, Athanase Dorémus confirmed what Calistus Munbar had said. In

his opinion there was a cloud on the horizon, and even
the menace of an approaching storm. Between the Starboardites and Larboardites a conflict of interests and self-
esteem was to be feared. The families of Tankerdon and
Coverley, the richest in the place, were betraying increasing
jealousy towards each other, and this would probably produce an explosion, if some means of conciliation could not
be found. Yes. An explosion!

"Providing it does not explode in the island, we have
nothing to be anxious about them," observed Pinchinat.

"At least, so long as we are on board!" added the
'cellist.

"Oh! It is firm enough, my dear compatriots," replied
Athanase Dorémus. "For the eighteen months it has
been afloat, no accident of any importance has happened
to it. Nothing but a few insignificant repairs, which did
not even require it to return to Madeleine Bay. Just
think, it is made of plates of steel!"

That answered everything, and if plates of steel did not
give an absolute guarantee in this world, to what metal
could you trust?

Pinchinat was then led to ask what the professor thought
of Governor Cyrus Bikerstaff.

"Is he of steel also?"

"Yes, Monsieur Pinchinat," replied Athanase Dorémus,
"he is gifted with great energy, and is a most able administrator. Unfortunately, in Milliard City it is not enough
to be made of steel."

"You must be made of gold," retorted Yvernès.

"Just so; or if you are not, you are of no account!"

That was the case exactly. Cyrus Bikerstaff, notwith
standing his high position, was only a servant of the
company. He presided at the proceedings of the municipality, he had to receive the customs, to watch over the
public health, to keep the roads clean, to superintend the
plantations, to receive the revenue—in a word, to make
enemies on all sides. In Floating Island it was necessary
to be wealthy; Cyrus Bikerstaff was not wealthy.

In addition to this, his duties obliged him to maintain a conciliatory attitude between both parties, to risk nothing that might be agreeable to one that was not agreeable to the other. A policy that was not easy.

Already ideas were evidently getting about that might bring the two sections into conflict. If the Starboardites had settled on Floating Island solely with a view to peaceably enjoy their riches, the Larboardites began to hanker after business. They were asking why Floating Island should not be used as an immense merchant vessel and carry cargo to every part of Oceania, why all industries were forbidden in the island? In short, although they had been here less than two years, these Yankees, with Tankerdon at the head, were beginning to long to do a trade again. Although they had not stated this in so many words, Cyrus Bikerstaff could not help being anxious about it. He hoped, however, that the future would not grow worse, and that intestine dissension would not trouble an island made expressly for the tranquillity of its inhabitants.

In taking leave of Athanase Dorémus, the quartette promised to visit him again. As a rule, the professor went in the afternoon to the casino to which nobody came. There, not wishing to be accused of unpunctuality, he waited preparing his lessons before the looking-glasses in the room.

The island gradually moved to the westward, and a little towards the north-west, so as to touch at the Sandwich Islands. In the latitudes bordering on the torrid zone the temperature is already high, and the inhabitants of Milliard City would have found it almost unbearable had it not been for the cooling sea breeze. Fortunately, the nights are fresh, and even in the dog-days the trees and lawns watered with artificial rain retained their attractive verdure. Every day, at noon, the position shown on the dials of the town hall was telegraphed to the different quarters. On the 17th of June, Floating Island was in 155° longitude west and 27° latitude north, and approaching the tropics.

"You might say it was the sun which towed us," remarked Yvernès, " or if you like it more elegantly, that we have for our team the horses of the divine Apollo ! "

The observation was as appropriate as it was poetical, but Sebastien Zorn received it with a shrug of his shoulders. It did not suit him to be towed—against his will.

"Well," he would never cease repeating, " we shall see how this adventure will end."

The quartette generally went into the park every day at the fashionable hour. On horse, on foot, in their carriages, all the notables of Milliard City were to be met with around the lawns. The ladies of fashion here showed their third daily toilette, of one colour throughout, from the hat to the boots, and usually of Indian silk, which was very fashionable this year. Often, too, they wore artificial silk made of cellulose, in which there is such a play of colour ; or even imitation cotton, made of pine or larch-wood defibrized and disintegrated.

This provoked Pinchinat to remark, " You will see that one day they will make fabrics of ivy-wood for faithful friends, and weeping willow for inconsolable widows."

In any case, the wealthy Milliardites would not have worn these fabrics if they had not come from Paris, nor these dresses if they had not borne the name of the king of dressmakers—of him who haughtily proclaimed the axiom : " Woman is only a question of dress."

Sometimes the King and Queen of Malecarlie would pass among these smart gentry. The royal couple, deprived of their sovereignty, inspired our artistes with real sympathy. What reflections occurred to them at seeing these august personages arm-in-arm. They were relatively poor amid this wealthy crowd, but they were evidently proud and honourable, like philosophers withdrawn from the cares of this world. It is true that the Americans of Floating Island were at heart much flattered at having a king for one of their citizens, and treated him with the respect due to his former position. The quartette respect-fully saluted their Majesties when they met them in the avenues of the town or the footpath of the park. The king and queen showed that they much appreciated these marks of deference that were so French. But their Majesties were of no more account than Cyrus Bikerstaff —perhaps less.

In truth, travellers who were frightened at a sea-voyage might well adopt this kind of navigation on a moving island. Under such circumstances, there could not be any anxiety as to the accidents of the sea. There was nothing to fear from storms. With ten million horse-power on its flanks, a Floating Island could never be detained by calms, and would be powerful enough to make headway against contrary winds. If there were any danger from collisions, the danger was not to the island. So much the worse for the vessels that hurled themselves at full speed or under full sail against its sides of steel. But there was not much fear of such encounters, owing to the electric light of its aluminium moons with which the atmosphere was filled during the night. As to storms, they were not worth talking about. The island was large enough to put a bridle on the fury of the waves.

And when their walks brought Pinchinat and Frascolin to the bow or stern of the island, either to the Prow or Stern Battery, they were both of opinion that there was a want of capes, promontories, points, creeks, and beaches. The shore was but a breastwork of steel kept in place by millions of bolts and rivets. And how a painter would have regretted the absence of those old rocks, rough as an elephant's skin, which the surf caresses with seaweeds as the tide comes in. Decidedly, you do not replace the beauties of nature by the marvels of industry. In spite of his permanent admiration, Yvernès was forced to admit that the imprint of the Creator was wanting on this artificial island.

During the evening of the 25th of June Floating Island

crossed the tropic of Cancer and entered the Torrid Zone
of the Pacific. At this hour, the quartette were giving
their second performance in the casino. Kindly note
that owing to the success of their first appearance, the
price of stalls was now increased by a third.

No matter! The room was still too small. The
dilettanti struggled for places. Evidently this chamber
music should be excellent for health, and no one could
entertain a doubt as to its therapeutic qualities. Again
examples of Mozart, Beethoven, Haydn, as before.
Immense success for the performers to whom Parisian
bravos would certainly have given greater pleasure. But
in their absence, Yvernès, Frascolin, and Pinchinat knew
how to be contented with Milliardite hurrahs, for which
Sebastien Zorn continued to profess the most complete
disdain.

"What more can we wish for?" said Yvernès, when
they crossed the tropic of Cancer.

"The tropic of Concert!" replied Pinchinat, taking
safety in flight.

And when they came out of the casino, whom should
they see among the poor beggars who could not afford
three hundred and sixty dollars for a stall? The King
and Queen of Malecarlie standing humbly at the door.

CHAPTER IX.

THERE exists in this portion of the Pacific a submarine mountain range extending from the west-north-west to the east-south-east for nine hundred leagues, if the abysses of two thousand fathoms which separate it from the other ocean lands were emptied away. Of this chain but seven summits appear above the waters: Nirhau, Kauai, Oahu, Molokai, Lanai, Kahulaui, and Hawaii. These seven islands, of unequal size, constitute the Hawaiian Archipelago, otherwise known as the Sandwich Islands.

Leaving Sebastien Zorn to grumble in his corner, and shut himself up in his complete indifference to all natural curiosities as if he were a violoncello in its box, Pinchinat, Yvernès and Frascolin reasoned in this way, and they were not wrong in doing so.

" I shall not be sorry to visit these Sandwich Islands ! If we have to cruise about the Pacific, we may as well have a few souvenirs to take away with us."

" The natives will be a change to us after the Pawnees, Sioux and other too civilized Indians of the Far West, and I shall not be sorry to meet a few real savages—cannibals."

" Are they cannibals still ? "

" Let us hope so," replied Pinchinat. " Their grandfathers ate Captain Cook, and if the grandfathers enjoyed the illustrious navigator, it is not likely that the grandchildren have lost the taste for human flesh ! "

It must be confessed that his highness spoke rather irreverently of the celebrated English sailor who discovered this archipelago in 1778.

The result of this conversation was that our artistes hoped that the chances of the voyage would bring them into the presence of natives more authentic than the specimens exhibited in the *Jardin d'Acclimatation*, and in any case in their native country, instead of that of their production. They experienced a certain impatience to get there, expecting every day that the look-outs at the observatory would signal the first heights of the Hawaiian Group.

This they did in the morning of the 6th of July. The news immediately spread, and the placard at the casino bore this notice telautographically inscribed, " Sandwich Islands now in sight."

It is true that the islands were still fifty leagues away ; but the highest summits of the group, those of the island of Hawaii, are over 4200 metres high, and in fine weather are visible at this distance.

Coming from the north-east, Commodore Ethel Simcoe steered for Oahu, having for its capital Honolulu, which is also the capital of the archipelago. This island is the third of the group in latitude. Nuhau, which is a vast cattle park, and Kauai being both to the north-west of it. Oahu is not the largest of the Sandwich Islands ; it measures only 1680 square kilometres, while Hawaii has an area of nearly 17,000. As to the other islands, their area is more than 3812 all together.

As a matter of course, our Parisian artistes had formed agreeable acquaintanceships with the chief functionaries of Floating Island. All of them, as well as the Governor, the Commodore, Colonel Stewart and Engineers Somwah and Watson, had done their best to make them welcome. They frequently visited the observatory, and remained for hours on the platform of the tower. One need not be astonished therefore that on this occasion Yvernès and Pinchinat, the most enterprising of the quartette, had come here, and that about ten o'clock in the morning, the lift hoisted them to the masthead, as his highness called it.

Commodore Ethel Simcoe was there already, and lending the two friends his telescope, told them to observe a point on the horizon to the south-west among the lower mists of the sky.

"That is Mauna Loa of Hawaii," said he; "or it is Mauna Kea, two superb volcanoes which in 1852 and 1855 precipitated on to the island a flood of lava covering seven hundred square metres, and whose craters in 1880 hurled forth seven hundred million cubic metres of eruptive substances."

"Famous!" replied Yvernès. "Do you think, Commodore, that we shall have the good luck to see such a spectacle?"

"I do not know, Monsieur Yvernès," replied Ethel Simcoe. "Volcanoes do not erupt to order."

"Oh! on this occasion only, and under distinguished patronage!" added Pinchinat. "If I were rich like Messrs. Tankerdon and Coverley, I would pay for eruptions when I liked."

"Well, we will talk to them about it," said the Commodore, smiling, "and I have no doubt they will do even the impossible to make themselves agreeable to you."

Thereupon Pinchinat asked what was the population of the Sandwich Islands. The Commodore told him that it had been two hundred thousand at the beginning of the century, and was then reduced to about half.

"Good! Mr. Simcoe, a hundred thousand savages, that is quite enough, and if only they have remained cannibals, and lost nothing of their appetite, they will make only a mouthful of all the Milliardites of Floating Island."

It was not the first time that the island had visited this archipelago. The preceding year it had been in these waters attracted by the salubrity of the climate. And in fact invalids went there from America, sent by the doctors, as the doctors send Europeans to breathe the humid air of the Pacific? Why not? Honolulu is not more than twenty-five days from Paris, and when you can there impregnate your lungs with an oxygen you can get nowhere else—

Floating Island arrived within sight of the group in the morning of the 9th of July. The island of Oahu lay about five miles off to the south-west. Above, pointing to the east, was Diamond Head, an ancient volcano dominating the roadstead behind, and another cone called the Punch Bowl by the English. As the Commodore observed, if this enormous cup were filled with brandy or gin, John Bull could have no difficulty in emptying it.

They passed between Oahu and Molokai. Floating Island, like a ship under the action of its rudder, was steered by its starboard and larboard screws. The floating island stopped after rounding the south-east cape of Oahu, at ten cables' lengths from the shore, its draught of water being considerable. As it was necessary for the purpose of keeping a clear berth to remain at some distance from the land, it did not moor in the strict sense of the word, that is to say, it did not use anchors, which would have been impossible, owing to the depth of a hundred metres and more. By means of the engines, which were kept working during the stay, it lay as motionless as the eight principal islands of the Hawaiian Archipelago. The quartette contemplated the heights which developed before their eyes. In the distance they could see nothing but masses of trees—clumps of orange trees, and other magnificent specimens of the temperate flora. To the west, through a narrow break in the reef, appeared a little lake, the Lake of Pearls, a sort of lacustrine plain pierced with ancient craters.

The aspect of Oahu was smiling enough, and the anthropophagi so desired by Pinchinat had nothing to complain of the theatre of their exploits. If they still abandoned themselves to their cannibalistic instincts, his Highness could wish for nothing more.

But this is what he suddenly exclaimed,—

" Great Heaven! what is it I see? "

" What do you see? " asked Frascolin.

" There. Steeples—"

"Yes—and towers—and palace façades !" said Yvernès.
" It cannot be possible that they ate Captain Cook,
there ! "

"We are not at the Sandwiches !" said Sebastien Zorn,
shrugging his shoulders. "The Commodore has made a
mistake as to the route."

"Assuredly," replied Pinchinat. No! Commodore
Simcoe had not gone astray. It was really Oahu, and
the town extending over many square kilometres was
Honolulu.

Evidently the quartette were mistaken. What changes
there had been since the great English navigator discovered
this group ! Missionaries had excelled each other in devotion and zeal. Not only had the original language
disappeared before the Anglo-Saxon tongue, but the
archipelago contained Americans, Chinese—for the most
part employed by the owners of the soil, from whom had
arisen a race of semi-Chinese, the Hapa-Paké—and even
Portuguese, owing to the line of vessels between the
Sandwich Islands and the Azores. Aborigines were still
to be found, however, and enough of them to satisfy our
four artistes, although these natives had been decimated
by leprosy, a malady of Chinese importation. But they
were hardly of the type of eaters of human flesh.

"O local colour !" exclaimed the first violin, " what
hand has wiped thee from the modern palette ! "

Yes ! Time, civilization, progress, which is a law of
nature, had almost effaced this colour ; and this had to be
recognized, not without regret, when one of the electric
launches of Floating Island passed the long line of reefs
and put Sebastien Zorn and his comrades ashore.

Between two lines of piles meeting at an acute angle
opened the harbour sheltered from the dangerous winds
by an amphitheatre of mountains. Since 1794 the reefs
which protect it from the ocean waves had risen more than
a yard in height.

Nevertheless, tnere was sufficient water for vessels

drawing from eighteen to twenty feet of water to come alongside the quays.

"What a deception!" murmured Pinchinat. "It is really deplorable that we should have to get rid of so many illusions when we travel."

"And we would do much better to stay at home," retorted the 'cellist.

"No!" exclaimed Yvernès, always enthusiastic. "What spectacle can be compared to that of this artificial island coming to visit the oceanic archipelagoes?"

Nevertheless, if the moral condition of the Sandwich Islanders had regrettably changed to the lively displeasure of our artistes, it was not the same with the climate. It is one of the most salubrious in these parts of the Pacific, notwithstanding that the group is in a region known as the Hot Sea. If the thermometer does not stand at a high level when the north-east trade winds are not in force, if the northern trades cause violent storms known as kouas, the mean temperature of Honolulu does not exceed twenty-one degrees centigrade. It would be bad taste to complain of this on the borders of the torrid zone ; and the inhabitants did not complain of it, and, as we have indicated, American invalids crowded into the archipelago.

But the more the quartette penetrated into the secrets of this archipelago, the more their illusions fell, fell like the leaves at the end of autumn. They pretended to have been mystified when they should have accused themselves of inviting this mystification.

"It is this Cálistus Munbar who has again taken a rise out of us," said Pinchinat, remembering what the superintendent had told them as to the Sandwich Islands being the last rampart of native savagery in the Pacific. And when they bitterly reproached him,—

"What would you have, my dear friends?" he replied, with a wink of his right eye. "The place has changed so since my last voyage that I no longer recognize it."

"Joker!" retorted Pinchinat, amusing himself with a dig in the superintendent's stomach.

There could be no doubt that if changes had taken place, they must have occurred with extraordinary rapidity. The Sandwich Islands had rejoiced in a constitutional monarchy, founded in 1837, with two chambers, that of the nobles and that of the deputies. The first was nominated by the proprietors of the land, the second elected by all the people who knew how to read and write, the nobles for six years, the deputies for two years.

Each chamber was composed of twenty-four members, who held their deliberations together in the presence of the royal ministry, formed of four of the king's councillors.

"And then," said Yvernès, "they had a king, a constitutional king, instead of a monkey in feathers, and to whom foreigners could offer their humble respects."

"I am sure," affirmed Pinchinat, "that his Majesty did not even wear rings in his nose, and that he was provided with false teeth by the best dentists in the New World."

"Ah! civilization, civilization!" repeated the first violin. "These Kanakas had no need of false teeth when they ate their prisoners of war."

Floating Island was prepared for a stay of ten days, and a number of its inhabitants took advantage of this to explore Honolulu and its environs. The Coverley and Tankerdon families, the chief notables of Milliard City, went ashore daily. On the other hand, although it was the second appearance of the island in these parts of Hawaii, the admiration of the Hawaiians was boundless, and they came in crowds to visit this marvel. It is true that the policy of Cyrus Bikerstaff made the admission of strangers difficult, and required that when evening came the visitors returned at the stated hour. Owing to these measures of security it would have been anything but pleasant for an intruder to remain on the Pearl of the Pacific without a permit, which was not easily obtained. There were thus nothing but good relations on both sides, but there were no official receptions between the two islands.

The quartette enjoyed several very interesting walks. The natives pleased our Parisians. Their character is well marked, their hue brown, their physiognomy gentle and proud. And although the Hawaiians were a republic, it is not unlikely that they regretted their former savage independence.

"The air of our country is free," says one of their proverbs, and they are none the less so.

And in fact, after the conquest of the archipelago by Kamehameha, after the representative monarchy established in 1840, each island had been administered by its own governor. At this period, under the republican *régime*, they were divided into districts and sub-districts.

"Come," said Pinchinat, "there is no want of prefects, sub-prefects, and counsellors of prefecture, with the constitution of the Year VIII."

"All I want is to get away!" replied Sebastien Zorn.

He would have been mistaken to have done so without admiring the chief places of Oahu. They are superb, if the flora is not rich. Along the shore there is an abundance of cocoa-nut trees and other palms, breadfruit trees, trilobas which yield the oil, castor-oil plants, daturas, indigo plants. The valleys, watered by the mountain streams, are carpeted with such encroaching vegetation as menervia, shrubs becoming arborescent, chenopodium, and halapepe, a sort of gigantic asparigines. The forest zone, prolonged to an altitude of two thousand metres, is covered with ligneous species, myrtles of lofty growth, colossal docks, and band-creepers, which intermingle like a many-branched thicket of serpents. As to the products of the soil which furnish items of commerce and exportation, there are rice, cocoa-nuts, and sugar-cane. Hence an important coasting trade between one island and another, so as to concentrate at Honolulu the products which are despatched to America. In the fauna there is little variety. If there is a tendency for the Kanakas to become absorbed in the more intelligent races, the species of animals show no sign of change. There are only pigs, fowls, and goats as domestic animals; there are no wild animals beyond a few pigs. There are mosquitoes, which are not easy to get rid of, a number of scorpions, and a few species of inoffensive lizards; birds that never sing, among others the "Oo," the *Drepanis pacifica*, of black plumage, with ornamental yellow feathers, of which was formed the famous mantle of Kamehameha, on which nine generations of natives had worked.

Man's task—a considerable one in this archipelago—has been to become civilized in imitation of the United States with his learned societies, his schools of compulsory education, which gained a prize at the Exposition of 1878, his rich libraries, his newspapers published in English and Kanaka. Our Parisians could not well be surprised at this, for the notables of the archipelago are most of them Americans, and their language is as current as their money. Only these notables freely attract to their service the Chinese of the Celestial Empire, contrary to what is done in Western America, to combat the infliction to which has been given the significant name of the "Yellow Plague."

After the arrival of Floating Island within sight of the capital of Oahu, many of the local boats often sailed round it. With this magnificent weather, this sea so calm, nothing could be pleasanter than an excursion of some twenty kilometres at a cable's length from the steel shore, over which the custom-house officers exercised such strict surveillance.

Among these excursion boats one could not help noticing a small vessel which every day persisted in sailing in Floating Island waters. It was a kind of Malay ketch, with two masts and a square stern, manned by twelve men under the orders of a captain of energetic appearance. The Governor, however, took no objection to this, although the practice might have seemed suspicious. These people, in fact, kept a constant watch on the island all round it hanging about from one port to the other, examining through the glasses every part of the coast. After all, supposing that their intentions were unfriendly, what could such a crew undertake against a population of ten thousand inhabitants ? So that there was nothing to be uneasy about in the proceedings of this ketch during the day and night, and the maritime administration of Honolulu was not appealed to in the matter.

The quartette bade farewell to the island of Oahu on the morning of the 10th of July. Floating Island got under way at the dawn, obediently to the impulsion of its powerful propellers. Turning quite round, it headed south-west, to come in sight of the other Hawaiian islands. Moving obliquely across the equatorial current running from east to west, it moved in an inverse direction to that in which the archipelago lies towards the north.

For the convenience of the inhabitants on the larboard side, Floating Island boldly entered between the islands Molokai and Kauai. Over the latter, one of the smallest of the group, rises a volcano of eighteen hundred metres, Nirhau, which is always giving forth a few fuliginous vapours. At the foot are rounded hills of coralline formation, dominated by a range of sand-hills, against which the echoes are reflected with metallic sonority when the surf beats fiercely on the shore. The night had come when the island entered the narrow channel ; but there was nothing to fear under the command of Ethel Simcoe. When the sun disappeared behind the heights of Lanai, the look-outs could not have noticed the ketch, which left the harbour after Floating Island, and endeavoured to keep in its wake. Besides, as we may again remark, why should any one have been uneasy at the presence of this Malay vessel ?

Next day, when the sun reappeared, the ketch was only a white speck on the horizon.

During the day the voyage was continued between Kahulaui and Maui. Owing to its extent, the latter, with Lahaina for its capital, a harbour renowned for its whalers, occupies the second place in the Sandwich Archipelago.

Haleahala, "the house of the sun," rises three thousand metres towards the sky.

The two following days were spent in coasting along the shores of the Great Hawaii, whose mountains, as we have said, are the highest in the group. It was in the Bay of Kealakeacua that Captain Cook, after being received as a god by the natives, was massacred in 1779, a year after discovering the archipelago, to which he gave the name of Sandwich in honour of the celebrated Minister of Great Britain. Hilo, the chief place of the island, which is on the eastern coast, was not sighted ; but a view was obtained of Kailu on the western shore. Hawaii possesses fifty-seven kilometres of railway, used principally in the transport of goods, and the quartette could perceive the white smoke of its locomotives.

" It only wanted that ! " said Yvernès.

Next morning the Pearl of the Pacific had left these regions, and the ketch rounded the extreme point of Hawaii, dominated by Mauna Loa, the Great Mountain, whose summit is lost in the clouds at a height of twelve thousand feet.

" Come," said Pinchinat, " we have been cheated—really cheated ! "

" You are right, said Yvernès; " we ought to have been here a hundred years earlier. But then we should not have been brought here on this admirable Floating Island ! "

" No matter. Having found natives in waistcoats and turn-down collars, instead of savages in feathers, as that rascal Calistus promised us, I regret the days of Captain Cook ! "

" And if these cannibals had eaten your Highness ? " said Frascolin.

"Well, I should have died with the consolation of having once in my life been loved for myself alone ! "

CHAPTER X.

SINCE the 23rd of June the sun had been moving towards the southern hemisphere, and it had become necessary to leave these regions, wherein the bad season would soon exercise its ravages. As the star of day in its apparent course was nearing the equinoctial line, the island should cross the line in its track. Beyond were pleasant climates, where, in spite of the names of October, November, December, January, and February, the months were no less agreeable than those of the warm season. The distance which separates the Hawaiian Archipelago from the Marquesas Islands is about three thousand kilometres, and Floating Island, being in haste to accomplish it, was driven at maximum speed.

Polynesia properly so-called is comprised within that wide extent of ocean bounded on the north by the Equator, on the south by the tropic of Capricorn. In that five millions of square kilometres there are eleven groups, composed of two hundred and twenty islands, a land surface of ten thousand kilometres, of which the islets can be counted in thousands. These are the summits of submarine mountains, of which the chain runs from the north-west to the south-east, to the Marquesas and Pitcairn, throwing out almost parallel ramifications.

If, in imagination, this vast basin were suddenly emptied, what an extraordinary country would be displayed to view! What Switzerland, what Norway, what Tibet, could equal it in grandeur? Of these submarine mountains, volcanic for the most part, some of madreporic origin are formed of calcareous or corneous matter secreted in concentric beds by the polyps, those radiated animalcules of such simple organization, endowed with immense productive power. Of these islands, some—the youngest—have the mantle of vegetation only at their summit; the others, draped in vegetation from head to foot, are the most ancient, even where their origin is coralline. There exists then a wide mountainous region buried in the waters of the Pacific. Floating Island moved above the mountains as an aerostat over the peaks of the Alps or the Himalaya. Only it was not the air, but the water that bore her up.

And as large displacements of atmospheric waves exist across space, so there are liquid displacements on the surface of this ocean. The main current flows from east to west, and under its lower beds are two counter currents from June to October, when the sun moves towards the tropic of Cancer. Besides these, on the borders of Tahiti there are four tides, which neutralize each other in such a way as to be almost imperceptible. The climate of these different archipelagoes is essentially variable. The mountainous islands stop the clouds, which pour their showers down on to them; the lower islands are drier, owing to the mists being driven away by the prevailing winds.

It would have been strange if the casino library did not possess a few charts relative to the Pacific. It had a complete collection, and Frascolin, the most serious of the quartette, often consulted them. Yvernès preferred to abandon himself to the surprises of the voyage, to the admiration provoked in him by this moving island, and did not seek to bother his brain with geographical notions. Pinchinat only cared to take matters on their amusing or fantastic side. For Sebastien Zorn the itinerary mattered little, inasmuch as it was taking him where he had never intended to go.

Frascolin was the only one to work at this Polynesia, studying the principal groups that compose it, the Low

Islands, the Marquesas, Paumotu, the Society Islands, the Cook Islands, the Friendly Islands, Samoa, the Austral Islands, Wallis Island, Fanning Island, the Tokelau Islands, the Phœnix Islands, the Penrhyn Islands, Easter Island, Sala y Gomez, etc., etc. He knew then that in most of this archipelago, even those under protectorates, the government is always in the hands of powerful chiefs, whose influence is never disputed, and that the poorer classes are entirely subject to the rich. He knew also that the natives are of all religions, Brahmin, Mahometan, Protestant, Catholic, Catholic being preponderant in the islands dependent on France owing to the pomp of its services. He knew that the native language, of which the alphabet is simple enough, owing to its being composed of from thirteen to seventeen characters, is much mixed with English, and will be finally absorbed by the Anglo-Saxon. He knew, in short, that in a general way from an ethnic point of view the Polynesian population tends to decrease, which is regrettable, for the Kanaka type—a word which signifies a man—is whiter under the Equator than in the groups distant from the equinoctial line, and is magnificent, Polynesia losing much by its absorption by the foreign races. Yes! He knew that and many other things which he learnt in the course of his conversations with Commodore Ethel Simcoe, and when his comrades asked him he was not at all embarrassed at having to reply to them.

And so Pinchinat nicknamed him the Larousse of the tropical zone.

Such were the principal groups amid which Floating Island was to bear its wealthy population. It justly deserved its name of the happy island, for in a certain way it offered all that could promote happiness. Why was it that this state of things was in danger of being troubled by the rivalries, the jealousies, the disagreements, by questions of influence and precedence which divided Milliard City into two camps, as it were into two sections— the camp of the Tankerdons and the camp of the Coverleys ? In any case, for the artistes who were quite dis-interested in the matter, the struggle promised to be interesting.

Jem Tankerdon was Yankee from his head to his feet, big in build, with a reddish goatee, lank hair, eyes bright in spite of his sixty years, the iris almost yellow like that of a dog's eye, the pupil glowing. He was tall in stature, powerful in the body, strong in the limbs. He was the trapper of the prairies, although the only traps he had set were those into which he had precipitated the millions of pigs in his slaughter-houses at Chicago. He was a violent man, whose position ought to have made him more care-ful, had not his early education been defective. He liked to show off his fortune, and, as people say, he had noisy pockets. And it seemed that he did not find them full enough, for he and a few others on the island were thinking of returning to business.

Mrs. Tankerdon was an American, a fairly good wife, very submissive to her husband, an excellent mother, gentle to her children, predestined to bring up a numerous family, and having in no way failed to fulfil her functions. If there were several millions to be shared amongst the direct heirs, why should there not be a dozen in the world ? And there were.

Of the whole family the attention of the quartette was directed only to the eldest son, who is destined to play a certain part in this history. Walter Tankerdon, most elegant in his person, of moderate intelligence, of pleasing manners and face, taking more after Mrs. Tankerdon than after the head of the family. Fairly well educated, having travelled in America and Europe, but recalled by his habits and tastes to the attractive life on Floating Island, he was familiar with every branch of sport, and the best player in the island at tennis, polo, golf and cricket. He was not too proud of the fortune which would be his some day, and he was a good-hearted fellow ; but as there were no poor in the island, he had no opportunity of being charitable. In short, it was to be desired that his brothers and sisters would resemble him. If these were not yet old enough to marry, he, who was nearly thirty, might think of doing so. Did he? We will see.

There existed a striking contrast between the Tankerdon family, the most important of the Larboard Section, and the Coverley family, the most considerable in the Starboard Section. Nat Coverley was of a much finer nature than his rival. That was due to the French origin of his ancestors. His fortune had not come from the entrails of the soil in the form of petroleum lakes, nor from the smoking entrails of the porcine race. No! It was industrial enterprises, railways and banking, which had made him what he was. All he wanted was to enjoy his wealth in peace, and—he made no secret of it—he would oppose to the utmost every attempt to transform the Pearl of the Pacific into an enormous workshop or an immense house of business.

Tall, well set up, his fine head grey-haired, wearing all his beard, the chestnut of which was streaked with a few silver threads. Somewhat cold in character, of distinguished manners, he occupied the first rank among the notables who in Milliard City kept up the traditions of good society in the Southern States. He loved the arts, understood painting and music, spoke easily the French language, which was much in use among the Starboardites, kept himself abreast of American and European literature, and when opportunity offered applauded in bravos and bravas which the ruder types of New England and the Far West applauded in hurrahs and hips.

Mrs. Coverley was ten years younger than her husband, and had just turned forty. She was an elegant, distinguished woman, belonging to one of the old demi-Creole families of Louisiana, a good musician, a good pianist, and it is not to be believed that a Reyer of the twentieth century would have proscribed the piano in Milliard City. In her house in Fifteenth Avenue the quartette had many an occasion to perform with her assistance, and they could but congratulate her on her artistic talents.

Heaven had not blessed the Coverleys as it had blessed the Tankerdons. Three daughters were the heiresses of an immense fortune, which Coverley did not brag about as his rival did. They were good-looking enough, and would find suitors enough among the nobility or the wealthy when the time came for them to marry. In America these remarkable dowries are not rare. A few years ago did we not hear of little Miss Terry, who, at the age of two years, was being sought for her 30,000,000*l.*? Let us hope that each girl would marry to her taste, and that to the advantage of being among the richest women in the States they would add that of being among the happiest.

Diana, or rather Di, as she was familiarly called, the eldest daughter of Mr. and Mrs. Coverley, was barely twenty. She was a very pretty girl, and possessed the physical and mental qualities of her father and mother. Beautiful blue eyes, magnificent hair, between chestnut and blonde, a colour fresh as the petals of the rose newly opened, an elegant and graceful figure, explained why Miss Coverley was the admired of the young men of Milliard City, who would probably not leave to strangers the task of winning this "inestimable treasure," as she might well be called in terms of mathematical accuracy. There was reason for supposing that Mr. Coverley would not see in difference of religion an obstacle to a union which seemed to assure the happiness of his daughter.

In truth, it was regrettable that questions of social rivalry separated the two leading families of Floating Island. Walter Tankerdon seemed to have been specially created to become the husband of Di Coverley.

But that was a combination not to be thought of. Rather cut the island in two, and let the Larboardites float away on one half, and the Starboardites on the other, than sign such a marriage contract.

"Providing that love does not enter into the matter!" said the superintendent, winking his eye behind his gold eye-glasses.

But it did not seem that Walter Tankerdon had any fancy for Di Coverley, and inversely—or at least if it were so, they both maintained a reserve which deceived the curious of the select world of Milliard City.

The island continued to descend towards the Equator, along the hundred and sixtieth meridian. Ahead of it extended that portion of the Pacific which offers the widest expanses destitute of islands and islets, and the depth of which reaches two leagues. During the 25th of July they passed over the basin of Belknap, an abyss of six thousand metres, from which the sounding apparatus brought up those curious molluscs or zoophytes, constituted in such a way as to support with impunity the pressure of masses of water estimated at six hundred atmospheres.

Five days afterwards Floating Island traversed a group of islands belonging to England, although they are occasionally called the American Islands. Leaving Palmyra and Samarang to starboard, it approached within two miles of Fanning, one of the numerous guano islands in these parts, the most important of the archipelago. The others are but emerged peaks, more barren than verdant, of which the United Kingdom has not made much up to now. But she has put her foot down in this place, and we know that the large foot of England generally leaves ineffaceable impressions.

Every day, while his comrades walked in the park or in the surrounding country, Frascolin, much interested by the details of this curious voyage, went to the Prow Battery. There he often met the Commodore. Ethel Simcoe gladly talked to him about the phenomena peculiar to these seas, and when they were of interest, the second violin did not omit to communicate them to his companions.

For instance, they could not restrain their admiration in presence of a spectacle which Nature gratuitously offered them during the night of the 30th of July.

An immense shoal of jelly-fish, covering several square

miles, had been signalled during the afternoon. Never
before had the islanders met with such masses of these
medusæ, to which certain naturalists have given the name
of oceanians. These animals, of very rudimentary organization, approach in their hemispherical form to the products
of the vegetable kingdom. The fish, greedy as they may
be, treat them as flowers, for none, it seems, feed on them.
The oceanians peculiar to the torrid zone of the Pacific
are of the shape of many-coloured umbrellas, transparent,
and bordered with tentacles. They do not measure more
than an inch or so; judge then of the milliards required to
form a shoal of such extent.

And when these numbers were mentioned in presence
of Pinchinat:

"They could not," remarked his Highness, "surprise
these notables of Floating Island, for the milliard is the
current coin."

At nightfall, many of the people went out to the fore-
castle, that is to say the terrace which looked down on
Prow Battery. The trams were invaded; the electric cars
were loaded with sight-seers. Elegant carriages conveyed
the leading nabobs. The Coverleys and the Tankerdons
elbowed each other at a distance. Mr. Jem did not salute
Mr. Nat, who did not salute Mr. Jem. The families were
fully represented. Yvernès and Pinchinat had the pleasure
of talking with Mrs. Coverley and her daughter, who
always gave them a hearty welcome. Perhaps Walter
Tankerdon felt a little annoyance at not being able to join
in the conversation, and perhaps also Miss Di would not
have been averse to his doing so. But what a scandal
that would have caused, and what allusions more or less
indiscreet on the part of the *Starboard Chronicle* or the
New Herald in their society article!

When the darkness is complete as far as it can be in
these tropical starlight nights, the Pacific seems to sleep
in its deepest depths. The immense mass of water is
impregnated with phosphorescent lights, illuminated by
rosy and blue reflections. not only in well marked luminous

lines along the crests of the waves, but as if the light were shed from innumerable legions of gleaming worms. This phosphorescence becomes so intense that it is possible to read by it as by the radiation of a distant aurora. It seems as if the Pacific dissolved the sunshine during the day and emitted it at night in luminous waves.

When the prow of Floating Island cut into the mass of medusæ, it divided it into two branches along its metal shore. In a few hours the island was girt by a belt of phosphorescent light. It was as it were an aureole, one of those glories of the middle ages which surround the heads of the saints. The phenomenon lasted until the birth of the dawn, the first hues of which extinguished it.

Six days afterwards the Pearl of the Pacific touched the imaginary great circle of our spheroid which cuts the horizon into equal parts. From it the poles of the celestial sphere could be simultaneously seen, the one in the north illuminated by the scintillations of the Pole Star, the other in the south decorated like a soldier's breast with the Southern Cross. From the different points on this equatorial line the stars appeared to describe circles perpendicular to the plane of the horizon. If you would enjoy nights and days of equal length, it is in these regions or in continents and islands traversed by the Equator that you should make your home.

It was the second time since its creation that Floating Island had passed from one hemisphere to another, crossing the equinoctial line, first in descending towards the south, then in ascending towards the north. The occasion of this passage was kept as a holiday. There would be public games in the park, religious ceremonies in the temple and cathedral, races of electric vehicles round the island. From the platform of the observatory there would be a magnificent display of fireworks, from which the rockets and serpents and Roman candles would rival the splendours of the stars of the firmament.

This, as you may have guessed, was in imitation of the fantastic scenes customary on ships when they cross the

Equator, a pendant to the baptism of the line.   And, as a
fact, this day was always chosen for the baptism of the
children born since the departure from Madeleine Bay, and
there was a similar baptismal ceremony with regard to
the strangers who had not before entered the southern
hemisphere.

"It will be our turn then," said Frascolin to his comrades,
"and we are going to receive baptism."

"Fancy!" replied Sebastien Zorn, with protesting gestures of indignation.

"Yes, my old bass scraper!" replied Pinchinat.   "They
will throw unblessed buckets of water on our head, seat
us on planks that see-saw, pitch us into surprise depths,
and Father Neptune will come on board with his company of buffoons to shave our faces with the black grease
pot."

"If they think," said Zorn, "that I will submit to this
masquerade—"

"We shall have to," said Yvernès.   "Every country has
its customs, and the guests must submit."

"Not when they are detained against their will!" said
the intractable chief of the quartette party.

He need not have excited himself about this carnival
with which many crews amuse themselves when crossing
the line!   He need have had no fear of Father Neptune!
He and his comrades would not be sprinkled with sea
water, but with champagne of the best brands.   They
would not be hoaxed by being shown the Equator previously drawn on the object glass of a telescope.   That
might do for sailors on board ship, but not for the serious
people of Floating Island.

The festival took place in the afternoon of the 5th of August.
With the exception of the custom-house officers, who were
never allowed to leave their posts, the State servants all
had a holiday.   All work was suspended in the town and
harbours.   The screws did not work.   The accumulators
possessed a voltage sufficient for the lighting and communications.   The island was not stationary, but drifted with

the current towards the line which divides the two hemi-
spheres of the globe. Chants and prayers were heard in
the churches, in the temple as at St. Mary's church, and
the organs played cheerily. Great rejoicings took place in
the park, where the sporting events were brought off with
remarkable enthusiasm. The different classes associated
together. The richest gentlemen, with Walter Tankerdon
at their head, did wonders at golf and tennis. When the
sun had dropped perpendicularly below the horizon,
leaving a twilight of only forty-eight minutes, the rockets
would take their flight across space, and a moonless night
would give the best of conditions for the display of
firework magnificence.

In the large room of the casino the quartette were bap-
tized, as we have said, and by the hand of Cyrus Bikerstaff.
The Governor offered them a foaming tankard, and the
champagne flowed in torrents. The artistes had their
full share of Cliquot and Roederer. Sebastien Zorn could
not have the bad taste to complain of a baptism which in
no way reminded him of the salt water he had imbibed in
the earliest days of his life.

To these testimonies of sympathy the quartette responded
by the execution of the finest works in their repertory :
the seventh quartette in F major, op. 59 of Beethoven ; the
fourth quartette in E flat, op. 10 of Mozart ; the fourth
quartette in D minor, op. 17 of Haydn ; the seventh quartette (andante, scherzo, capriccioso, and fugue), op. 18 of
Mendelssohn. Yes, all these marvels of concerted music,
and there was no charge for hearing them ! The crush at
the doors was tremendous, and the room was suffocating.
The pieces were encored and encored again, and the
Governor presented to the executants a medal in gold
encircled with diamonds respectable in the number of their
carats, having on one face the arms of Milliard City, and
on the other—

Presented to the Quartette Party
By the Company, the Municipality, and the People
of Floating Island.

And if all these honours did not reach to the very depths of the soul of the irreconcilable violoncellist, it was decidedly because he was a deplorable character, as his comrades told him.

" Wait for the end ! " he was content to reply, twisting his beard with a feverish hand.

It was at thirty-five minutes past ten in the evening— the calculation was made by the astronomers of Floating Island—that the line would be crossed. At that precise moment a salute would be fired from one of the cannon in the Prow Battery. A wire connected this gun with an electric apparatus arranged in the centre of the square of the observatory. Extraordinary satisfaction of self-esteem for the notable on whom devolved the honour of sending the current which would provoke the formidable detonation !

On this occasion the honour was sought by two important personages. These were, as may be guessed, Jem Tankerdon and Nat Coverley. Consequently, considerable embarrassment for Cyrus Bikerstaff. Difficult negotiations had been taking place between the town hall and the two sections of the city. No agreement had been arrived at. At the Governor's invitation, the services of Calistus Munbar had been called in. Despite his well-known diplomatic adroitness, he had failed. Jem Tankerdon would not give way to Nat Coverley, who would not give way to Jem Tankerdon. An explosion was expected.

It did not promise to be long in coming when the two chiefs met in the square. The apparatus was but five paces away from them. They had but to touch the button.

Aware of the difficulty, the crowd, much interested in this question of precedence, had invaded the garden. After the concert, Sebastien Zorn, Yvernès, Frascolin, and Pinchinat had come to the square, curious to observe the phases of this rivalry, which, considering the dispositions of the Larboardites and Starboardites, was of exceptional gravity for the future.

The two notables advanced towards the apparatus, without the slightest inclination of the head.

"I think, sir," said Jem Tankerdon, "that you will not contest this honour."

"That is exactly what I expect from you, sir," replied Nat Coverley.

"I shall not allow any one to deprive me of it."

"Nor shall I allow any one to deprive me of it."

"We shall see, then!" said Jem Tankerdon, taking a step towards the instrument.

Nat Coverley also took a step. The partisans of the two notables began to mingle. Ill-sounding provocations broke out in the ranks. Doubtless Walter Tankerdon was ready to maintain the rights of his father; but when he caught sight of Miss Coverley standing a little way off, he was visibly embarrassed.

As to the Governor, although the superintendent was at his side, ready to act as buffer, he was in intense distress at not being able to unite in a single bouquet the white rose of York and the red rose of Lancaster. And who knows if this deplorable competition might not have consequences as regrettable as the roses had in the fifteenth century for the English aristocracy?

But the moment was approaching when the prow of Floating Island would cut the equinoctial line. Calculated precisely to a quarter of a second of time, the error could not be greater than eight metres. The signal would soon be sent from the observatory.

"I have an idea," murmured Pinchinat.

"What?" asked Yvernès.

"I will give a whack on the instrument, and that will put matters right."

"Don't do that!" said Frascolin, stopping his Highness with a vigorous grip.

No one knew how the matter would have ended if a detonation had not suddenly taken place.

The report was certainly not from the Prow Battery. It came from a gun out at sea, which had been heard distinctly.

The crowd paused in suspense. What could be the

meaning of this discharge of a gun which did not belong to the island's artillery ?

A telegram from Starboard Harbour almost immediately gave the explanation.

Two or three miles off, a ship in distress had signalled its presence and demanded assistance.

Fortunate and unexpected diversion ! There was no more thought of touching the button nor saluting the crossing of the Equator. There was no time. The Equator was crossed, and the charge remained in the cannon. All the better for the honour of the Tankerdons and Coverleys.

The public evacuated the square, and, as the trams were not working, proceeded rapidly on foot to Starboard Harbour.

Immediately the signal had been heard, the harbour master had taken measures for the rescue. One of the electric launches moored in the wet dock had gone out. And at the moment the crowd arrived, the launch had brought back the crew from the ship, which had soon afterwards foundered in the Pacific.

The ship was the Malay ketch which had followed Floating Island since its departure from the Sandwich Archipelago.

CHAPTER XI.

In the morning of the 29th of August, the Pearl of the Pacific reached the Marquesas Islands, lying between 7° 55' and 10° 30' south latitude, and 141° and 143° 6' longitude west of the meridian of Paris. It had traversed a distance of three thousand four hundred kilometres since leaving the Sandwich group.

If this group is called after Mendana, it is because the Spaniard of that name discovered its southern portion in 1595. If it is called Revolution Islands, it is because it was visited by Captain Marchand in 1791, in its north-western part. If it is called the Nuka Hiva Archipelago, it is because that is the name of the largest island in it. And yet, as a matter of justice, it ought to bear the name of Cook, for that celebrated navigator surveyed it in 1774.

This was what Commodore Ethel Simcoe remarked to Frascolin, who thought the observation very reasonable, adding,—

"We might also call it the French Archipelago, for we are not without a few marquises in France."

In fact, a Frenchman has the right to regard this group of eleven islands or islets as one of his country's squadrons moored in the waters of the Pacific. The largest are vessels of the first class, Nuka-Hiva and Hiva-Oa; the moderate ones are cruisers of different ranks, Hiavu, Uapvu, Uahuka; the little ones are despatch boats, Motane, Fatu-Hiva, Taou-Ata; while the islets and atolls will do for the launches and boats. It is true, these islands could not move about like Floating Island.

It was on the 1st of May, 1842, that the Commander of

the naval station of the Pacific, Vice-Admiral Dupetit-Thouars, took possession of this archipelago in the name of France. It is separated by from a thousand to two thousand leagues from the coast of America, New Zealand, Australia, China, the Moluccas, and the Philippines. Under these conditions, was the act of the Vice-Admiral to be praised or blamed ? He was blamed by the Opposition and praised by the Government. It is none the less true that France has there an insular domain where its whaling vessels can shelter and re-victual, and to which the Panama Canal, if it is ever open, will give very considerable commercial importance. This domain should be completed by the taking possession or declaration of a protectorate over the Paumotu Islands and the Society Islands, which form its natural prolongation. As British influence extends over the north-western regions of this immense ocean, it is good that French influence should counterbalance it in the regions of the south-east.

"But," asked Frascolin of his complaisant cicerone, "have we military forces there of any strength ?"

"Up to 1859," replied the Commodore, "there was a detachment at Nuka-Hiva. Since the detachment has been withdrawn the care of the flag has been confided to the missionaries, and they will not leave it undefended."

"And now ?"

"You will only find at Taio-Hae a resident, a few gendarmes, and native soldiers, under the orders of an officer who fulfils the functions of a justice of the peace."

"In the native law-suits ?"

"For the natives and the colonists."

"Then there are colonists at Nuka-Hiva ?"

"Yes ; twenty-four."

"Not enough to form an orchestra, Commodore, nor even a harmony, and hardly a fanfare !"

The archipelago of the Marquesas extends over a hundred and ninety-five miles in length and forty-eight miles in width, covering an area of thirteen thousand superficial kilometres, and its population consists of twenty-four thousand natives. That gives one colonist to each thousand inhabitants.

Is this population destined to increase when a new route of communication is made through the two Americas? The future will show. But as far as concerns the population of Floating Island, the number of its inhabitants had been increased several days before by the rescue of the Malays of the ketch, which took place in the evening of the 5th of August.

They were ten in number, in addition to their captain, a man of energetic face and figure. This captain was about forty years of age, and his name was Sarol. His sailors were stoutly-built fellows of the Malay race, natives of the furthest islands of Western Malaysia. Three months before Sarol had brought them to Honolulu with a cargo of coprah. When Floating Island had come to stay there for ten days, its appearance had excited their surprise, as it excited surprise in every archipelago it visited. If they did not visit it, permission to do so being very difficult to obtain, it will not be forgotten how their ketch was often at sea observing it at close quarters, and coasting along it within half a cable's length of its perimeter.

The continual presence of this vessel had excited no suspicion, and neither did its departure from Honolulu a few hours after Commodore Simcoe. Besides, what was there to be uneasy about in this vessel of a hundred tons with not a dozen men on board?

When the report of the gun attracted the attention of the officer at Starboard Harbour, the ketch was within two or three miles. The launch was fortunate enough to bring off the captain and his crew.

These Malays spoke English fluently, in which there was nothing astonishing on the part of natives of the Western Pacific, where, as we have mentioned, British preponderance is unquestioned. They could thus describe the circumstances of their being in distress, and tell how they would have been lost in the depths of the ocean if the launch had been a few minutes later.

According to these men, twenty-four hours before, during the night of the 4th of August, the ketch had been run into by a steamer at full speed. Although his lights were all showing, Captain Sarol had not been noticed. The collision had been so slight for the steamer that she seemed to feel nothing of it, and continued her voyage, unless—which is, unfortunately, not too rare—she had gone off at full speed " to avoid costly and disagreeable claims."

But the blow, insignificant for a vessel of heavy tonnage with her iron hull driven at considerable speed, was terrible for the Malay vessel. Cut down just before the mizen mast, it was hardly intelligible that she did not immediately sink. She remained, however, at the water level, the men clinging on to the deck. If the weather had been bad the wreck could not have resisted the waves. By good luck the current took them towards the east, and they arrived within sight of Floating Island.

At the same time, when the Commodore questioned Captain Sarol he could not help manifesting his astonishment that the ketch, half submerged, had been able to drift within sight of Starboard Harbour.

"Neither do I understand it," replied the Malay. " Your island cannot have moved very far during the last twenty-four hours."

"That is the only explanation possible," replied Commodore Simcoe. "It does not matter after all, we have been able to rescue you, that is the main point."

It was true. Before the launch had got a quarter of a mile away the ketch had gone down head foremost.

Such was the story Captain Sarol told to the officer who had rescued him, then to the Commodore, then to the Governor, Cyrus Bickerstaff, after he had been given all the assistance that he and his crew seemed to be in urgent need of.

Then arose the question as to sending these men home. They were bound for the New Hebrides when the collision occurred. Floating Island was going south-east, and could not change its route. Cyrus Bikerstaff proposed

to put the captain and his men ashore at Nuka-Hiva,
where they could wait for a merchant ship bound for the
New Hebrides.

The captain and his men looked at one another. They
seemed greatly distressed. This proposal was hard on
poor fellows, without resources, despoiled of all they possessed with the ketch and its cargo. To wait at the
Marquesas was to chance having to wait an interminable
time, and how would they get a living?

"Mr. Governor," said the captain in a suppliant tone,
"you have rescued us, and we don't know how to show our
gratitude. But yet we beg you will assure our return
under better circumstances."

"And in what manner?" asked Cyrus Bikerstaff.

"At Honolulu it was said that Floating Island after
going south was to visit the Marquesas, Paumotu, the
Society Islands, and then make for the west of the
Pacific."

"That is true," said the Governor, "and very probably
we shall get as far as the Fijis before returning to Madeleine Bay."

"The Fijis," continued the captain, "are an English
archipelago, where we should easily find a ship to take us
to the New Hebrides, which are not far off, and if you
could keep us until then—"

"I cannot promise you anything with regard to that,"
said the Governor. "We are forbidden to give passages
to foreigners. You must wait till we reach Nuka-Hiva.
I will consult the administration by cable, and if they consent we will take you on to Fiji, whence you could get
home more easily."

That is the reason why the Malays were on Floating
Island when it came within sight of the Marquesas on the
29th of August.

This archipelago is situated in the belt of the trade winds,
as are also the Paumotu and Society Islands, which owe
to these winds a moderate temperature and a salubrious
climate.

It was off the north-west of this group that Commodore Simcoe appeared in the early hours of the morning. He first sighted a sandy atoll which the maps called Coral Islet, and against which the sea, driven by the currents, beats with extreme violence.

This atoll being left to port, the look-outs now signalled the first island, Fetuhuhu, very steep, surrounded by perpendicular cliffs four hundred metres in height. Beyond is Hiau, six hundred metres high, of a barren aspect on this side, while on the other it is fresh and verdant, and has two creeks practicable for small vessels.

Frascolin, Yvernès, and Pinchinat, leaving Sebastien Zorn to his chronic ill-humour, took their places on the tower, in company with Ethel Simcoe and several of his officers.

One need not be astonished that this name of Hiau had excited his Highness to emit several strange onomatopes.

"Assuredly," said he, "it is a colony of cats which inhabits that island with a tom for chief."

Hiau was left to port. There was no intention of stopping there, and the course was continued towards the principal island of the group, to which it had given its name, and which was now to be temporarily increased by this extraordinary Floating Island.

Next morning, that of the 30th of August, at daybreak our Parisians returned to their port. The heights of Nuka-Hiva had been visible the evening before. In fine weather the mountain chains of this archipelago can be seen from a distance of eighteen or twenty leagues, for the altitude of certain summits exceeds twelve hundred metres, and they lie like a gigantic backbone along the length of the islands.

"You will notice," said the Commodore to his guests, "a peculiarity common to all this archipelago. The summits are singularly bare, and the vegetation which begins about two-thirds up the mountain slopes penetrates to the very bottom of the ravines and gorges, and spreads magnificently down to the white beaches of the coast."

"And yet," said Frascolin, "it seems that Nuka-Hiva is an exception to the general rule, at least as regards the verdure of the intermediate zones. It appears barren!"

"Because we are approaching it from the north-west," said the Commodore, "but when we turn at the south, you will be surprised at the contrast. Everywhere, verdant plains, forests, cascades of three hundred metres."

"Eh!" exclaimed Pinchinat, "a mass of water falling from the top of the Eiffel Tower, that is worth considering! Niagara should be jealous."

"Not at all," said Frascolin, "it prides itself on its width, and its fall extends for nine hundred metres, from the American shore to the Canadian. You know that well, Pinchinat, for we have visited it."

"That is so, and I beg to apologize to Niagara," replied his Highness.

That day Floating Island coasted along about a mile away from the island. Always the barren slopes rising to the central plateau of Tovii, rocky cliffs which seemed to have no break in them. Nevertheless, according to the navigator Brown, there are good anchorages, which, in fact, have recently been discovered.

In short, the aspect of Nuka-Hiva, the name of which evokes such pleasant landscapes, is rather mournful. But, as has been justly observed by Dumoulin and Desgraz, the companions of Dumont d'Urville during his voyage to the South Pole and in Oceania, "all its natural beauties are confined to the interior of its bays, into the valleys formed by the ramifications of the chain of mountains which rise in the centre of the island."

After following this desert shore beyond the acute angle projecting to the west, Floating Island gradually changed its direction by diminishing the speed of its starboard screws, and rounding Cape Tchitchagoff, so called by the Russian navigator Krusenstern. The coast then runs in, describing an elongated curve, in the course of which a narrow inlet gives access to the port of Taiva or Akaui, one of the creeks of which offers a shelter against the most terrible storms of the Pacific.

Commodore Simcoe did not stop there. To the south are two other bays, that of Anna Maria or Taio-Hae in the centre, and that of Comptroller or Taipis on the other side of Cape Martin, the extreme south-westerly point of the island. Is was off Taio-Hae that they were to make a stay of twelve days.

A little distance from the shore of Nuka-Hiva the sea is of great depth. Near the bays there is anchorage at a depth of forty or fifty fathoms. It was thus easy for the Commodore to bring up very close to Taio-Hae Bay, which he did in the afternoon of the 31st of August.

As soon as they arrived in sight of the port, reports were heard on the right, and a circling smoke appeared above the cliffs to the east.

"Hallo!" said Pinchinat. "Are they firing the guns to welcome our arrival?"

"Not so," said the Commodore. "Neither the Tais nor the Happas, the two principal tribes of the island, possess artillery capable of firing the simplest salutes. What you hear is the noise of the sea plunging into the depths of a cavern half-way up Cape Martin, and the smoke is the spray hurled aloft from it."

The island of Nuka-Hiva has many names—we might say many baptismal names—given it by its successive godfathers: Federal Island by Ingraham, Beaux Island by Marchand, Sir Henry Martin Island by Hergert, Adam Island by Roberts, Madison Island by Porter. It measures seventeen miles from east to west and ten miles from north to south, its circumference being about fifty-four miles.

Its climate is healthy; its temperature that of the tropical zone moderated by the trade winds. At this anchorage Floating Island would not be subject to the formidable tempests and pluvial cataracts which occur during the winter, for it was not going to be there from April to October, when the easterly and south-easterly winds,

known to the natives as tuatuka, prevail. It is in October
that the heat is greatest, the months of November and
December being the driest. At other times the prevailing
winds range from east to north-east.

For the population of the Marquesas Islands, we must
reject the exaggerations of their early discoverers, who
estimated it at a hundred thousand. Élisée Reclus, rely-
ing on official documents, says that it does not exceed
six thousand for the whole group, and that the great
majority are in Nuka-Hiva. If at the time of Dumont
d'Urville the Nuka-Hivans numbered eight thousand,
divided into Tais, Happas, Taionas, and Taipis, the number
must have continued to decrease. Whence results this
depopulation? From the extermination of natives by
wars, the carrying off of the males to the plantations of
Peru, the abuse of strong liquors, and, it must also be confessed, to the evils which conquest brings, even when the
conquerors belong to civilized races.

During their stay here the Milliardites made numerous
visits to Nuka-Hiva, and the principal Europeans, by the
Governor's permission, had free access to Floating Island.

On their side, Sebastien Zorn and his comrades undertook several long excursions, the pleasure of which amply
paid them for their fatigues.

The bay of Taio-Hae describes a circle, cut by the
narrow inlet, in which Floating Island could not have
found room, so much is this bay cut up by the two sandy
beaches. These beaches are separated by a sort of hill
with rugged escarpments, where still exist the remains of
a fort, built here by Porter in 1812. It was at this period
that this sailor made the conquest of the island, the
American camp occupying the eastern beach—a capture
which was not ratified by the Federal Government.

In place of a town, on the opposite beach, our Parisians
found a small village; the Marquesan habitations being,
for the most part, scattered under the trees. But what
admirable valleys ran up from it, among others that of Taio-
Hae, in which the Nuka-Hivans had placed most of their

dwellings. It was a pleasure to explore beneath the clumps óf cocoa-nut trees, bananas, casuarinas, guavas, breadfruit trees, hibiscus, and other species rich in over-flowing sap. The tourists were hospitably received in the huts, where a century earlier they might have appreciated banana cakes and mei pastry and breadfruit, and the yellowish fecula of the taro, sweet when fresh and sour when stale, and the edible roots of the tacca. As to the hanu, a species of large ray which was eaten raw, and filets of shark, esteemed most highly the higher they are, our tourists declined to taste them.

Athanase Dorémus occasionally went with them on their walks. The year before this good man had visited this archipelago and was able to act as guide. Perhaps he was not very strong in natural history or botany, perhaps he confounded the superb *Spondia cytherea*, whose fruits resemble the apple, with the *Pandanus odoratissimus*, which justifies this superlative epithet ; with the casuarina, whose bark is as hard as iron ; with the hibiscus, whose bark yields the garments worn by the natives ; with the papaw tree ; with the *Gardenia florida?* It is true that the quartette had no necessity to have recourse to his some-what suspicious knowledge, when the Marquesan flora displayed its magnificent ferns, its superb polypodies, its China roses, red and white, its grasses, its solanaceous plants, among others tobacco, its labiates in violet clusters, which form the cherished finery of the Nuka-Hivans, its castor-oil plants a dozen feet high, its dracænas, its sugar-canes, its oranges, its lemon trees of recent importation, which had succeeded marvellously in a soil impregnated by summer heat and watered by the many mountain streams.

One morning when the quartette had ascended beyond the village of Tais along the banks of a torrent to the summit of the chain, and beneath their feet and before their eyes lay spread the valleys of the Tais, the Taipis, and the Happas, a shout of admiration escaped them. If they had had their instruments with them they could not have resisted their desire to reply by the execution of some lyric masterpiece to this spectacle of one of the masterpieces of nature. Doubtless the executants would have had but a few birds for their audience! But how beautiful is the kurukuru pigeon which flies at these heights, how charming the little salangane, which beats the air with so capricious a wing, and the tropic-bird, the habitual visitor to these Nuka-Hivan gorges. Besides, no venomous reptile was to be feared in the depths of these forests. There was no fear of the boas, barely two feet long, as inoffensive as a common snake, nor of the simquas, whose blue tail is indistinguishable among the flowers.

The natives are of a remarkable type. There is a sort of Asiatic character about them, on account of which they are assigned a very different origin to that of the other races of Oceania. Their extremities are well shaped, their face oval, their forehead high, their black eyes with long lashes, their nose aquiline, their teeth white and regular, their colour neither black nor red, but brown like that of the Arabs, a physiognomy marked by cheerfulness and gentleness.

Tattooing had almost disappeared—tattooing obtained not by cutting into the flesh, but by prickings, dusted with carbon and the aleurite triloba, and now replaced by the cotton cloth of the missionaries.

"Very fine, these men," said Yvernès, "but not so much so as when they were simply clothed in their skins, wore their own hair, and brandished bows and arrows!"

This remark was made during an excursion to Comptroller Bay in the Governor's company. Cyrus Bikerstaff had expressed a wish to take his guests to this bay, divided into several harbours like Valetta, and doubtless in the hands of the English Nuka-Hiva would become a Malta of the Pacific Ocean. In this district the Happas are principally found, among the gorges of a fertile country, with a small river fed by a noisy cascade. This was the chief theatre of the struggle between Porter, the American, and the natives.

The remark of Yvernès required a reply, and the Governor made answer :

"Perhaps you are right, Monsieur Yvernès. The Marquesans must have looked well in their cotton drawers, with the maro and pareo of brilliant colours, the alm bun, a kind of flying scarf, and the tiputa, a sort of Mexican poncho. It is certain that the modern costume hardly becomes them. What would you have? Decency is the consequence of civilization! At the same time, as our missionaries endeavour to instruct the natives, they encourage them to clothe themselves in a more or less rudimentary fashion."

"Are they not right?" asked Frascolin.

"From the point of view of the proprietors, yes! From the hygienic point of view, no! Since they have become more decently clothed, the Nuka-Hivans and other islanders have undoubtedly lost their native vigour, and also their natural cheerfulness. They get weary, and their health suffers. Formerly they knew nothing of bronchitis, pneumonia, phthisis—"

"And since they have not gone stark naked they have caught colds," remarked Pinchinat.

"As you say! And that has been an important cause of the decay of the race."

"From which I conclude," said his Highness, "that Adam and Eve did not sneeze until the day they wore shirts and pants, after being chased from the terrestrial Paradise—and that has given us, their degenerate and responsible children, diseases of the chest."

"It seems to us," remarked Yvernès, "that the women are not as good-looking as the men in this archipelago."

"As in the others," replied Cyrus Bikerstaff, "and yet here perhaps you see the most perfect type of the Oceanians. But is not that a law of nature common to the races which approach the savage state? Is it not also so in the animal kingdom, where the fauna, from the point of view of physical beauty, shows us almost invariably the males superior to the females?"

"Well," exclaimed Pinchinat, "we must come to the Antipodes to make observations of that kind. Our lovely Parisians would never admit it."

There are only two classes in the Nuka-Hiva population, and they are subject to the law of the taboo. This law was invented by the strong against the weak, by the rich against the poor, so as to protect their privileges and their goods. The taboo has white for its colour, and tabooed objects, sacred places, funereal monuments, the houses of the chiefs, the lower class are not allowed to touch. Hence a tabooed class, to which belong the priests, the sorcerers or touas, the akarkis or civil chiefs, and a non-tabooed class, to which are relegated the greater part of the women and the poorer people. Besides, not only is it not allowed to lift the hand against an object protected by the taboo, but it is even forbidden to look at it.

"And this rule," said Cyrus Bikerstaff, "is so strict in the Marquesas, as in Paumotu and the Society Islands, that I would advise you never to infringe it."

"You understand, my brave Zorn," said Frascolin. "Keep a watch on your hands and a watch on your eyes."

The violoncellist was content to shrug his shoulders like a man whom these things in no way interested.

On the 5th of September, Floating Island left its moorings at Tacoahe. It left to the east the island of Hua-Huna (Kahuga), the most easterly of the first group, of which they only perceived the distant verdant heights, and which has no beach, its circumference being formed of steep cliffs. It need hardly be mentioned that in passing along these islands Floating Island reduced its speed, for such a mass driven at a full rate would produce a sort of tide that would hurl small craft on to the shore and inundate the coast. A few miles further was Uapou, of remarkable aspect, for it bristles with basaltic peaks. Two creeks, one named Possession Bay and the other Bon Accueil Bay, indicate that their names had been given by Frenchmen. It was there in fact that Captain Marchand hoisted the flag of France.

Beyond Ethel Simcoe entered the regions of the second
group, standing towards Hiva-Oa, Dominica, according to
its Spanish designation. The longest of the archipelago,
of volcanic origin, it measures fifty-six miles round. Its
cliffs could be distinctly observed, cut in blackish rock,
and the cascades which fall from the central hills covered
with rich vegetation.

A strait three miles in width separates this island from
Taou-Ata. As Floating Island could not find space
enough to pass, it had to round Taou-Ata by the west,
where the Bay of Madre de Dios—Resolution Bay of
Cook—received the first European vessels. This island is
less easy of access than its rival Hiva-Oa. Perhaps then,
war being more difficult between them, the inhabitants
could not come into touch with one another, and decimate
themselves with their accustomed energy.

After sighting to the eastward Motane, a sterile island,
without shelter, without inhabitants, the Commodore moved
on towards Fatu-Hiva. This in truth is but an enormous
rock, where the birds of the tropical zone swarm, a sort
of sugar-loaf measuring three miles in circumference.

Such was the third islet in the south-east, of which
the Milliardites lost sight in the afternoon of the 9th of
September. In conformity with its itinerary, Floating
Island then steered south-west for the Paumotu Archipelago, and passed through the centre of that group.

The weather continued favourable, this month of September corresponding to that of March in the northern
hemisphere.

In the morning of the 11th of September the launch
from Larboard Harbour picked up one of the floating
buoys, to which was attached one of the cables from
Madeleine Bay. The end of this copper wire, of which
a sheath of gutta-percha assured the complete insulation,
was connected with the instruments in the observatory,
and telephonic communication established with the
American coast.

The council of administration of the Floating Island

Company was consulted concerning the shipwrecked crew of the Malay ketch. Would they authorize the governor to give them a passage to the Fijis, whither they could return to their country quickly and cheaply?

The reply was favourable. Floating Island even received permission to cruise to the New Hebrides, so as to land the crew there, if the notables of Milliard City considered that it would not be inconvenient to do so.

Cyrus Bikerstaff conveyed this reply to Captain Sarol, who in the name of his companions begged the Governor to transmit their thanks to the administrators at Madeleine Bay.

CHAPTER XII.

REALLY the quartette would have been guilty of revolting ingratitude to Calistus Munbar if they had not thanked him for having, somewhat treacherously perhaps, brought them on to Floating Island. What mattered the means employed by the superintendent to make them the welcome, petted, and handsomely paid guests of Milliard City! Sebastien Zorn never ceased from sulking, for you can never change a hedgehog with his prickly spines into a cat with soft fur. But Yvernès, Pinchinat, and Frascolin could not dream of a more delicious existence. An excursion with neither danger nor fatigue across these wonderful waters of the Pacific. Taking no part in the rivalry between the two camps, accepted as the island's soul of song, welcomed always by the Tankerdons and the chiefs of the Larboard section, as they were by the Coverleys and most distinguished families of the Starboard section, treated with honour by the Governor and his assistants at the town hall, by Commodore Simcoe and his officers at the observatory, by Colonel Stewart and his militia, giving their services at the temple and at the ceremonies in the cathedral, finding good friends in both ports, in the workshops, among the functionaries and servants of the State, could our compatriots, we ask any reasonable person, regret the time when they were travelling from city to city of the Federal Republic, and who is the man who would be sufficiently his own enemy not to envy them?

"You will kiss my hands!" the superintendent had told them at their first interview.

And if they had not done it, if they would never do it, it was because it is never necessary to kiss a masculine hand.

One day Athanase Dorémus, most fortunate of mortals as he was, said to them, "I have been two years on Floating Island, and I am sorry it is not to be sixty, if I could be certain that in sixty years I shall still be here."

"Won't you have too much of it," asked Pinchinat, "if you are to become a centenarian?"

"Ah! Monsieur Pinchinat, be sure that I shall attain the century! Why do you want people to die on Floating Island?"

"Because they die everywhere."

"Not here, sir, no more than they do in the celestial paradise."

What could be said to that? However, there were from time to time a few ill-advised people who took upon themselves to die even in this enchanted island. And then the steamers took away their remains to the distant cemetery at Madeleine Bay. Decidedly it is written that we cannot be completely happy in this world below.

But at the same time there were a few black spots on the horizon. It must even be admitted that these black spots were gradually taking the form of electrified clouds, which before long would bring storm and tempest. Disquieting was this regrettable rivalry between the Tankerdons and the Coverleys—a rivalry which was approaching an acute stage. Their partisans made common cause with them. Were the two sections to fight each other some day? Was Milliard City threatened with troubles, outbreaks, revolutions? Would the council of administration have an arm energetic enough, and Governor Cyrus Bikerstaff have a hand firm enough to keep the peace between these Capulets and Montagues of Floating Island? We can hardly say. Everything is possible with rivals whose self-esteem is apparently boundless.

Since the scene at the crossing of the line the two millionaires had been avowed enemies. Their friends supported them. All communication had ceased between the two sections. When they saw each other from afar they avoided each other, and if they met, what an exchange of menacing gestures and fierce looks! A rumour had spread that the old merchant of Chicago and a few of the Larboardites were going to found a trading business, that they were asking the company for permission to build a huge establishment, that they were going to import a hundred thousand pigs, and that they would slaughter them and salt them and sell them in the different archipelagoes of the Pacific.

After that it can easily be believed that the house of the Tankerdons and the house of the Coverleys were two powder magazines. It wanted but a spark to blow them up, and the island with them. Do not forget that the island was afloat above the deepest depths. It is true that this explosion would be only an explosion in a figurative sense, but the consequences would probably be that the notables would clear out. That proceeding would compromise the future and the financial position of the Floating Island Company.

All this was full of menacing complications, if not of actual catastrophes. And who knows if the latter were not to be feared?

In fact, if the authorities of the island had been less asleep in deceptive security, they might have done well to keep a watch on Captain Sarol and his Malays. Not that these people had said anything suspicious, being but slightly loquacious, living apart, keeping themselves clear of all connections, rejoicing in a state of happiness they would regret in their savage New Hebrides. Were there any grounds for suspecting them? Yes and no. But a more watchful observer would have noticed that they were exploring every part of Floating Island, that they were constantly making notes of Milliard City, the position of its avenues, the situation of its palaces and its houses, as if they were making an exact plan of it. They were met with in the park and the country. They were frequently either at Larboard Harbour or Starboard Harbour, observing the arrival and departure of the ships. They were seen to take long walks exploring the coast, where the custom-house officers were on duty day and night, and visiting the batteries at the bow and stern of the island. After all, what could be more natural? These out-of-work Malays could not employ their time better than in such walks, and what was there suspicious in that?

The Commodore gradually moved towards the southwest at reduced speed. Yvernès, as if he had been transformed since he had become a Floating Islander, abandoned himself to the charm of the voyage. So did Pinchinat and Frascolin. What delightful hours were passed at the casino during the fortnightly concerts and the evenings when the crowd struggled for admission at prices that could only be paid in gold. Every morning, thanks to the newspapers of Miliard City, provided with fresh news by the cables and with facts a few days old by the steamers, they were informed of everything of interest that was happening in both continents in society, science, arts, and politics. And from the last point of view it was noticeable that the English press of all parties never ceased to complain about the existence of this moving island which had chosen the Pacific as the theatre of its excursions. But such recriminations were treated with contempt at Floating Island as in Madeleine Bay.

Let us not forget to mention that for some weeks now Sebastien Zorn and his comrades had been reading under the heading of foreign intelligence that their disappearance had been mentioned by the American journals. The celebrated Quartette Party, so well received in the States of the Union, so expected by those who had not yet had the pleasure of listening to them, could not vanish without a good deal of fuss being made about their disappearance. San Diego had not seen them on the appointed date, and San Diego had raised a cry of alarm. Inquiries had been

made, and it had been ascertained that the French artistes
were on Floating Island after being carried off from the
coast of Lower California. As they had not protested
against their capture, there had been no exchange of
diplomatic notes between the Company and the Federal
Republic. When it pleased the quartette to reappear on
the scene of their successes they would be welcome.

It goes without saying that the two violins and the alto
had imposed silence on the violoncello, who would not
have been sorry to be the cause of a declaration of war
which would have brought about a contest between the
new continent and the Pearl of the Pacific.

Besides, our instrumentalists had many times written to
France since their departure from Madeleine Bay. Their
families, relieved of all fears for their safety, frequently sent
them letters, and the correspondence continued as regularly as the postal service between Paris and New York.

One morning—that of the 17th of September—Frascolin,
installed in the library of the casino, felt a very natural
desire to consult the map of this archipelago of Paumotu to
which they were bound. As soon as he opened the atlas,
as soon as his eye lighted on these regions of the Pacific,
he exclaimed :

"A thousand treble strings! How can Ethel Simcoe
get through this chaos? Never will he find a passage
through this mass of islets and islands. There are hundreds of them! A regular heap of pebbles in the middle
of a pond. He will touch, he will run aground, he will
hook his machine on to this point, he will knock it in on
this. We shall end by remaining fixed in this group,
which is more numerous than our Morbihan in Brittany."

The judicious Frascolin was right. Morbihan has only
three hundred and sixty-five islands—as many as there
are days in the year—and in this Paumotu Archipelago
there are quite double as many. It is true that the sea
which beats on them is circumscribed by a girdle of coral
reefs, the circumference of which, according to Elisée
Reclus, is not less than six hundred and fifty leagues.

Nevertheless, in looking at the map of this group, one would feel astonished that a ship, and more than all such a peculiar vessel as Floating Island, should dare to venture through this archipelago. Comprised between the seventeenth and twenty-eighth parallels of south latitude, and between the hundred and fortieth and hundred and forty-seventh meridians of west longitude, it is composed of hundreds of islands and islets—seven hundred at the least —ranging from Mata-Hiva to Pitcairn.

It is not surprising, then, that this group has received several names, among others that of the Dangerous Archipelago and the Evil Sea. Thanks to that geographical prodigality of which the Pacific Ocean has the privilege, it is also called the Low Islands, the Tuamotou Islands, which means the distant isles, the Southern Islands, the Isles of the Night, the Mysterious Islands. As to the name of Paumotu or Pamautou, which signifies the subject islands, a deputation from the archipelago assembled in 1850 at Papaete, the capital of Tahiti, protested against this designation. But although the French Government, deferring to this protest in 1852, chose among all these names that of Tuamotu, it is more convenient to speak of them here under their better-known name of Paumotu.

Dangerous as the navigation might be, the Commodore did not hesitate. He was so accustomed to these seas that every confidence was to be placed in him. He manœuvred his island as if it were a canoe. He could spin it round within its own length. He was said to treat it as if it were a sculling boat. Frascolin need have no fear for Floating Island; the capes of Paumotu would not even be grazed by its hull of steel.

In the afternoon of the 19th the look-outs at the observatory reported the first appearance of the heights of the group twelve miles away. If a few rise some fifty metres above the level of the sea, seventy-four of them rise but a yard or so, and would be under water twice a day if the tides were not almost imperceptible. The others are but atolls surrounded by breakers, coral banks of absolute aridity, mere reefs leading on to the larger islands of the archipelago.

It was on the east that Floating Island approached the group and was to reach Anaa Island, which Farakava has replaced as the capital, owing to Anaa having been partially destroyed by the terrible cyclone of 1878, in which a large number of its inhabitants perished, and which extended its ravages to the island of Kaukura.

The first island passed was Vahitahi, three miles away. The most minute precautions were taken in these parts, the most dangerous of the archipelago, on account of the currents and the extensions of the reefs towards the east. Vahitahi is but a mass of coral flanked by three wooded islands, of which that to the north is occupied by the principal village.

Next morning they sighted the island of Akiti, with its reefs carpeted with prionia, with purslane, a creeping plant of yellowish hue, and with hairy borage. It differs from the others in that it possesses no interior lagoon. If it is visible for some distance away, it is because its height is rather above that of the average of the group.

The following day another island of rather more importance, Anranu, was sighted, the lagoon of which communicates with the sea by two channels on the north-west coast.

While the Floating Islanders were content to wander indolently amidst the archipelago, which they had visited the preceding year, admiring its wonders as they passed, Pinchinat, Frascolin, Yvernès would have been glad of a few stoppages, that they might explore these islands, due to the work of polyparies, that is to say artificial, like Floating Island.

"Only," said the Commodore, "ours has the power of movement."

"A little too much so," replied Pinchinat, "for it stops nowhere."

"It will stop at the islands of Hao, Anaa, and Farakava, and you will have plenty of time to explore them."

When asked as to the mode of formation of these islands, Ethel Simcoe answered in the terms of the theory most generally adopted; that is, that in this part of the Pacific the ocean bed has gradually sunk about thirty metres. The zoophytes, the polyps, have formed on its sunken summits a solid foundation for their coral constructions. Little by little these constructions have risen stage by stage, owing to the work of the infusorians, who cannot work at great depths. They have reached the surface, they have formed this archipelago, the islands of which can be classed as barrier reefs, fringing reefs, and atolls— the Indian name of those provided with interior lagoons. Then the fragments dashed up by the waves have formed a vegetable mould; seeds have been brought by the wind; vegetation has appeared on their coral rings; the calcareous margin is clothed with herbs and plants, and dotted with shrubs and trees under the influence of our intertropical climate.

"And who knows," asked Yvernès in a burst of prophetic enthusiasm, "if the continent swallowed up by the waters of the Pacific will not appear again at its surface, reconstructed by these myriads of microscopic animalcules? And then on these regions, now ploughed by sailing ships and steamers, there will run at full speed express trains which will connect the old with the new world—"

"Take the handle off—take the handle off, my old Isaiah!" replied the disrespectful Pinchinat.

As the Commodore had said, Floating Island stopped on the 23rd of September off the island of Hao, which it was able to get rather near to, owing to the great depth of water. Its boats took several visitors through the passage, which on the right is sheltered by a curtain of cocoa-nut trees. The principal village is six miles away on the top of a hill. The village consists of from two to three hundred inhabitants, for the most part pearl fishers, employed as such by the merchants at Tahiti. There abound the pandanus and the mikimiki myrtle, which were the first trees of a soil whence now rises the sugar-cane, the

pineapple, the taro, the prionia, the tobacco, and above all
the cocoa-nut tree, of which the immense palm groves of
the archipelago contain more than forty thousand.

One might say that this "tree of providence" succeeds
almost without culture.   Its nut serves as the customary
food of the natives, being superior in nutritive substances to
the fruits of the pandanus.   With it they fatten their pigs,
their poultry, and also their dogs, whose chops and steaks
are much in demand.   And then the cocoa-nut gives a
valuable oil.   When scraped, reduced to pulp, and dried in
the sun, it is submitted to pressure in a very rudimentary
machine.   Ships take cargoes of these "copperas" to the
continent, where the factories treat them in more profitable
fashion.

It is not at Hao that an idea of the people of Paumotu
can be gained.   The natives there are not numerous, but
where the quartette could observe them to advantage was
in the island of Anaa, before which Floating Island arrived
in the morning of the 27th of September.

Anaa shows its wooded masses of superb aspect from
but a short distance.   One of the largest islands of the
archipelago, it is eighteen miles in length by nine in
breadth, measured at its madreporic base.

We have said that in 1878 a cyclone ravaged this island
and necessitated the transport of the capital of the
archipelago to Farakava.   That is true, although in this
wonderful climate it was presumable that the devastation
would be repaired in a few years.   In fact, Anaa has
become as flourishing as ever, and possesses fifteen hundred
inhabitants.   It is, however, inferior to Farakava, its rival,
for a reason which is of importance ; the communication
between the sea and the lagoon being through a narrow
channel troubled with whirlpools.   At Farakava, on the
contrary, the lagoon has two wide openings to the north
and south.   At the same time, although the principal
market for cocoa-nut oil has been removed to Farakava,
Anaa, which is more picturesque, always attracts the
preference of visitors.

As soon as Floating Island had taken up its position in
a favourable spot, a number of the Milliardites went ashore.
Sebastien Zorn and his comrades were among the first,
the violoncellist having consented to take part in the
excursion.

At first they went to the village of Tuahora, after studying the way in which the island had been formed—a
formation common to all the islands of this archipelago.
Here the calcareous margin, the width of the ring, if you
like, is from four to five metres, very steep towards the
sea and sloping gently towards the lagoon, the circumference of which encloses about a hundred miles, as at
Rairoa and Farakava. On this ring are massed thousands of
cocoa-nut trees, the principal, if not the only wealth of the
island, the branches of which shelter the huts of the natives.

The village of Tuahora is traversed by a sandy road of
dazzling whiteness. The French resident in the archipelago no longer lives at Anaa, since it has ceased to be
the capital ; but his house is there protected by a small
fortification. On the barracks of the little garrison, confided to the care of a sergeant of marines, floats the
tricolour. The houses of Tuahora are not undeserving
of praise. They are not huts, but comfortable and
salubrious dwellings, sufficiently furnished, and built for the
most part on coral foundations. Their roofs are of the
leaves of the pandanus, the wood of this valuable tree
being used for the doors and windows. Occasionally they
are surrounded with kitchen gardens, which the hand of
the native has filled with vegetable soil, and their appearance is really enchanting.

If these natives, with their lighter colour, their less expressive physiognomy, their less amiable character, are of
a type less remarkable than those of the Marquesas, they
yet offer fine specimens of the people of equatorial
Oceania. Being intelligent and laborious workers, they
may perhaps oppose more resistance to the physical
degeneracy which menaces the Pacific Islanders.

Their principal industry, as Frascolin noticed, was the

fabrication of cocoa-nut oil; hence the considerable quantity of cocoa-nut trees in the palm gardens of the archipelago. These trees reproduce themselves as easily as the coralligens at the surface of the atoll. But they have one enemy, and the Parisian excursionists discovered it one day when they were stretched on the beach of the interior lake, whose green waters contrasted with the azure of the surrounding sea.

At first their attention, and then their horror was provoked by a sound of creeping among the herbage.

What did they see ? A crustacean of enormous size.

Their first movement was to jump up, their second to look at the animal.

"The ugly beast !" said Yvernès.

"It is a crab," said Frascolin.

A crab it was, the crab called "birgo" by the natives. Its front claws form two strong pincers or shears with which it opens the nuts on which it chiefly feeds. These birgos live in a kind of cave dug deeply in among the roots, the fibres of cocoa-nut being heaped up to form a bed. During the night more particularly they seek about for fallen nuts, and even catch hold of the trunk and branches to shake the fruit down. The crab must have been seized with wolfish hunger, as Pinchinat said, to have left his dark retreat in broad daylight.

They let the animal alone, for the operation promised to be extremely curious. He found a large nut among the bushes, he tore off gradually the fibres with his pincers ; then when the nut was bare, he attacked the hard skin, knocking it, hammering it at the same place. When he had made the opening the birgo picked out the interior substance, using his hind pincers, which are very narrow at the end.

"It is certain," observed Yvernès, "that nature has created this birgo for opening cocoa-nuts."

"And that nature created the cocoa-nut for feeding the birgo," added Frascolin.

"Well, suppose we frustrate the intentions of nature by

preventing this crab from eating this nut, and this nut from being eaten by this crab?" proposed Pinchinat.

"I beg you will not disturb him," said Yvernès. "Do not even to a birgo give a bad impression of Parisians on their travels."

They consented, and the crab, who had doubtless given an angry look at his Highness, gave a grateful glance at the first violin of the Quartette Party.

After a stay of sixty hours at Anaa, Floating Island moved off towards the north. It passed through the thicket of islets and islands, Commodore Simcoe following the channel with perfect sureness of hand. It need hardly be said that under these circumstances Milliard City was rather abandoned by its inhabitants for the shore, and especially that part of it about Prow Battery. Islands were constantly in view, or rather baskets of verdure which seemed to float on the surface of the waters. It looked like a flower market on one of the Dutch canals. Numerous canoes tacked about at the entrances to the harbours, but were not permitted to enter, the custom-house officers having received formal notice with regard to this. Numbers of native women came swimming towards the island, when it went close to the madreporic cliffs. If they did not accompany the men in the canoes, it was because their vessels are tabooed to the Paumotuan fair sex, and they are forbidden to enter them.

On the 4th of October Floating Island stopped off Farakava, at the opening of the southern passage. Before the boats were got ready to take visitors ashore the French Resident presented himself at Starboard Harbour, whence the Governor gave orders to conduct him to the town hall.

The interview was very cordial. Cyrus Bikerstaff put on his official manner—which he kept for ceremonies of this nature. The resident, an old officer of infantry of marine, was in no way behind him. Impossible to imagine anything more serious, more dignified, more proper, more wooden on both sides!

The reception over, the Resident was invited to look round Milliard City, Calistus Munbar doing the honours. As Frenchmen, the Parisians and Athanase Dorémus asked to accompany the superintendent.

Next day the Governor went to Farakava, to return the visit, and did so in the style of the day before. The quartette landed and went to the residency. It was a very simple habitation, occupied by a garrison of twelve old sailors, and from the mast was displayed the flag of France.

Although Farakava has become the capital, it cannot compare with its rival, Anaa. The principal village is not as picturesque under the verdure of the trees, and the people move about more.

Besides the manufacture of cocoa-nut oil, the centre of which is at Farakava, the natives are employed in pearl fishing. The mother-o'-pearl trade obliges them to frequent the neighbouring island of Toau, which is specially devoted to this industry. Bold divers, these natives do not hesitate to plunge to depths of twenty and thirty metres, accustomed as they are to support such pressures without inconvenience and to hold their breath for more than a minute.

A few of these fishermen were authorized to offer the products of their fishery, mother-o'-pearl or pearls, to the notables of Milliard City. Assuredly it was not jewels that these opulent dames were in want of. But these natural productions in their rough state were not easily procurable, and the opportunity presenting itself, the fishers were able to sell at unheard-of prices. The moment Mrs. Tankerdon bought a pearl of great price, Mrs. Coverley must have another. Fortunately there was no opportunity of outbidding one another on some one thing different to anything else, for no one knows when the bidding would have stopped. Other families took heart to imitate their friends, and that day the Farakavans had a good time.

After twelve days, on the 13th of October, the Pearl

of the Pacific started early. In leaving the capital of the
Paumotu it had reached the western limit of the archipelago. Commodore Simcoe had no longer to be anxious
regarding such a wonderful maze of isles and islets, reefs
and atolls. He had come out of it without a scratch.
Beyond extended that portion of the Pacific which over a
space of four degrees separates the Paumotu group from
the Society Islands. It was in heading south-west that
Floating Island, driven by the million horses of its engines
proceeded towards the island so poetically celebrated by
Bougainville, as the enchantress Tahiti.

CHAPTER XIII.

THE Society Islands, otherwise the Tahiti Archipelago
are comprised between the fifteenth and seventeeth degrees
of south latitude and the hundred and fiftieth and hundred
and fifty-sixth west longitude. The area of the archi-
pelago is two thousand two hundred superficial kilometres.
There are two groups; first the Windward Islands,
Taiti or Tahiti Tahau, Tapamanoa, Moorea or Simeo,
Tetiaroa, Meetia, which are under the protectorate of
France; and secondly the Leeward Islands, Tubuai,
Manu, Huahmi, Kaiateathao, Bora-Bora, Moffy-Iti,
Maupiti, Mapetia, Bellinghausen, Scilly, governed by
native sovereigns. Cook, their discoverer, called them
the Society Islands, in honour of the Royal Society of
London. Situated some two hundred and fifty marine
leagues from the Marquesas, this group, according to the
most recent census, contains but forty thousand inhabitants.

Coming from the north-east, Tahiti is the first of the
Windward Islands to be sighted by navigators. And it
was Tahiti that the look-outs of the observatory reported
at a great distance, thanks to Mount Maiao or Diadem,
which rises for a thousand two hundred and thirty-nine
metres above the level of the sea.

The voyage was accomplished without incident. Aided
by the trade winds, Floating Island crossed these admirable waters above which the sun moves as it descends
towards the tropic of Capricorn. Still two months and a
few days more and it would reach the tropic and return

towards the equatorial line, and Floating Island would have it in its zenith during several weeks of burning heat ; then the island would follow it as a dog follows his master, keeping it at the regulation distance.

It was the first time the Milliardites were to put in at Tahiti. The preceding year their voyage had begun too late ; they had not gone so far to the westward, and after leaving Paumotu they had steered for the equator. Yet this archipelago of the Society Islands is the most beautiful in the Pacific. As they passed through it our Parisians would realize all that was enchanting in the moving island, free to choose its anchorages and its climate.

"Yes ; but we shall see what will be the end of this absurd adventure ! " was the invariable conclusion of Sebastien Zorn.

"May it never finish ! That is all I ask ! " exclaimed Yvernès.

Floating Island arrived in sight of Tahiti at dawn on the 17th of October. It was the north shore of the island that was seen first. During the night the lighthouse on Point Venus had been sighted. During the day they could reach Papaete, situated in the north-west, beyond the point. But the council of notables had assembled under the presidency of the governor. Like every well-balanced council it was divided into two camps. One section with Jem Tankerdon wished to go west; the other with Nat Coverley wished to go east. Cyrus Bikerstaff, having a vote when the sides were equal, decided to reach Papaete by passing round the south of the island. This decision could but satisfy the quartette, for it would allow of their admiring in all its beauty this Jewel of the Pacific, the New Cythera of Bougainville.

Tahiti possesses an area of a hundred and four thousand two hundred and fifteen hectares, about nine times that of Paris. Its population, which in 1875 comprised seven thousand six hundred natives, three hundred French and eleven hundred foreigners, is now but seven thousand,

In shape it is exactly like a flask turned upside down, the body of the flask being the principal island, joined to the mouth, represented by the peninsula of Tatarapu, by the narrow isthmus of Taravao.

It was Frascolin who made this comparison in studying the large scale map of the archipelago, and his comrades thought it so good that they christened Tahiti " the Flask of the Tropics."

Administratively, Tahiti is divided into six sections, subdivided into twenty-one districts, since the establishment of the protectorate on the 9th of September, 1842. It will be remembered what difficulties occurred between Admiral Dupetit-Thouars, Queen Pomare, and England at the instigation of that abominable trafficker in bibles and cotton goods who called himself Pritchard, and was so humorously caricatured in the Guêpes of Alphonse Karr.

But that is ancient history, quite as much fallen into oblivion as the performances of the famous Anglo-Saxon apothecary.

Floating Island could venture without danger within a mile of the shore of the Flask of the Tropics. This flask reposes on a coral base, whose foundations descend sheer down into the depths of the ocean. But before approaching so near, the Milliardites were able to contemplate its imposing mass, its mountains more generously favoured by nature than those of the Sandwich Islands, its verdant summits, its wooded gorges, its peaks rising like the pinnacles of some vast cathedral, its belt of cocoa-nut trees watered by the white foam of the surf on the ridge of breakers.

During the day the course lay along the western side ; the sightseers, glasses in hand, gathered in the environs of Starboard Harbour, watching the thousand details of the shore. The district of Papenoo, the river of which they saw across, the wide valley from the base of the mountains, and which falls into the sea where there is a break of several miles in width ; Hitiia, a safe port from which millions and millions of oranges are exported to San Francisco ; Mahaeua, where the conquest of the island was completed in 1845, after a terrible battle with the natives.

In the afternoon, they had arrived off the narrow isthmus of Taravao. In rounding the peninsula the Commodore approached close enough for the fertile fields of the Tautira district, the numerous water-courses of which make it one of the richest in the archipelago, to be admired in all its splendour. Tatarapu, reposing on its plate of coral, lifts majestically the rugged cones of its extinct craters. As the sun sinks on the horizon, the summits grow purple for the last time, and the colours fade into the hot transparent mist. Soon it is no more than a confused mass from which the evening breeze arises laden with the fragrance of oranges and lemons, and after a short twilight the darkness is profound.

Floating Island then rounded the extreme south-east point of the peninsula, and next morning at daybreak was moving up the western side of the island.

The district of Taravao, much cultivated, and thickly populated, displayed its fine roads among the orange woods which link it to the district of Papeiri. At the highest point is a fort, commanding both sides of the isthmus, defended by a few cannon, whose muzzles project from the embrasures like gargoyles of bronze. Below is Port Phaeton.

" Why has the name of that presumptuous driver of the solar chariot lighted on this isthmus ? " asked Yvernès.

The day was spent in coasting at slow speed along the more varied contours of the coralline substructure which distinguishes the west of Tahiti. New districts rose into view—Papeiri with its marshy plains, Mataiea with its excellent harbour of Papeiriri, then a wide valley watered by the river Vaihiria, and at the head this mountain of five hundred metres, as a sort of washstand supporting a basin half a kilometre in circumference. This ancient

crater, doubtless full of fresh water, did not appear to have
any communication with the sea.

After the district of Ahauraono, devoted to vast cotton
fields, after the district of Papara, which is principally
given over to agriculture, Floating Island, beyond Point
Mara, opened the wide valley of Paruvia, cut off from the
Diadem, and watered by the Punarnu.   Beyond Tapuna,
Cape Tatao and the mouth of the Faa, the Commodore
headed slightly to the north-east, cleverly avoiding the
islet of Motu-Uta, and at six o'clock in the evening
stopped before the gap giving access to the Bay of
Papaete.

At the entrance lay in capricious windings through the
coral reef the channel buoyed with obsolete guns up to
Point Fareute.   Ethel Simcoe, thanks to his charts, had
no need for the services of the pilots who cruise in whale-
boats off the entrance of the channel.   A boat, however,
came out, with a yellow flag at its stern.   This was the
quarantine boat, bound for Starboard Harbour.   People
are strict at Tahiti, and no one can land before the health
officer accompanied by the harbour master has given free
pratique.

Landing at Starboard Harbour, the doctor put himself
in communication with the authorities.   It was only mere
formality.   Sick there were none, either in Milliard City
or its environs.   In any case epidemic maladies, cholera,
influenza, yellow fever, were absolutely unknown.   A
clear bill of health was given according to custom.   But
as the night was rapidly closing in, landing was postponed
until the morning, and Floating Island slept until daybreak.

At dawn there were reports of cannon.   It was Prow
Battery saluting with twenty-one guns the group of the
Windward Islands and Tahiti the capital of the French
Protectorate.   At the same time, on the observatory
tower, the red flag with the golden sun rose and fell three
times.

Immediately an identical salvo was given by the

Ambuscade Battery at the head of the main passage into Tahiti.

Starboard Harbour was crowded from the earliest hour. The trams had brought a considerable crowd of tourists, on their way to the capital of the archipelago. Doubt not that Sebastien Zorn and his friends were as impatient as any. As the boats were not numerous enough to take all this crowd, the natives were busy offering their services to cross the six cables' length which separated Starboard Harbour from the port.

At the same time it was necessary for the Governor to be the first to land. He must have the customary interview with the civil and military authorities of Tahiti, and pay the no less official visit to the Queen.

Consequently about nine o'clock Cyrus Bikerstaff and his assistants, Barthélemy Ruge, and Hubley Harcourt, all in full uniform, the chief notables of both sections, among others Nat Coverley and Jem Tankerdon, Commodore Simcoe and his officers in brilliant uniforms, Colonel Stewart and his escort, took their places in the boats and were rowed towards Papaete.

Sebastien Zorn, Frascolin, Yvernès, Pinchinat, Athanase Dorémus, and Calistus Munbar occupied another boat with a certain number of functionaries.

Canoes and native boats formed in procession behind the official world of Milliard City, worthily represented by its Governor, its authorities, its notables, of whom the two chief were rich enough to buy Tahiti right out, and even the Society Islands, including their sovereign.

This harbour of Papaete is an excellent one, and of such depth that ships of heavy tonnage can anchor there. There are three channels into it : the main channel on the north, seventy metres wide and eighty long, narrowed by a small bank marked with buoys, the Tanoa channel on the east, and Tapuna channel on the west.

The electric launches majestically skirted the beach dotted with villas and country houses, and the quays at which the vessels were moored. The landing took place at

the foot of an elegant fountain which serves as a watering-
place and is fed by the streams from the neighbouring
mountains, on one of which is a semaphore.

،Cyrus Bikerstaff and his suite landed amid a large crowd
of the French, native and foreign population, who welcomed the Pearl of the Pacific as the most extraordinary
of the marvels made by the genius of man.   After the first
outbursts of enthusiasm the procession moved towards the
palace of the Governor of Tahiti.

Calistus Munbar, superb in his state costume, which
he only wore on ceremony days, invited the quartette
to follow him, and they were only too happy to accept the
superintendent's invitation.

The French protectorate not only embraces the island
of Tahiti and the island of Moorea, but also the neighbouring group.   The chief is a commandant-commissioner, having under his orders an "ordonnateur" who
manages the troops, the shipping, the colonial and
local finances and the judicial administration.   The
general secretary of the commissioner has charge of
the civil affairs of the country.   Several Residents are
located in the islands, at Moorea, at Farakava in the
Paumotus, at Taio-Hahè, at Nuka-Hiva, and a justice of
the peace, whose jurisdiction extends over the Marquesas.
Since 1861 there has been a consultative committee for
agriculture and trade, which sits once a year at Papaete.
There also are the headquarters of the artillery and the
engineers.   The garrison comprises detachments of colonial
gendarmerie, artillery, and marine infantry.   A curé and
a vicar appointed by the government, and nine missionaries scattered among the islands, assure the practice of the
Catholic religion.   In truth the Parisians might believe
themselves in France, in a French port, and there was
nothing displeasing to them in that.

As to the villages on the different islands, they are
administered by a sort of native municipal council presided over by a tarana, assisted by a judge, a chief mutoi,
and two councillors elected by the inhabitants.

Under the shade of beautiful trees the procession marched towards the palace of the government. On every side were cocoa-nut trees of superb growth, miros with rosy foliage, bancoulias, clumps of orange trees, guava trees, caoutchoucs, etc. The palace stood amid this charming verdure, which rose as high as its roof, which was decorated with charming mansardes; its front was of considerable elegance and embraced a ground floor and one storey. The principal French functionaries were here assembled, and the colonial gendarmerie formed a guard of honour.

The commandant-commissioner received Cyrus Bikerstaff with a graciousness that he certainly would not have met with in the English archipelagoes of these parts. He thanked him for having brought Floating Island into the waters of this archipelago. He hoped that the visit would be renewed every year, regretting that Tahiti could not return the compliment. The interview lasted half an hour, and it was agreed that Cyrus Bikerstaff might expect the authorities next day at the town hall.

"Do you intend to remain some time at Papaete?" asked the commandant-commissioner.

"A fortnight," replied the Governor.

"Then you will have the pleasure of seeing the French naval division which is expected here at the end of the week."

"We shall be happy to do them the honours of our island."

Cyrus Bikerstaff presented the members of his suite, his assistants, Commodore Ethel Simcoe, the commandant of the militia, the different functionaries, the superintendent of fine arts, and the artistes of the Quartette Party, who were welcomed as they ought to be by a compatriot.

Then there was a slight embarrassment with regard to the delegates of the sections of Milliard City. How was he to avoid giving offence to Jem Tankerdon and Nat Coverley, those two irritable personages who had the right—

"To march both at once," said Pinchinat.

The difficulty was evaded by the commandant-commissioner himself. Knowing the rivalry between the two famous millionaires, he was of such perfect tact, so rigid in his official correctness, and acted with such diplomatic address, that the matter passed over as if it had been all arranged.

It is needless to say that Sebastien Zorn, Yvernès, Pinchinat, and Frascolin had intended to leave Athanase Dorémus, who was already out of breath, to get back to his house in Twenty-Fifth Avenue. They hoped to spend as much time as possible at Papaete, in visiting the environs, making excursions into the principal districts, even as far as the peninsula of Tatarapu, even to exhaust to the last drop this Flask of the Pacific.

Having decided on this, they informed Calistus Munbar, who could but approve of the plan.

"But," he said, "you had better wait a couple of days before starting on your journey."

"And why not to-day?" asked the impatient Yvernès.

"Because the authorities of Floating Island wish to pay their respects to the Queen, and you will have to be presented to her and her court."

"And to-morrow?" said Frascolin.

"To-morrow the commandant-commissioner of the archipelago is to return the visit he has received from the authorities of Floating Island, and it is the proper thing—"

"For us to be there," replied Pinchinat. "Well, Mr. Superintendent, we shall be there, we shall be there."

Leaving the palace of the Government, Cyrus Bikerstaff and his procession directed their steps to the palace of her Majesty. It was a simple promenade under the trees, which did not take more than a quarter of an hour.

The royal dwelling is very agreeably situated amid masses of verdure. It is a quadrilateral in two storeys, with a chalet-like roof overhanging two tiers of verandahs. From the upper windows the view embraces the large plantations which extend up to the town, and beyond is a large section of sea. In short a charming house, not luxurious, but comfortable.

The Queen had lost nothing of her prestige in passing under the rule of a French protectorate. If the flag of France is displayed from the masts of the vessels moored in the port of Papaete or anchored in the roadstead, on the civil and military edifices of the city, at least the standard of the sovereign displays over her palace the ancient colours of the archipelago—red and white stripes, horizontal, with a tricolour in the upper canton.

It was in 1706 that Quiros discovered the island of Tahiti, to which he gave the name of Sagittaria. After him Walter in 1767, Bougainville in 1768, completed the exploration of the group. At the time of the first discovery Queen Oberea was reigning, and after her death the celebrated dynasty of the Pomares appeared in the history of Oceania.

Pomare I. (1762-1780) having reigned under the name of Otoo, the Black Heron, changed it for that of Pomare.

Her son, Pomare II. (1780-1819), favourably welcomed in 1797 the first English missionaries, who converted him to the Christian religion ten years afterwards. This was a period of dissensions and internecine war, and the population of the archipelago gradually decreased from a hundred thousand to sixteen thousand.

Pomare III., son of the preceding, reigned from 1819 to 1827, and his sister Aimata, born in 1812, became Queen of Tahiti and the neighbouring islands. Having no children by Tapoa, her first husband, she repudiated him to marry Ariifaaite. From this union there was born in 1849 Arione, the heir presumptive, who died at the age of thirty-five. From the following year afterwards the Queen presented four children to her husband, who was the finest man in the islands—a daughter, Teriimaevarua, princess of the island of Bora-Bora since 1860 ; Prince Tamatoa, born in 1842, King of the island of Raiatea, who was overthrown by his subjects revolting against his brutality; Prince Teriitapunui, born in 1846, afflicted with lameness, and Prince Tuavira, born in 1848, who finished his education in France.

The reign of Queen Pomare was not absolutely peaceful. In 1835 the Catholic missionaries began a struggle with the Protestant missionaries. Being sent out of the country, they were brought back by a French expedition in 1838. Four years afterwards the protectorate of France was accepted by the five chiefs of the island. Pomare protested, the English protested. Admiral Dupetit-Thouars proclaimed the deposition of the Queen in 1843. But the admiral having been disavowed to a certain extent, Admiral Bruat was sent to bring the matter to a conclusion.

Tahiti submitted in 1846, and Pomare accepted the protectorate by the treaty of June 19th, 1847, receiving the sovereignty of the islands of Raiatea, Huahine and Bora-Bora. There were further troubles in 1852; an outbreak overthrew the Queen, and a republic was even proclaimed. At last the French Government reinstated the sovereign, who abandoned three of her crowns; in favour of her eldest son that of Raiatea and Tahaa, in favour of her second son that of Huahine, and in favour of her daughter that of Bora-Bora.

In these days it is one of her descendants, Pomare IV., who occupies the throne of the archipelago.

The complaisant Frascolin continued to justify his title of the Larousse of the Pacific which Pinchinat had given him. These historical and biographical details he gave to his comrades, declaring that it was always better to know the people among whom they went and to whom they spoke. Yvernès and Pinchinat replied that he was right in instructing them as to the genealogy of the Pomares, and Sebastien Zorn observed that it was a matter of indifference to him.

The sensitive Yvernès became entirely steeped in the charm of this poetic Tahitian nature. To his memory returned the enchanting narratives of the voyages of

Bougainville and Dumont-D'Urville. He did not hide his emotion at the thought that he was to find himself in the presence of this sovereign of New Cythera, of a real Queen Pomare, whose name—

"Signifies ' right of coughing,'" said Frascolin.

"Good!" exclaimed Pinchinat, "as if you were to say the goddess of catarrh, the empress of coryza! Beware, Yvernès, and don't forget your handkerchief."

Yvernès was furious at this unseasonable attempt at wit, but the others laughed so heartily that he finished by joining in with them.

The reception of the Governor of Floating Island, his assistants, and the delegation of the notables took place in great state. The honours were rendered by the mutoi, the chief of the gendarmerie, with whom were some of the native auxiliaries.

Queen Pomare IV. was about forty years of age. She wore, like her family who surrounded her, a ceremonial costume of pale rose, the colour preferred by the Tahitian populace. She received the compliments of Cyrus Bikerstaff with an affable dignity, if such an expression is permissible, which would not have disgraced a European monarch. She replied graciously and in very correct French, for our language is current in the Society Archipelago. She had besides a very great wish to see this Floating Island, of which there had been so much talking in the Pacific, and hoped that its stay would not be the last. Jem Tankerdon was the object of particular attention —much to the disgust of Nat Coverley. This was because the royal family are of the Protestant religion, and Jem Tankerdon was the most notable personage of the Protestant section of Milliard City.

The Quartette Party were not forgotten in the presentations. The Queen deigned to inform its members that she would be charmed to hear them and applaud them. They bowed respectfully, affirming that they were at her Majesty's command, and the superintendent would arrange for the Queen to be gratified.

After the audience, which lasted for half an hour, the honours given to the procession as it entered the royal palace were repeated as it retired.

The visitors returned to Papaete. A halt was made at the military club, where the officers had prepared a luncheon in honour of the Governor and his companions. The champagne flowed, toasts succeeded, and it was six o'clock when the launches left the Papaete quays for Starboard Harbour.

In the evening, when the Parisian artistes found themselves in the casino,—

"We have a concert in view," said Frascolin. "What shall we play to her Majesty? Will she understand Mozart or Beethoven?"

"We will play Offenbach, Varney, Lecoq, or Audran!" replied Sébastien Zorn.

"Not at all! The bamboula is plainly suggested!" said Pinchinat, indulging in the characteristic hip motions of this negro dance

CHAPTER XIV.

THE island of Tahiti was destined to become a stopping place for Floating Island. Every year, before pursuing its route towards the tropic of Capricorn, its inhabitants would sojourn in the neighbourhood of Papaete. Received with sympathy by the French authorities as well as by the natives, they showed their gratitude by opening wide their gates, or rather their ports. Soldiers and civilians crowded on to the island, exploring the country, the park, the avenues, and probably no incident would happen to alter this satisfactory state of affairs. At the departure, it is true, the Governor's police would have to assure themselves that the population had not been fraudulently increased by the intrusion of a few Tahitians, not authorized to take up their abode on his floating domain.

It followed, that by reciprocity, every latitude was given to the Milliardites to visit the islands of the group, when Commodore Simcoe called at one or the other of them.

In view of the stay here, a few rich families had rented villas in the environs of Papaete, and secured them in advance by telegraph. They intended to take up their quarters there, as the Parisians do in the neighbourhood of Paris, with their servants and horses, so as to live the life of large landowners, as tourists, excursionists, sportsmen even although they had little taste for sport. In short, they would have a little country life without having anything to fear from the salubrious climate, the temperature of which ranges between thirty and forty degrees centigrade between April and December the other months

of the year constituting the winter in the southern
hemisphere.

Among the notables who left their mansions on the
island for their country houses ashore were the Tankerdons
and the Coverleys. Mr. and Mrs. Tankerdon, their sons
and their daughters, departed next day for a picturesque
chalet on the heights of Tatao Point. Mr. and Mrs.
Coverley, Miss Diana and her sisters left their palace in
Fifteenth Avenue for a delightful villa, hidden beneath the
big trees of Venus Point. Between these habitations there
was a distance of several miles, which Walter Tankerdon
perhaps thought a little too long. But it was not in his
power to bring these two points of the Tahitian coast any
nearer. Besides, there were carriage roads, conveniently
arranged to place them in direct communication with
Papaete.

Frascolin remarked to Calistus Munbar that if they
started in the morning, the two families could not be
present at the visit of the commandant to the Governor.

"Well, so much the better!" replied the superintendent,
his eyes brightening with diplomatic acuteness. "That
will avoid any conflict between them. If the representative of France paid his first visit to the Coverleys, what
would the Tankerdons say, and if he went to the Tankerdons, what would the Coverleys say? Cyrus Bikerstaff
must be glad of their departure."

"Is there no reason for hoping that the rivalry of these
families will end?" asked Frascolin.

"Who knows?" replied Calistus Munbar.

"It may perhaps depend on the amiable Walter and
the charming Diana."

"Up to the present, however," observed Yvernès, "it
does not seem that this heir and this heiress—"

"Good! good!" replied the superintendent. "It wants
an opportunity, and if chance does not bring it about, we
may have to take the place of chance—for the good of our
beloved island."

And Calistus Munbar performed a pirouette on his heels,

which would have been applauded by Athanase Dorémus, and would not have been disavowed by a marquis in the days of Louis Quatorze.

In the afternoon of the 20th of October, the commander and his staff landed at Starboard Harbour. They were received by the Governor with the honours due to their rank. There was a salute from both batteries. Cars decorated with the French and Milliardite colours took the procession to the capital, where the rooms at the town hall were prepared for this interview. On the road there was a flattering reception from the population, and before the steps of the municipal palace an exchange of official speeches of regulation length.

Then came a visit to the temple, the cathedral, the observatory, the two electric works, the two harbours, the park, and finally a circular trip on the trams round the coast. On the return a luncheon was served in the grand hall of the casino. It was six o'clock when the commandant and his staff embarked for Papaete amid the thunders of the artillery of Standard Island, taking away with him a pleasing remembrance of this reception.

The next morning, the 21st of October, the four Parisians landed at Papaete. They had invited no one to accompany them, not even the professor of deportment, whose legs were not suited for lengthy peregrinations. They were free as the air—like schoolboys on a holiday, happy to have under foot a real soil of rocks and vegetable mould.

In the first place they must visit Papaete. The capital of the archipelago is incontestably a pretty town. The quartette took a real pleasure in wandering about under the lovely trees which shaded the houses on the beach, and the offices and trading establishments near the harbour. Then passing up one of the streets abutting on the quay, where a railway on the American system was working, our artistes ventured into the interior of the city.

There the streets are wide, as well planned with rule and square as the avenues of Milliard City, among gardens

of verdure and freshness. Even at this early hour there
was a constant passing and re-passing of Europeans and
natives, and this animation, which would be greater after
eight o'clock in the evening, would last all through the
night. You understand that the tropical nights, and
particularly Tahitian nights, are not made to spend in bed,
although the beds of Papaete are composed of a network
of cocoa fibre, a palliasse of banana leaves, and a mattress
of tufts of the silk cotton tree, to say nothing of the net
protecting the sleeper against the irritating attacks of
mosquitoes.

As to the houses, it is easy to distinguish those which
are European from those which are Tahitian. The former,
built almost entirely of wood, are raised a few feet on
blocks of masonry, and leave nothing to be desired in the
way of comfort. The latter, of which there are not many
in the town, scattered here and there under the shade of
the trees, are made of jointed bamboos covered with mat-
ting, which renders them clean, airy and agreeable.

But the natives ?

"The natives!" said Frascolin to his comrades.
"There are no more here than at the Sandwich Islands; we
shall not find those gallant savages, who, before the conquest, dined on a human cutlet, and reserved for their
sovereign the eyes of a vanquished warrior roasted according to the recipe of Tahitian cookery!"

"Ah, is that it?" asked Pinchinat. "Then there are
no more cannibals in Oceania. What! we shall have
voyaged thousands of miles without meeting one of
them!"

"Patience!" remarked the violoncellist, beating the air
with his right hand like Rodin in the Mysteries of Paris;
"we may find one, if it is only to gratify your foolish
curiosity."

The Tahitians are of Malay origin, very probably, and
of the race known as Maori. Raiatea, the Holy Island, was
the cradle of their kings—a charming cradle washed by
the limpid waters of the Pacific in the Windward group.

Before the arrival of the missionaries, Tahitian society comprised three classes : those of the princes, privileged persons who were recognized as possessing the gift of performing miracles ; chiefs, or owners of the soil, of little consideration, and reduced to servitude by the princes ; the common people, possessing nothing, or when they did possess it, having nothing beyond a life interest in the land.

All this has been changed since the conquest, and even before, under the influence of the English and Catholic missionaries. But that which has not changed is the intelligence of the natives, their lively speech, their cheerful disposition, their unfailing courage, their physical beauty. The Parisians could not help admiring this in the town and in the country.

" What fine men ! " said one.

" And what fine girls ! " said another.

Men of a stature above the average, their skin copper-coloured as if impregnated with the ardour of their blood, their proportions as admirable as those of antique statues, their faces gentle and prepossessing. These Maories are truly superb, with their large bright eyes, their rather thick but well-cut lips. Their tattooing for war purposes is disappearing with the occasions which formerly rendered it necessary.

The more wealthy natives clothe themselves in European fashion, and yet they look well with shirts cut to the figure, vest of pale rose stuff, trousers falling over the boots. But these did not attract the attention of the quartette. No ! To the trousers of modern cut, our tourists preferred the pareo of cotton, coloured and striped, draped from the belt to the ankle, and in place of the high hat, and even the Panama hat, the headdress common to both sexes, the hei, composed of leaves and flowers.

The women are still the poetic and graceful Otaheitans of Bougainville. The white petals of the tiara, a sort of gardenia, mingle with the black mats unrolled on their shoulders their heads covered with the light hat made of the epidermis of a cocoa-nut, but of which the sweet name of revareva "seems to come from reverie," as Yvernès said. Add to the charm of this costume, with its colours like those of a kaleidoscope modifying at every move-ment, the gracefulness of the walk, the freedom of the attitudes, the sweetness of the smile, the penetration of the look, the harmonious sonorousness of the voice, and you will understand why, as soon as one of our artistes exclaimed, "What fine men!" the others should have answered in chorus,—

"And what fine girls!"

When the Creator had fashioned such marvels of beauty, would it have been possible for Him not to have given them a frame worthy of them? And what could be imagined more delightful than the Tahitian landscapes, in which the vegetation is so luxuriant under the in-fluence of the running streams and abundant dews of the night?

During their excursions across this island, and in the neighbourhood of Papaete, the four Parisians did not cease to admire this world of vegetable wonders. Leaving the borders of the sea, which are more suited to culti-vation, where the forests are replaced by plantations of lemon trees, orange trees, arrowroot, sugar-cane, coffee-plants, cotton trees, fields of yams, manioc, indigo, sorghum, and tobacco, they ventured under the masses of trees in the interior up to the foot of the mountains, whose summits rose above the dome of foliage. Everywhere were elegant cocoa-nut trees of magnificent growth, miros or rosewood trees, casuarinas or ironwood trees, tiairi or bancoulias, puraus, tamanas, ahis or santals, guava trees, mango trees, taccas, whose roots are edible, and also the superb taro, the precious breadfruit tree, high in the stem, slender and white, with large brownish-green leaves, amid which are groups of large fruits, with chiselled bark, and of which the white pulp forms the principal food of the natives.

The tree which with the cocoa-nut is the commonest is the guava tree, which grows all the way up the mountains, and whose name in the Tahitian tongue is tuava. It grows in thick forests, while the puraus form gloomy thickets, difficult to get through, when you are imprudent enough to venture among them.

There were no dangerous animals. The only native quadruped is a sort of pig. As to the horses and cattle, they have been imported into the island, where they prosper like the sheep and goats. The fauna is much less rich than the flora, even with the birds included. There are pigeons and swallows as at the Sandwich Islands. There are no reptiles. There are centipedes and scorpions. And for insects there are wasps and mosquitoes.

)The products of Tahiti are mainly cotton and sugarcane, the cultivation of which is largely developed, to the detriment of tobacco and coffee; besides these there are cocoa-nut oil, arrowroot, oranges, nacre and pearls. This is, however, enough for an important trade with America, Australia, and New Zealand, with China in Asia, with France and England in Europe, to a value of three million two hundred thousand francs of imports, counterbalanced by four millions and a half of exports.

The excursions of the quartette extended to the peninsula of Tabaratu. A visit to Fort Phaeton introduced them to a detachment of marine infantry, who were delighted to welcome their compatriots.

At an inn near the harbour, kept by a colonist, Frascolin stood treat. To the natives of the neighbourhood, to the mutoi of the district, there were glasses round of French wine, which the innkeeper did not forget to charge for. In return the locals offered their entertainers some of the products of the country, such as the preparation from a species of banana known as fei, of beautiful yellow colour, yams prepared in a succulent fashion, maiore, which is the breadfruit cooked to bursting in a hole full of hot stones, and finally a confection sourish in flavour, made from grated cocoa-nut, and which, under the name of taiero, is kept in bamboo twigs.

This luncheon was very jolly. The party smoked many

hundreds of cigarettes made of tobacco leaf dried at the fire, and rolled within a pandanus leaf. Only, instead of imitating the Tahitian men and women, who pass them from mouth to mouth after taking a few whiffs, the French-men preferred to smoke them in French fashion. And when the mutoi offered his, Pinchinat thanked him with a " mea maitai," that is to say "very well," with such a grotesque intonation that it put the whole crowd into good humour.

In the course of their excursions it need not be said that the quartette returned every evening to Papaete or to Floating Island. Everywhere, in the villages, in the scattered habitations, among the colonies, among the natives, they were received with as much sympathy as comfort.

On the 7th of November they decided to visit Point Venus, an excursion undertaken by every tourist worthy of the name.

They started at dawn, crossing the river Fantalina by the bridge. They ascended the valley up to the noisy cascade, double that of Niagara in height, but much narrower, which falls with superb uproar from a height of 200 feet. In this way they arrived, by following the road along the flank of Paharahi Hill, on the edge of the sea, at the hillock to which Captain Cook gave the name of Tree Cape—a name justified at that time by the presence of an isolated tree, since dead of old age. An avenue planted with magnifi-cent trees led them from the village of Paharahi to the lighthouse at the extreme end of the island.

It was in this place, half-way up a verdant hill, that the Coverley family had fixed their residence. There was no apparent reason for Walter Tankerdon, whose villa was on the other side of Papaete, to be in the neighbourhood of Point Venus. The young man was, however, on horse-back, close to the cottage of the Coverleys, and he ex-changed a salute with the quartette, and asked them if they intended to return to Papaete that evening.

"No, Mr. Tankerdon," replied Frascolin. " We have

received an invitation from Mrs. Coverley, and it is probable that we shall spend the evening at the villa."

"Then, gentlemen, I bid you good-bye," said Walter Tankerdon."

And it seemed as if the young man's face darkened as if a cloud had for a moment veiled the sun.

He then spurred his horse and went off at a gentle trot, giving a glance at the villa, which stood out white among the trees.

"Eh!" said Pinchinat. "Perhaps he would like to have accompanied us, this charming cavalier?"

"Yes," added Frascolin, "and it is evident that our friend Munbar may be right. He did not seem happy at not being able to meet Miss Coverley."

"That proves that millions do not bring happiness," replied Yvernès, like a great philosopher.

During the afternoon and evening a delightful time was spent with the Coverleys. At the villa the quartette met with as warm a welcome as at the house in the Fifteenth Avenue. A sympathetic meeting in which art was agreeably mingled. The music was excellent—at the piano, be it understood. Mrs. Coverley played a few new pieces, Miss Coverley sang like a true artiste, and Yvernès, who had a fine voice, mingled his tenor with her soprano.

We do not know why—perhaps designedly—Pinchinat slipped into the conversation that he and his comrades had met Walter Tankerdon in the neighbourhood of the villa. Was this clever on his part, or had he done better to have been silent? No, and if the superintendent had been there he could not but have approved of his Highness. A slight smile, almost imperceptible, flitted across Miss Coverley's lips, her beautiful eyes sparkled, and it seemed when she sang again as though her voice had become more penetrating.

Mrs. Coverley looked at her for a moment, and was content to say, while Mr. Coverley frowned:

"You are not tired, my child?"

" No, mother."

" And you, Monsieur Yvernès ? "

" Not the least in the world, madam. Before my birth I ought to have been a chorister boy in one of the chapels of Paradise."

The evening came to an end, and it was nearly midnight when Mr. Coverley thought the time had come to retire to rest.

Next morning the quartette, enchanted at their simple and cordial reception, went back again down the road to Papaete.

The stay at Tahiti could not last longer than a week ; according to the programme which had been laid down in advance, Floating Island would then resume its route to the south-west. And without doubt there would have been nothing to distinguish this last week, during which the quartette completed their excursions, if a very pleasant incident had not happened on the 11th of November. The division of the French squadron of the Pacific was signalled in the morning by the semaphore on the hill behind Papaete.

At eleven o'clock a cruiser of the first class, the *Paris*, escorted by two cruisers of the second class and a gunboat, dropped anchor in the roadstead.

The regulation salutes were exchanged, and the rear-admiral, whose flag was flying on the *Paris*, landed with his officers.

After the official salutes, in which the Floating Island batteries took part, the rear-admiral and the commandant of the Society Islands returned each other's visits.

It was fortunate for the ships of the divisions, their officers and crews, to have arrived in the roadstead of Tahiti while Floating Island was there. Here were new opportunities for receptions and festivities. The Pearl of the Pacific was open to the French sailors, who crowded to admire its wonders. For two days the uniforms of our navy mingled with the Milliardite costumes. Cyrus

Bikerstaff did the honours at the observatory, the superintendent did the honours at the casino and the other
establishments under his superintendence.

It was under these circumstances that an idea occurred
to that astonishing Calistus Munbar, a genial idea, the
realization of which would never be forgotten, and this
idea he communicated to the Governor, who adopted it at
the advice of his council of notables.

Yes! A grand festival was decreed for the 15th of
November. Its programme included a set dinner and a
ball given in the rooms of the town hall.

By this time all the Milliardites would have returned to
the island, for the departure would take place two days
afterwards.

The high personages of both sections would not fail to
be present at this festival in honour of Queen Pomare IV.,
the Tahitians, native or European, and the French
squadron.

Calistus Munbar was entrusted with the management of
the festival, and his imagination and zeal could be relied
on. The quartette offered their services, and it was agreed
that a concert should figure among the most attractive
features of the programme.

As far as the invitations were concerned, the Governor
undertook to send them out.

In the first place Cyrus Bikerstaff went in person to
Queen Pomare and the princes of her court to assist at the
festivities, and the Queen deigned to reply by accepting the
invitation. There were similar thanks on the part of the
commandant and the chief French functionaries, and of
the rear-admiral and his officers, who showed themselves
deeply sensible of the kindness.

In short a thousand invitations were issued. It must
be understood that the thousand guests could not sit down
at the municipal table. No! Only a hundred : the royal
personages, the officers of the squadron, the authorities of
the protectorate, the chief functionaries and council of

notables and superior clergy of Floating Island. But there would be in the park, refreshments, games, and fireworks, with which to satisfy the populace.

The King and Queen of Malecarlie were not forgotten, that need scarcely be said. But their Majesties, averse to all pomp, living retired in their modest habitation in the Thirty-Second Avenue, thanked the Governor for an invitation they regretted to be unable to accept.

" Poor sovereigns ! " said Yvernès.

The great day arrived, and the island was decked with the French and Tahitian colours mingled with the Milliardite colours.

Queen Pomare and her court, in gala costume, were received at Starboard Harbour amid a salute from the island's artillery, replied to by the guns of Papaete and the guns of the fleet.

About six o'clock in the evening, after a promenade in the park, all the great ones went to the municipal palace, which was superbly decorated. What a splendid sight was the monumental staircase, every step of which cost at least ten thousand francs, like that at Vanderbilt's house in New York ! And in the splendid dining-hall the guests sat down at the tables.

The code of precedence was observed by the Governor with perfect tact. There was no reason for conflict between the great rival families of the two sections. Everyone was contented with the places reserved for them, among others Miss Coverley, who found herself opposite Walter Tankerdon. That was as much as the young people could expect, for they could not be brought much nearer.

There is no need to say that the French artistes had nothing to complain of(They were placed at the table of honour, a new proof of esteem and sympathy for their talent and for themselves.

As to the bill of fare of this memorable repast, studied, meditated, and composed by the superintendent, it proved that even from the culinary point of view Milliard City had nothing to fear from old Europe.

Here is this bill of fare, as printed in gold on vellum by Calistus Munbar:—

Le potage à la d'Orléans,
La crême comtesse,
Le turbot à la Mornay,
Le filet de bœuf à la Napolitaine,
Les quenelles de volaille à la Viennoise,
Les mousses de foie gras à la Trévise.
Sorbets.
Les cailles rôties sur canapé,
La salade provençale,
Les petits pois à l'anglaise,
Bombe, macédoine, fruits,
Gâteaux variés,
Grissins au parmesan.
Vins :
Château d'Yquem.—Château-Margaux.
Chambertin.—Champagne.
Liqueurs variées.

At the table of the Queen of England, of the Emperor of Russia, of the German Emperor, or the President of the French Republic, was there ever any better combination for an official dinner, and could the most famous cooks of both continents have produced a better one?

At nine o'clock the guests went to the casino for the concert. The programme contained four items :—

Fifth quartette in A major : Op. 18, Beethoven.

Second quartette in D minor : Op. 10, Mozart.

Second quartette in D major : Op. 64 (2nd part), Haydn.

Twelfth quartette in E flat. Onslow.

This concert was a fresh triumph for the Parisian executants so fortunately embarked—no matter what the recalcitrant violoncellist might say—on Floating Island.

Meanwhile Europeans and strangers took part in the different games in the park. Open-air dances were organized on the lawns, and—why should we not admit it ?—there was dancing to the music of accordions, which are instruments much in vogue among the natives of the

Society Islands. French sailors have a weakness for this pneumatic apparatus, and as the men on leave from the *Paris* and other ships of the squadron had landed in great numbers, accordions became the rage. Voices joined in, and ship songs responded to the " himerre," which are the popular and favourite airs of the Oceanic peoples.

Besides, the natives of Tahiti, men and women, have a decided taste for singing and dancing in which they excel. On this occasion they many times repeated the figures of the "repanipa," which may be considered a national dance, of which the measure is marked by beating the tambourine. Thus dancers of all kinds, natives and foreigners, enjoyed themselves immensely, thanks to the stimulus of refreshments of all kinds provided by the municipality.

At the same time there were dances of more select arrangement and composition, at which, under the direction of Athanase Dorémus, the families gathered in the saloons of the town hall. The Milliardite and the Tahitian ladies tried to surpass each other in their dresses, but we need not be surprised at the former, who were faithful customers of the Parisian dressmakers, easily eclipsing even the most elegant Europeans of the colony. The diamonds rippled on their heads, their shoulders, their necks, and it was amongst them only that the contest was of any interest. But who would dare say if Mrs. Coverley or Mrs. Tankerdon were the more dazzling? Certainly not Cyrus Bickerstaff, always so careful to preserve a perfect equilibrium between the two sections of the island.

In the quadrille of honour there figured the sovereign of Tahiti and her august spouse, Cyrus Bikerstaff and Mrs. Coverley, the rear-admiral and Mrs. Tankerdon, the commodore and the first lady of honour to the Queen. At the same time other quadrilles were formed, in which the couples took part according to their tastes and sympathies. All this was charming, and yet Sebastien Zorn kept himself apart in an attitude, if not of protest, at least of disdain, like the two snarling Romans in the famous picture of the

Décadence. But Yvernès, Pinchinat, Frascolin waltzed and danced polkas and mazurkas with the prettiest Tahitians and the most delightful young ladies of Floating Island. And who knows if, this evening, a few weddings were not decided as a finish to the ball—which would doubtless give a little more work to the civil officials ?

Besides, what was the general surprise when chance made Walter Tankerdon Miss Coverley's cavalier in a quadrille ? Was it chance, or had not that astute diplomatist, the superintendent, managed to assist it in some way ? In any case it was the event of the evening, great perhaps in its consequences, if it marked a first step towards the reconciliation of these two powerful families.

After the fireworks on the large lawn, dancing was resumed in the park and at the town hall, and continued until daylight.

Such was the memorable festival, of which the remembrance would be perpetuated through the long and happy series of ages that the future—it was hoped—had in store for Floating Island.

Two days afterwards the stay terminated and Commodore Simcoe gave orders to get under way at dawn. The roar of cannon saluted the departure of the island as it had saluted its arrival, and it returned the salutes gun for gun from both Tahiti and the naval division.

The direction was north-west, so as to pass in review the other isles of the archipelago. Thus it coasted along the picturesque outline of Moorea, bristling with superb peaks ; Raiatea, the Holy Island, the cradle of the native royalty ; Bora-Bora, dominated by a mountain a thousand metres high ; then the islets of Motu-Iti, Mapeta, Tubuai, Manu, the heads of the Tahitian chain stretched across these regions.

On the 19th of November, as the sun descended towards the horizon, the last summits of the archipelago disappeared.

Floating Island then steered south-west, as shown by the charts displayed on the windows of the casino.

And who at this moment would notice Captain Sarol, as, with a gloomy look in his eye and a fierce expression on his face, with a menacing hand he showed his Malays the route to the New Hebrides, situated twelve hundred leagues to the westward ?

END OF THE FIRST PART.

Part II.

CHAPTER I.

FOR six months, Floating Island, after leaving Madeleine Bay, had been voyaging from archipelago to archipelago across the Pacific. Not an accident had occurred in the course of this marvellous journey. At this period of the year the equatorial regions are calm, the trade winds blowing steadily between the tropics. Even if there had been a storm, the solid basis which bore Milliard City, the two harbours, the park and the country, would not have experienced the least shock. The squall would have passed, the tempest would have abated. Hardly would it have been noticed on the surface of the Pearl of the Pacific.

That which was rather to be feared under these circumstances was the monotony of too uniform an existence. But our Parisians would have been the first to agree that there was none of this. On this immense desert of ocean oasis succeeded oasis, such as the groups they had already visited, the Sandwich Isles, the Marquesas, Paumotu, the Society Islands, such as those they would explore before turning northwards, the Cook Islands, Samoa, Fiji, the New Hebrides, and others perhaps. So many stopping places, so many opportunities of exploring these countries so interesting from an ethnographic point of view.

As far as the Quartette Party were concerned how could they think of complaining even if they had the time? Perhaps they might consider themselves separated from the rest of the world. Were not the postal services with the two continents regular? Not only did the petroleum ships bring their cargoes for the wants of the electric works almost to the day, but there was not a fort-night without steamers unloading at Starboard Harbour or Larboard Harbour, their cargoes of all sorts and the batches of newspapers with which the inhabitants filled up their leisure time.

The salaries of the artistes were paid with a punctuality that bore witness to the inexhaustible resources of the Company. Thousands of dollars found their way into their pockets, and accumulated there, and they would be rich, very rich at the expiration of such an engagement. Never had instrumentalists been made so much of, and they could not regret the results, "relatively mediocre," of their tour across the United States of America.

"Come," said Frascolin one day to the violoncellist, "have you got over your prejudices against Floating Island?"

"No," replied Sebastien Zorn.

"And yet," added Pinchinat, "we shall have a good bag when the campaign is over?"

"To have a good bag is not everything, you must be sure of carrying the bag away with you."

"And you are not sure?"

"No."

What answer could there be to that? And yet there was nothing to fear for the said bag, as the instalments in the form of bills had been sent to America, and paid into the Bank of New York. The best thing to do was to leave the obstinate man alone to his unjustifiable suspicions.

In fact, the future appeared more settled than ever. It seemed as though the rivalry of the two sections had entered on a period of appeasement. Cyrus Bikerstaff and his assistants had reason to congratulate themselves. The superintendent assumed more airs than ever since "the great event of the ball at the town hall." Yes! Walter Tankerdon had danced with Miss Coverley. Were people to conclude that the estrangement between the families had become easier? It was certain that Jean Tankerdon and his friends no longer spoke of making Floating Island an industrial and commercial island. In the best society the incident at the ball was much spoken of. A few perspicacious persons saw in it a reconciliation, perhaps a union which might put an end to dissensions private and public.

And if these previsions were realized, a young man and a young woman assuredly worthy of one another would accomplish their dearest wish we have every reason to believe.

There was no doubt that Walter Tankerdon had not remained insensible to the charms of Miss Coverley. He had been so for a year already. Under the circumstances he had confided the secret of his feelings to no one. Miss Coverley had guessed it, she had understood him, and had been pleased at his discretion. Perhaps she had clearly read her own heart—and was this heart ready to respond to Walter's? She had let no sign of it appear. She was as distant as her dignity and the estrangement between the families demanded.

But an observer might have remarked that Walter and Miss Coverley never took part in the discussions which occasionally arose in the mansion in the Fifteenth Avenue or in that in the Nineteenth. When the intractable Jean Tankerdon abandoned himself to some fulminating diatribe against the Coverleys, his son would bow his head, remain silent, and retreat. When Nat Coverley stormed against the Tankerdons his daughter lowered her eyes, her pretty face turned pale, and she tried to turn the conversation, without succeeding, it is true. That these two personages saw nothing is the common lot of fathers over whose eyes Nature has put a

bandage. But—at least Calistus Munbar affirmed it—
neither Mrs. Coverley nor Mrs. Tankerdon were in a similar
state of blindness. The mothers had not eyes to see
nothing, and this state of mind in their children was a
subject of constant apprehension, as the only remedy
possible was inapplicable. They felt that in face of the
enmity between the rivals, in face of their self-esteem,
constantly injured by questions of precedence, any reconciliation, any union was inadmissible. And yet Walter
and Di loved one another. Their mothers had found that
out.

More than once the young man had been asked to make
his choice among the marriageable girls of the Larboard
section. There were many charming ones amongst them,
perfectly educated, with fortunes almost equal to his own,
and whose families would have been delighted at such a
union. His father had spoken to him pretty plainly on
the subject, and so had his mother, though not so press-
ingly. Walter had always refused, giving as a reason that
he had no desire to be married. But the old Chicago
merchant would not listen to this—when you can get
hundreds of millions as a wedding present you ought not
to remain unmarried. If his son could not find a girl to
his taste on Floating Island—among his own circle—well,
let him travel through America or through Europe. With
his name, his fortune, to say nothing of his appearance,
he would have only too many to choose from—would he
like a princess of the imperial or royal blood ? Thus said
John Tankerdon. Each time his father brought him to
the foot of the wall, Walter declined to clear it, to go in
search of a wife abroad. And once when his mother said
to him,—

" My dear child, is there any girl here that you like ? "

" Yes, mother," he replied.

And as Mrs. Tankerdon did not ask which girl, her son
did not think it necessary to tell her.

A similar state of affairs existed in the Coverley family.
That the old New Orleans banker wished to marry his

daughter to one of the young fellows visiting the house, where the receptions were very fashionable, could not be doubted. If none of them were agreeable to her, well, her father and mother would willingly have consented to her marriage with a foreigner. They would visit France, Italy, England. Miss Coverley's answer was that she did not wish to leave Milliard City. She was very well on Floating Island; she only asked to be left there. Mr. Coverley was very uneasy at this reply, the real motive of which escaped him.

Besides, Mrs. Coverley had not put the question to her daughter as bluntly as Mrs. Tankerdon had to Walter, as need scarcely be said, and it is presumable that Miss Coverley would hardly have dared to reply with the same frankness—even to her mother.

This was how matters stood. Although neither of them could doubt the state of their feelings, and they had often exchanged looks, they had never said a word to each other. If they had met, it was only at official entertainments, at the receptions of Cyrus Bikerstaff, at some ceremony at which the Milliardite notables felt it necessary to be present, if only to maintain their position. Under these circumstances Walter Tankerdon and Miss Coverley maintained complete reserve, being so placed that any imprudence might have the most unfortunate consequences.

Judge then of the effect produced by the extraordinary incident at the Governor's ball, an incident in which many endeavoured to see a scandal, and of which the whole town was talking next day. The superintendent had asked Miss Coverley to dance with him : he was not there at the opening of the quadrille; that artful Munbar ! Walter Tankerdon, had offered himself in his place, and the lady had accepted him as her partner.

That explanation would be asked for regarding this fact, of such importance to the fashionable world of Milliard City, was probable, even certain. Mr. Tankerdon would question his son; Mr. Coverley would question his daughter on the subject. What would Miss Coverley

say ?   What would Walter say ?   Had Mrs. Coverley and
Mrs. Tankerdon interfered, and what had been the result ?
With all his ferret-like perspicacity, all his diplomatic
acuteness, Calistus Munbar could not discover.   When
Frascolin asked him about it, he was content to reply with
a wink of his right eye, which was worth nothing, for he
knew absolutely nothing.   The interesting thing to notice
was that, since this memorable day, whenever Walter met
Mrs. Coverley and Miss Coverley, he bowed respectfully,
and the girl and her mother returned his salute.

According to the superintendent this was " an immense
step in advance."

In the morning of the 25th of November an event
happened which had nothing to do with the position of the
two preponderating families of Floating Island.

At daybreak the look-out at the observatory reported
several large vessels steering south-west.   These ships
were in line, keeping their distances.   Evidently they
formed a division of one of the Pacific squadrons.

Commodore Simcoe telegraphically informed the
governor, who gave orders for salutes to be exchanged
with the ships of war.

Frascolin, Yvernès, and Pinchinat went to the observatory tower, in the hope of seeing this exchange of international courtesy.

The glasses were directed at these ships, to the number
of four, which were from five to six miles distant.   There
was no flag at their peaks, and the Frenchmen could not
recognize their nationality.

" Nothing indicates to what navy they belong ? " said
Frascolin to the officer.

" Nothing," he replied ; " but from their appearance they
are evidently British.   Besides, in these parts we hardly
ever meet with any men-of-war that are not either English,
French, or American."

The ships were approaching at very moderate speed,
and if they did not change their course they would pass
very close to Floating Island.

A good many sight-seers went out to the Prow Battery to watch the approach of the ships.

An hour later the vessels were within two miles of them. From their large funnels the smoke poured forth, which the westerly breeze bore to the furthest limits of the horizon.

When they were within a mile and a half, the officer was able to announce that they formed the British West Pacific division—Great Britain possessing or having under its protection certain archipelagoes in these parts, such as Tonga, Samoa, and Cook's Islands.

In the morning of the 29th of November the look-outs caught sight of the first heights of Cook's Archipelago, situated in 20 deg. south latitude and 160 deg. west longitude. Known as the Mangaia Islands and the Hervey Islands, and then named after Cook, who landed here in 1770, it is composed of the Islands of Mangaia, Rarotonga, Watson, Mittri, Hervey, Palmerston, Hagemeister, &c. Its population, of Maori origin, decreased from twenty thousand to twelve thousand, is formed of Malay Polynesians, whom the European missionaries have converted to Christianity. The islanders, pertinacious as to their independence, have always resisted foreign invasion. They believe they are still their own masters, although they have gradually submitted to the protecting influence—we know what that means—of the British.

The first island of the group to be met with was Mangaia, the most important and the most peopled—in fact the capital of the archipelago. The plan of campaign allowed of a stay here of a fortnight.

Was it then in this archipelago that Pinchinat was to make the acquaintance of veritable savages—savages like those of Robinson Crusoe, whom he had vainly sought in the Marquesas, in the Society Islands, and at Nuka Hiva? Was his Parisian curiosity about to be satisfied? Would he see absolutely authentic cannibals?

"My dear Zorn," said he one day to his comrade, "if there are not cannibals here, there are none anywhere else!"

" I might say what does that matter to me ? But let me ask why nowhere else ? "

" Because an island which is called Mangaia could only be peopled by cannibals."

And Pinchinat had only just time to evade the punch that his miserable attempt at a pun deserved.

But whether there were cannibals or not at Mangaia, his Highness was not to have the chance of entering into communication with them.

In fact, when Floating Island had arrived within a mile of Mangaia, a canoe put out and came alongside the pier at Starboard Harbour. It bore the minister, a German, who, more than the Mangaian chiefs, exercises his provoking tyranny over the archipelago. In this island —measuring thirty miles in circumference, peopled by four thousand inhabitants — which is carefully cultivated, rich in plantations of taros, in fields of arrowroot and yams, it was this gentleman who owned the best lands. His was the most comfortable house in Ouchora, the capital of the island, at the foot of a hill crowded with breadfruit trees, cocoanut trees, mangotrees, bourras, pimentos, to say nothing of a flower-garden, in which coleas, gardenias, and pæonies were in full bloom. His power was due to the mutois, those native policemen before whom their Mangaian Majesties have to bow.

When this fat little man landed, the officer of the port went to meet him, and salutes were exchanged.

" In the name of the King and Queen of Mangaia," said the minister, " I present the compliments of their Majesties to his Excellency the Governor of Floating Island."

" I am under orders to accept them, and to thank you," replied the officer, " until our Governor goes in person to present his respects."

" His Excellency will be welcome," said the minister. " The sanitary state of Floating Island leaves nothing to be desired, I suppose ? "

" Never has it been better."

" There might, however, be a few slight epidemics, influenza, typhus, smallpox—"

" Not even a cold, sir. Will you then give us a clean bill, and as soon as we are at our moorings we can enter into communication in all due form."

" That," said the minister, not without a certain hesitation, " can only be done if the epidemic—"

" I tell you there is no trace of one."

" Then the inhabitants of Floating Island intend to land."

" Yes, as they have recently done in the other groups to the eastward."

" Very well, very well," replied the stout little man. " Be sure they will be heartily welcome, from the moment that no epidemic—"

" None, I tell you."

" Let them land then in large numbers. The inhabitants will do their utmost to make them welcome, for the Mangaians are hospitable. Only—"

" Only ? "

" Their Majesties, in accordance with the advice of the chiefs, have decided that at Mangaia, as at the other islands of the archipelago, strangers must pay a landing tax."

" A tax ? "

" Yes, two piastres. It is very little, you see ; two piastres for every person landing on the island."

It was very evident that the minister was the author of this proposal, which the king and queen and council of chiefs had readily adopted, and of which a fair share was reserved for his Excellency. As in the groups of the Eastern Pacific there had never been such a tax heard of before, the officer of the port could not help expressing his surprise.

" Are you in earnest ? " asked he.

" Quite in earnest," affirmed the minister, " and in default of payment we shall not let anybody—"

"All right!" replied the officer.

Then bowing to his Excellency, he stepped into the telegraphic office, and reported the matter to the Commodore. Ethel Simcoe put himself in communication with the Governor. Was it advisable for Floating Island to stop off Mangaia under the circumstances?

The reply was not long in coming. After conferring with his assistants, Cyrus Bikerstaff refused to submit to this vexatious tax. Floating Island would not stop at Mangaia, nor at any island of the archipelago. The greedy minister would get nothing by his proposition, and the Milliardites would, in the neighbouring archipelagoes, visit natives less rapacious and less exacting.

Orders were sent to the engineers to give the rein to their million horses, and that is why Pinchinat was deprived of the pleasure of shaking hands with cannibals —if there were any. But they do not eat each other now in Cook's Islands—which is perhaps regrettable.

Floating Island crossed the wide arm which projects up to the group of four islands, the line of which lies northward. A number of canoes were seen, some fairly well built and rigged, others merely dug out of the trunk of a tree, but manned with hardy fishermen who venture in pursuit of the whales so numerous in these seas.

These islands are very verdant, very fertile. When off Mangaia, there could be seen its rocky coasts, bordered by a bracelet of coral, its houses of dazzling whiteness, rough cast with quicklime made from the coral reefs, its hills clothed with the sombre verdure of tropical vegetation, their altitude not exceeding two hundred metres.

Next morning Commodore Simcoe sighted the wooded heights of Rarotonga. Near the centre rises a volcano, fifteen hundred metres high, whose summit emerges from a crown of brushwood. Among the foliage is a white building with Gothic windows. This is the Protestant temple, built amid large forests of mape trees, which descend to the shore. The trees—of great height, and much branched and with curious trunks—are crooked and

gnarled, like the old apple-trees of Normandy or the old
olive-trees of Provence.

Cyrus Bikerstaff did not think it convenient to land at
this island, and he was supported by the council of
notables, who were accustomed to be received like kings
on their travels.

At the end of the day no more of the island could be
seen than the peak of the volcano, rising like a pillar on
the horizon. Myriads of sea birds landed without permission and flew over Floating Island, but when night
came they flew off to regain the islets incessantly lashed
by the surges to the north of the archipelago.

Then a meeting was held, presided over by the
Governor, in which it was proposed to modify the route of
Floating Island. Continuing to the westward along the
twentieth parallel, as had been decided, they would pass
the Tonga Islands and the Fijis. But what had happened
at Cook's Islands was not very encouraging. Would it
not be better to make for New Caledonia and the Loyalty
Archipelago, where the Pearl of the Pacific would be
received with French urbanity ? Then after the December
solstice they could return towards the Equator. It is
true this would take them away from the New Hebrides,
where they had promised to land the shipwrecked crew of
the ketch.

During this deliberation as to a new route, the Malays
were evidently a prey to very intelligible anxiety, for if
the change were adopted their return home would be difficult. Captain Sarol could not conceal his disappointment,
or even his anger, and anyone who had heard him speaking to his men would probably have thought his irritation
rather suspicious.

"You see," he said, " they will drop us at the Loyalties
or at New Caledonia. And our friends are expecting us
at Erromango. Our plans were so well arranged for
the New Hebrides ! Is this stroke of fortune to escape
us ?"

Fortunately for the Malays—unfortunately for Floating

Island—the proposal for changing the route was not carried. The campaign would be proceeded with according to the programme arranged at the departure from Madeleine Bay. Only, so as to make up for the fortnight which was to have been spent at Cook's Islands, it was decided to go to Samoa, steering north-west so as to touch at the Tonga Islands.

When this decision was known the Malays could not hide their satisfaction.

After all, what could be more natural, and had they not reason to be glad that the council of notables had not renounced its plan of putting them ashore at the New Hebrides ?

CHAPTER II.

IF the horizon of Floating Island seemed to be clearer in one respect, inasmuch as relations were much less acute between the Larboardites and Starboardites owing to the feelings mutually experienced by Walter Tankerdon and Di Coverley, so that the governor and superintendent believed that the future would not be complicated by intestine quarrels, the Pearl of the Pacific was none the less in danger of its existence. It was difficult to see how it could escape a catastrophe which had been so long in preparation. The farther it went towards the west the nearer it became to the regions where its destruction was certain. And the author of this criminal machination was no other than Captain Sarol.

In fact it was not by mere accident that the Malays had come to the Sandwich Islands. The ketch had put in at Honolulu with the intention of waiting for Floating Island at its annual visit. To follow it after its departure, to cruise in its waters without exciting suspicion, to be received as a shipwrecked crew, as they could not obtain admittance as passengers, and then, under pretext of being returned to their own country, to direct it towards the New Hebrides, had been Captain Sarol's plan all through.

We know how this plan in its first developments had been put into execution. The collision between the ketch and the other vessel was imaginary. No ship had run into them in the vicinity of the Equator. It was the Malays who had scuttled their ship, but in such a way that they could keep it afloat until the arrival of the assistance demanded by the signal of distress, and then sink when the launch from Starboard Harbour had taken off the crew. In this manner no suspicion could exist with regard to the collision, and no one could doubt they were a shipwrecked crew when their ship was seen to sink, so that a shelter could not well be denied them.

It is true that the governor might not care to keep them. Perhaps there were regulations forbidding strangers to reside on the island? Perhaps it might be decided to land them on the nearest archipelago? That was a risk to run, and Captain Sarol ran it. But after the favourable opinion of the company it was resolved to keep the ship-wrecked crew on the island, and take them within sight of the New Hebrides.

Such had been the course of events. For four months Captain Sarol and his ten Malays had been living at liberty on Floating Island. They had been exploring it throughout and penetrating all its secrets, and had neglected nothing in this respect. That suited them exactly. For a moment they had reason to fear that the itinerary would be modified by the council of notables, and they had been anxious to such an extent that their anxiety might seem suspicious. Fortunately for their plans, the itinerary had not been altered. In another three months Floating Island would arrive among the New Hebrides, and then would take place a catastrophe unequalled among disasters of the sea.

This archipelago of the New Hebrides is dangerous to navigation, not only by reason of the reefs which are scattered about it, and the rapidity of the currents, but also on account of the native ferocity of a part of its population. Since the epoch when it had been discovered by Quiros in 1706, since it had been explored by Bougainville in 1768, and by Cook in 1773, it had been the theatre of horrible massacres, and its evil reputation was enough to justify the fears of Sebastien Zorn regarding the result of this maritime campaign. Kanakas, Papuans, Malays, are there mingled with Australian blacks—perfidious, dastardly, refractory to every attempt at civilization. A few of the islands of the group are regular nests of rascals, and their inhabitants only live by piracies.

Captain Sarol, a Malay by birth, belonged to this class of pirates, whalers, sandalwood traders, slave dealers, who, as has been noticed by Doctor Hagon in his voyage in the New Hebrides, infest these regions. Audacious, enterprising, well acquainted with these archipelagoes of ill-repute, thoroughly master of his trade, having more than once been in command of bloodthirsty expeditions, this Sarol was no novice, and his deeds had made him notorious in this part of the Western Pacific.

A few months before, Captain Sarol and his companions having for their accomplices the murderous population of the Island of Erromango, one of the New Hebrides, had prepared an attempt which, if it succeeded, would enable them to live as respectable people wherever they pleased. They knew the reputation of this Floating Island, which the year before had voyaged in the tropics. They knew what incalculable riches were to be found in this opulent Milliard City. But as it was not likely to venture so far to the west, it was necessary to allure it within sight of this savage Erromango, where everything was prepared for assuring its complete destruction.

On the other hand, although they would be reinforced by the natives of the neighbouring islands, these New Hebrideans had no intention of attacking Floating Island when in the open sea as if it were an ordinary merchant vessel, nor of boarding it from a fleet of canoes. Thanks to the sentiments of humanity the Malays had been able to take advantage of, without awaking suspicion, Floating Island would arrive in the neighbourhood of Erromango. She would anchor a short distance from the island. Thousands of natives would invade her by surprise. They would throw her on the rocks. They would smash her. They would hand her over to pillage, to massacre. In truth this horrible plot had many chances of success. In return for the hospitality accorded to Captain Sarol and his accomplices, the Milliardites were advancing to a supreme catastrophe.

On the 9th of December, Commodore Simcoe reached the hundred and seventy-first meridian, at its intersection with the fifteenth parallel. Between this meridian and the hundred and seventy-fifth lies the group of Samoa, visited by Bougainville in 1768, by La Perouse in 1787, by Edwards in 1791. Rose Island was first sighted in the north-west—an inhabited island which did not even deserve the honour of a visit.

Two days afterwards the island of Manona was sighted, flanked by the two islets of Olosaga and Ofou. Its highest point rises seven hundred and sixty mètres above sea level. Although it contains about two thousand inhabitants, it is not the most interesting island of the archipelago, and the governor gave no order to stop at it. It was better to stay a fortnight at the islands of Tetuila, Upolu, Savai, the most beautiful of the group. Manona rejoices in a certain celebrity in maritime annals. It was on its shores at Ma Oma that many of Cook's companions perished, at the head of a bay which still retains its well justified name of Massacre Bay.

Twenty leagues separate Manona from Tetuila, its neighbour. Floating Island approached it during the night of the 14th of December. That evening the quartette, who were walking in the vicinity of Prow Battery, had "smelt" Tetuila, although it was still several miles away. The air was laden with the most delicious perfumes.

"It is not an island," said Pinchinat, "it is Piver's shop, it is Lubin's manufactory, it is a fashionable perfumer's warehouse."

"If your Highness does not object," observed Yvernès, "I prefer to compare it to a casket of perfumes."

"Well, a scent-box, then," replied Pinchinat, who had no wish to oppose the poetic flights of his comrade.

And in truth it seemed as though a current of perfumes were being borne by the breeze over the surface of these wonderful waters. These were the emanations of that

scented tree to which the Kanakas of Samoa have given
the name of moussooi.

At sunrise, Floating Island was coasting along Tetuila,
at about six cables' length from its northern shore. It
looked like a basket of verdure, or rather tier upon tier of
forests, rising to the summits, of which the highest exceeds
seventeen hundred metres. A few islets lay in front of it,
among others that of Amru. Hundreds of elegant canoes
manned by powerful, half naked natives, working their
paddles to a Samoan song in two-four time, were acting
as an escort. From fifty to sixty men were in some of
them. This is no exaggeration for these long vessels, which
are strongly enough built to go far out to sea. Our
Parisians then understood why the early Europeans had
given this archipelago the name of Navigators' Islands.
But its true geographical name is Hamoa, or preferably
Samoa.

Savai, Upolu, Tetuila, stretching from north-west to
south-east; Olosaga, Ofou, Manona, scattered to the south-
east, such are the principal islands of this group of volcanic
origin. Its total area is about two thousand eight hundred
square kilomètres, and it has a population of thirty-five
thousand six hundred inhabitants. It is necessary therefore to reduce the estimates of the first explorers by one
half.

Be it observed that none of these islands could offer
such favourable climatic conditions as Floating
Island. The temperature ranges between twenty-six and
thirty-four degrees centigrade. July and August are the
coldest months, and the highest temperature occurs in
February. From December to April the Samoans are
deluged with abundant rains, and this is also the period
when occur the storms and hurricanes so fruitful of
disasters.

The trade, which is chiefly in the hands of the English,
and in a minor degree of the Americans and Germans,
amounts to about eighteen hundred thousand francs of
imports and nine hundred thousand francs for exports. It

consists mainly of agricultural products, cotton—the cultivation of which increased every year—and coprah, that is, the dried kernel of the cocoanut.

The population, which is of Malayo-Polynesian origin, contains about three hundred whites and a few thousand labourers from different islands of Melanesia. Since 1830 the missionaries have converted the Samoans to Christianity, but they retain a few of the practices of their ancient religious rites. The great majority of the natives are Protestants, owing to the influence of Germany and England. Nevertheless Catholicism has a few thousand converts, which the Mariste Fathers are doing their best to increase in number with a view of opposing Anglo-Saxon proselytism.

Floating Island stopped at the south of Tetuila, at the opening of Pago—Pago roadstead. This is the real port of the island, whose capital is Leone, situated in the central portion. This time there was no difficulty between Cyrus Bikerstaff and the Samoan authorities. Free pratique was accorded. It is not at Tetuila but at Upolu that the sovereign of the archipelago resides, and where the English, American, and German residencies are established. There were no official receptions. A certain number of Samoans took advantage of the opportunity of visiting Milliard City and its environs, while the Milliardites were assured that the population of the group would give them a cordial welcome.

The port is at the head of the bay. The shelter it offers against the winds from the offing is excellent and its access easy. Ships of war often put in there.

Among the first to land we need not be astonished at meeting Sebastien Zorn and his three comrades, accompanied by the superintendent, who had asked to join them. Calistus Munbar was as usual delightful and in high spirits. He had ascertained that an excursion to Leone in carriages drawn by New Zealand horses had been arranged among three or four families of notables. As the Coverleys and Tankerdons were going, perhaps there might be a meeting between Walter and Di, which would anything but displease him.

During the walk with the quartette he began talking about this great event in his usual grandiose way.

"My friends," he said, "we are in a regular comic opera. With a lucky accident we shall arrive at the end of the piece. A horse runs away—a carriage upsets—"

"An attack of brigands!" said Yvernès.

"A general massacre of the excursionists!" added Pinchinat.

"And that might happen!" growled the violoncellist in a funereal voice, as if he were down in the depths of his fourth string.

"No, my friends, no!" said Calistus Munbar. "Don't let us go as far as a massacre! We need not go to that. Let us have a nice sort of accident, in which Walter Tankerdon will be lucky enough to save the life of Miss Coverley."

"And then a little music from Boieldieu or Auber!" said Pinchinat, working his hand as if he were turning the handle of a barrel-organ.

"And so," said Frascolin, "you are still thinking of this marriage?"

"Think of it, my dear Frascolin! I dream of it night and day! I am losing my good humour, though I do not look like it! I am getting thinner, though you would not think so! I shall die if it does not take place."

"It will," said Yvernès, in a voice of prophetic sonority, "for God does not at present require the death of your Excellency."

And they entered a native inn, and drank to the health of the future couple in several glasses of cocoa milk, while they ate some luscious bananas.

Quite a joy to the eyes of the Parisians was this Samoan population in the streets of Pago-Pago, and amid the trees which surrounded the harbour. The men are of a stature above the average, their colour of a yellowish brown, their heads round, their bodies powerful, their limbs muscular, their faces gentle and jovial. Perhaps there was too much tattooing on their arms and bodies and even on their thighs, which were imperfectly hidden under a petticoat of grass and leaves. Their hair was black, straight or waved, according to the taste of native dandyism. But under the coating of white lime with which it was plastered it formed a wig.

"Savages in the style of Louis XV.!" said Pinchinat. "They only want the cloak, the sword, the breeches, the stockings, the red-heeled shoes, the plumed hat, and the snuff-box, to figure at the receptions at Versailles."

The Samoans, women or girls, are as rudimentarily clothed as the men, tattooed on the hands and breast, their heads garlanded with gardenias, their necks ornamented with collars of red hibiscus, fully justifying the admiration with which they were described by the early navigators—at least, such as were young. But they were distant, and of rather affected prudery. Graceful and smiling, they enchanted the quartette, wishing them the *kalofa*, that is, the good morning, in a sweet and melodious voice.

An excursion, or rather a pilgrimage, which our tourists had wished for, and which they performed on the morrow, gave them the opportunity of traversing the island from one shore to the other. One of the country carriages took them to the opposite coast at França Bay, the name of which recalls a remembrance of France. There, on a monument of white coral, raised in 1884, is a plate of bronze bearing in engraved letters the never-to-be-forgotten names of Commandant De Langle, the naturalist Lamanon, and nine sailors, the companions of La Perouse, who were massacred here on the 11th of December, 1787.

Sebastien Zorn and his comrades returned to Pago-Pago through the interior of the island. What wonderful masses of trees, interlaced with lianas, cocoanut-trees, wild bananas, and many native species suitable for cabinet-making. Over the country stretched fields of taro, sugar-cane, coffee plantations, cotton plantations, cinnamon-trees. Everywhere orange-trees, guava-trees, mangoes, avocado-trees, and climbing-plants, orchids and arborescent shrubs. A flora astonishingly rich from this fertile soil, fertilized by a humid and warm climate. The Samoan fauna, reduced to a few birds, a few almost inoffensive reptiles, contains among its mammals only a small rat, the sole representative of the rodents.

Four days afterwards, on the 18th of December, Floating Island left Tetuila without any such providential accident as had been desired by the superintendent. But it was evident that the state of affairs between the two families continued to improve.

Hardly a dozen leagues separate Tetuila from Upolu. In the morning of the next day Commodore Simcoe passed in succession, at a distance of a quarter of a mile, the three islets of Nom-tua, Samusu, Salafuta, which defend the island as if they were detached forts. He took Floating Island along with great ability, and in the afternoon reached his moorings in front of Apia.

Upolu is the most important island of the archipelago, with its sixteen thousand inhabitants. Here Germany, America, and England have established their representatives, united in a sort of council for the protection of the interests of their nations. The sovereign of the group reigns amid his court at Malinuu, at the eastern extremity of Apia Point.

The aspect of Upolu is similar to that of Tetuila, a mass of mountains, dominated by the peak of Mount Mission, which constitutes the backbone of the island. These ancient extinct volcanoes are covered with thick forests, which clothe them up to their craters. At the foot of these mountains are plains and fields, joining on to the alluvial strip along the shore, in which the vegetation is in all the luxuriant variety of the tropics.

In the morning, the governor and his assistants and a few notabilities landed at the fort of Apia. Their object was to pay an official visit to the representatives of Germany, England, and the United States of America, this composite municipality in whose hands are concentrated the administrative services of the archipelago.

While Cyrus Bikerstaff and his suite visited the residents, Sebastien Zorn, Frascolin, Yvernès, and Pinchinat, who had landed with them, occupied their leisure by visiting the town.

And at first sight they were struck with the contrast presented by the European houses with the huts of the old Kanaka village, in which the natives obstinately persist in living. These dwellings are comfortable, healthy, charming in a word. Scattered along the banks of the Apia river, their low roofs are sheltered under an elegant sunshade of palm trees. There was no lack of animation in the harbour. This is the most frequented harbour of the group, and the headquarters of the Commercial Company of Hamburg, which owns a fleet employed in the local service between Samoa and the neighbouring islands.

But if the influence of the English, Americans, and Germans preponderates in this archipelago, France is represented by Catholic missionaries, whose devotion and zeal keep them in good repute among the Samoans. Genuine satisfaction, profound emotion even, seized our artists when they perceived the little church of the Mission, which has not the Puritan severity of the Protestant chapels, and a little beyond, on the hill, a school-house, on which the tricolour was flying.

They walked in this direction, and a few minutes afterwards they were being welcomed in the French quarters. The Maristes gave them a patriotic welcome. Three fathers were in residence, employed in the services of the Mission, which includes two others at Savai, and a certain number of sisters stationed in the islands.

What a pleasure it was to converse with the Superior, already advanced in years, who had lived in Samoa for a long time. He was so happy to welcome his fellow-countrymen, and what was more—artistes of his nation. The conversation was varied with refreshing drinks of which the Mission possesses the recipe.

"But first," said the old man, "do not think, my dear sons, that the islands of our archipelago are in a savage state. It is not here that you will find natives who practise cannibalism."

"We have not met with any up to the present," said Frascolin.

" To our great regret," added Pinchinat.

"Why do you regret ? "

" Excuse me, father, that is the confession of a curious Parisian ! It is for love of local colour ! "

" Oh ! " said Sebastien Zorn, " we are not at the end of our campaign yet ; and we may see more than we want to of these cannibals mentioned by our comrade."

" That is possible," replied the Superior. " Among the approaches to the Western groups, the New Hebrides, the Solomons, navigators can only venture with extreme prudence ; but in Tahiti, the Marquesas, the Society Islands, as at Samoa, civilization has made remarkable progress. I know that the massacre of the companions of La Perouse has given the Samoans the reputation of being ferocious aborigines, devoted to the practice of cannibalism ; but there has been a great change since then, owing to the influence of the religion of Christ. The natives of these times are looked after by the police, rejoicing in a European Government, with two chambers in the European style—and revolutions."

" In European style ? " observed Yvernès.

" As you say, my dear son, the Samoans are not exempt from political dissensions."

" We have them on Floating Island," replied Pinchinat. "We are even expecting to have a dynastic war between two royal families."

" In fact, my friends, there has been a struggle between King Tupua, who is descended from the ancient sovereigns of the archipelago, and whom we supported with our influence, and King Malietoa, the man of the English and Germans. Much blood was shed, particularly in the great battle of December, 1887. These kings saw themselves successively proclaimed and dethroned, and finally Malietoa was declared sovereign by the three powers, in conformity

with the arrangements stipulated by the court of Berlin—
Berlin !"

And the old missionary could not restrain a convulsive
movement as the name escaped from his lips.

"You see," said he, "up to now the influence of the
Germans has been the dominating one at Samoa. Nine-
tenths of the cultivated lands are in their hands. In the
environs of Apia, at Suluafata, they have obtained from
the Government a very important concession in the
proximity of the port, which could serve as a victualling
station for their ships of war. Quick-firing guns have been
introduced by them. But all that will end some day."

"To the advantage of France ?" asked Frascolin.

"No ; to the advantage of the United Kingdom !"

"Oh !" said Yvernès. "England or Germany !"

"No, my dear child," replied the Superior; "there is a
notable difference."

The conversation ended, after the Superior had given
divers details as to the customs of the Samoans. He
added that if the majority belonged to the Wesleyan
religion, Catholicism seemed to be making more progress
every day. The church of the Mission was already too
small for their services, and the school required early
enlargement. He appeared very happy, and his guests
rejoiced with him.

The stay of Floating Island at the island of Upolu lasted
three days.

The missionaries came to return the visit they had
received. The French artistes took them through Milliard
City, and they were struck with wonder. And why should
we not say that in the room at the casino the quartette
party entertained the Father and his colleagues with a few
selections from their repertory ? He wept with emotion,
did the good old man, for he adored classical music, and to
his great regret had never had an opportunity of hearing
it at the festivals of Upolu.

The day before the departure, Sebastien Zorn, Frascolin,
Pinchinat, Yvernès, accompanied this time by the professor

of dancing and deportment, went to bid farewell to the missionaries The parting was most affectionate—the parting of people who had only known each other for a few days, and would never see each other again. The old man gave them his benediction and embraced them, and they retired in deep emotion.

Next day, the 23rd of December, Commodore Simcoe got under way at dawn, and Floating Island moved off amid a procession of canoes, who were to escort it to the neighbouring island of Savai.

This island is separated from Upolu by a strait of some seven or eight leagues. But the port of Apia being situated on the northern shore, it is necessary to coast along this shore all day before reaching the strait.

According to the itinerary arranged by the Governor, it was not intended to make the tour of Savai, but to manœuvre between it and Upolu, so as to run down southwest to the Tonga Archipelago. For this reason Floating Island advanced at very moderate speed, it being undesirable to venture during the night through this strait, which is flanked by the small islands of Apolinia and Manono.

At daybreak Commodore Simcoe manœuvred between these two islands, of which one, Apolinia, contains only two hundred and fifty inhabitants, and the other, Manono, a thousand. These natives have the reputation of being the bravest and most honest Samoans in the archipelago.

From this place Savai could be admired in all its splendour. It is protected by impregnable cliffs of granite against the attacks of the sea which the hurricanes, tornadoes and cyclones of the winter season make more formidable. Savai is covered with thick forests, dominated by an ancient volcano twelve hundred metres high, dotted with gleaming villages beneath the domes of gigantic palm trees, watered by tumultuous cascades, penetrated by deep caverns, from which escaped the violent echoes of the beating of the waves on the shore.

And, if legend is to be believed, this island is the cradle

of the Polynesian races, of which its eleven thousand inhabitants have retained the purest type. Its real name is Savaiki, the famous Eden of the Maori divinities.

Floating Island slowly moved away, and lost sight of its last heights in the evening of the 24th of December.

CHAPTER III.

SINCE the 21st of December, the sun in its apparent movement, after stopping on the tropic of Capricorn, recommenced its course towards the north, abandoning these regions to the inclemencies of winter, and bringing spring again to the northern hemisphere.

Floating Island was not more than a dozen degrees from the tropic. In descending to the islands of Tonga-Tabou, it reached the extreme latitude fixed by the itinerary, and continuing its course to the north, remained in the most favourable climatic conditions. It is true it could not avoid a period of extreme heat while the sun was in the zenith, but this heat would be tempered by the sea breeze, and would diminish as the distance of the sun increased.

Between Samoa and the principal island of Tonga-Tabou there are eight degrees—about nine hundred kilometres. There was no need to increase the speed. Floating Island skimmed over this ever beautiful sea, which the atmosphere hardly troubled with storms, that were as rare as they were short-lived. It was enough to be at Tonga-Tabou in the first days of January, to remain there a week, and then to proceed to Fiji. From there Floating Island would run up to the New Hebrides, and there land the Malay crew; then heading north-east, it would regain the latitude of Madeleine Bay, and its second cruise would be at an end.

Life at Milliard City continued amid unchanging calm. Always this existence, as in one of the large towns of

America or Europe—constant communications with the
new continent by steamers or telegraphic cables, the usual
family visits, the manifest tendency towards reconciliation
between the two rival sections, the walks and games, the
concerts of the quartette always in favour among the
dilettanti.

Christmas, so dear to Protestants and Catholics, was
celebrated with great pomp at the temple and at St.
Mary's church, as in the mansions, the hotels, and the
houses of the commercial quarter. This solemnity meant
a general holiday throughout the island during the week
which ended on the 1st of January.

In the meantime, the newspapers of Floating Island,
the *Starboard Chronicle* and the *New Herald*, did not
cease from offering their readers the latest news, home
and foreign. An item of news, published simultaneously
by both papers, caused a good deal of comment.

In the papers for the 26th of December it was stated
that the King of Malecarlie had been to the town hall,
where the Governor had given him an audience. What was
the object of this visit? Rumours of all sorts flew about
the town, and they would doubtless have been based on
the most unlikely hypotheses, if the newspapers next
day had not contained positive information on this
subject.

The King of Malecarlie had asked for a place in
the Observatory, and the company had acceded to his
request.

"Well," exclaimed Pinchinat, "you must live in Milliard City to see a thing like that; a sovereign, with a
glass at his eye, watching the stars on the horizon."

"A star of the earth interrogating his brothers in the
firmament!" replied Yvernès.

The news was authentic, and this is why His Majesty
was under the necessity of asking for the appointment.

He was a good king, this King of Malecarlie, and the
princess his wife was a good queen. They had done all
the good they could in one of the minor states of Europe,

being of enlightened liberal minds, without pretending that their dynasty, although it was one of the most ancient on the old continent, was of divine origin. The king was well informed in scientific matters, a great admirer of art, and passionately fond of music. A learned man and a philosopher, he was in no way blind with regard to the future of European sovereignties, and he was always prepared to leave his kingdom as soon as his people wanted him no more. Having no direct heir, he in no way injured his family when the time came for him to abandon his throne and lay aside his crown.

This time had come three years before. But there had been no revolution in the kingdom of Malecarlie, or at least no blood had been shed. By mutual agreement the contract was broken between his Majesty and his subjects. The king became a man, his subjects became citizens, and he left without more fuss than if he had been a tourist who had taken his ticket at the railway station, leaving his government to be replaced by another.

Vigorous still at sixty years of age, the king rejoiced in a constitution, better perhaps than that which his old kingdom had given itself. But the health of the queen was rather precarious, and required a climate free from sudden changes of temperature. This approach to uniformity of climatic conditions it was difficult to meet with elsewhere than on Floating Island, since it appeared that she was not able to submit to the fatigue of running from latitude to latitude after fine weather. It seemed as though the invention of the Floating Island Company offered these advantages, as the wealthiest men in the United States had made it the town of their adoption.

That is why, as soon as Floating Island had been constructed, the King and Queen of Malecarlie had resolved to take up their abode in Milliard City. Permission to do so had been granted them on condition that they lived as simple citizens, without any distinction or privilege.

There was not much chance of their Majesties wishing

to live otherwise. They rented a small house in the Thirty-ninth Avenue, in the Starboard Section, surrounded by a garden which opened on to the large park. There lived the two sovereigns in retirement, mixing in no way with the rivalries and intrigues of the rival sections, and content with their humble existence. The king occupied himself in astronomical studies, for which he had always had a great taste. The queen, a sincere Catholic, lived a semi-cloistral life, having not even the opportunity of devoting herself to charitable works, inasmuch as misery was unknown on the Pearl of the Pacific.

Such is the story of these ancient masters of the kingdom of Malecarlie—a story which the superintendent related to our artistes, adding that this king and this queen were the best people it was possible to meet, although their fortune was relatively very small.

The quartette, greatly affected at this fall from high estate, born with such philosophy and resignation, felt respectful sympathy for the dethroned sovereigns. Instead of taking refuge in France, that country of kings in exile, their Majesties had made choice of Floating Island as wealthy people make choice of Nice or Corfu, for reasons of health. They were not, of course, exiles ; they had not been driven from their kingdom ; they could live there, they could return there, if they chose to do so, as simple citizens. But they had no thought of doing so, and were content with this peaceful existence, conforming to the laws and regulations of Floating Island.

That the King and Queen of Malecarlie were not rich was true enough, compared with the majority of the Milliardites, and relatively to the wants of life in Milliard City. What could you do with two hundred thousand francs of income, when the rent of a small house was fifty thousand ? The ex-sovereigns were not wealthy compared with the emperors and kings of Europe, who do not make much of a figure compared with the Goulds, Vanderbilts, Rothschilds, Astors, Mackays, and other deities of finance. Although they indulged in no luxuries, confining themselves only to necessaries, they were not easy in their circumstances. But the queen's health was so well suited by this residence in the island, that the king had no thought of leaving it. Thus he wished to increase his income by his work, and a situation becoming vacant at the observatory—a situation of which the salary was very high—he had applied for it to the Governor. Cyrus Bickerstaff, after consulting the general administration at Madeleine Bay, had granted the appointment to the sovereign, and that is why the newspapers had announced that the King of Malecarlie had been appointed astronomer of Floating Island.

What a subject for conversation in other countries! There they talked about it for a couple of days and thought no more of it. It appeared quite natural that a king should seek in work the possibility of continuing this tranquil existence at Milliard City. He was a scientific man ; they would profit by his science. There was nothing in that but what was honourable. If he discovered some new star, planet, or comet, they would give it his name, which would figure with honour among the mythological names with which the official annuals swarm.

As they were walking in the park, Sebastien Zorn, Pinchinat, Yvernès, and Frascolin were talking about this event. In the morning they had seen the king going to his office, and they were not yet sufficiently Americanized to accept the situation as an every-day occurrence. Then they chatted about this matter, and Frascolin observed :

"It seems that if his Majesty had not been capable of doing the work of an astronomer, he would have had to give lessons like a professor of music."

"A king going out teaching !" exclaimed Pinchinat.

"Certainly, and at the price his rich pupils would pay him for his lessons—"

"They say he is a very good musician," observed Yvernès.

"I am not surprised at his being enthusiastic over

music," added Sebastien Zorn ; " for we have seen him at the door of the casino, during our concerts, owing to his not being able to afford a stall for the queen and himself."

" Well, fiddlers, I have an idea ! " said Pinchinat.

" An idea of his Highness's," replied the violoncellist, " is sure to be a queer one."

" Queer or not, old Sebastien," said Pinchinat, " I am sure you will approve of it."

" Let us hear this idea," said Frascolin.

" To give a concert at their Majesties', to them alone in their drawing-room, and to play the best pieces in our repertory."

" Well," said Sebastien Zorn, " your idea is not a bad one."

" Confound it, I have many like that in my head, and when I shake it—"

" It sounds like a rattle ! " said Yvernès.

" My dear Pinchinat," said Frascolin, " let us be content to-day with your proposal. I am certain it would be a great pleasure to this good king and this good queen."

" To-morrow, we will write and ask for an audience," said Sebastien Zorn.

" Better than that ! " said Pinchinat. " This very evening let us call at the royal habitation with our instruments, like a band of musicians come to give them a morning greeting—"

" You mean a serenade," said Yvernès, " for it will be at night."

" Be it so, first violin, severe but just ! Do not let us juggle with words ! Is it agreed ? "

" Agreed."

It was really an excellent idea. The king would no doubt appreciate this delicate attention, and be happy to hear the French artistes.

When the day closed in, the Quartette Party, laden with their violin cases and the violoncello box, left the casino in the direction of Thirty-ninth Avenue, situated at the extremity of the Starboard Section.

It was a very quiet house, having a small court in front with a verdant lawn. On one side were the domestic offices, on the other the stables, which were not used. The house consisted of a ground floor entered from a flight of steps, and a story surmounted by a mezzanine window and a mansard roof. On the right and left two magnificent nettle trees shaded the double footpath which led to the garden. Beneath the trees in the garden, which did not measure two hundred superficial metres, extended a lawn. There was no comparison between this cottage and the mansions of the Coverleys, Tankerdons, and other notables of Milliard City. It was the retreat of a sage who lived in retirement, of a learned man, a philosopher. Abdolonymus would have been satisfied with it when he left the throne of the kings of Sidon.

The king of Malecarlie had for his only chamberlain a valet, and the queen for a maid of honour had but her lady's maid. Add to this an American cook, and you have all the household of the deposed sovereigns, who once on a time were brother to brother with the emperors of the old continent.

Frascolin touched an electric bell. The valet opened the gate.

Frascolin expressed the wish of himself and comrades to present their respects to his Majesty, and begged the favour of being admitted.

The servant asked them to enter, and they stopped before the flight of steps.

Almost immediately the valet returned to inform them that the king would receive them with pleasure. They were introduced into the vestibule, where they put down their instruments, then into the drawing-room, where their Majesties entered at the same instant. That was all the ceremonial of this reception.

The artistes bowed respectfully before the king and queen. The queen, very simply dressed in dark coloured stuff, wore no headdress, but her abundant hair whose grey locks gave a charm to her rather pale face and somewhat weary look. She sat in an arm-chair near the window which opened on to the garden, beyond which were the trees of the park.

The king, standing, replied to the greeting of the visitors, and asked them to say what motive had brought them to this house, which was away on the outskirts of Milliard City.

The quartette felt somewhat affected as they looked at this sovereign whose appearance was one of inexpressible dignity. His look was keen under his almost black eyebrows—the profound look of a scientific man. His white beard fell large and silky on his chest. His face, of which a charming smile tempered the rather serious expression, could but arouse the sympathy of those who approached him.

Frascolin acted as spokesman, his voice trembling slightly.

"We thank your Majesty," said he, "for having deigned to welcome artistes who desire to offer you their respectful homage."

" The queen and I thank you, gentlemen, and we are sensible of your compliment. To this island, where we hope to end so troubled an existence, it seems as though you had brought a little of the fine air of your France. Gentlemen, you are not unknown to a man who, though busy with science, is passionately fond of music, that art in which you have acquired such good reputation in the artistic world. We know the successes you have obtained in Europe, in America. In the applause which welcomed the Quartette Party to Floating Island we have taken part —at a distance, it is true. And we have had one regret, that at not having yet heard you as you deserve to be heard."

The king gave a sign for his guests to sit down, while he stood before the mantelpiece, the marble of which supported a magnificent bust of the queen, when young, by Franquetti.

To come to business, Frascolin had only to reply to the last sentence uttered by the king.

"Your Majesty is right," said he, "and the regret expressed is fully justified as concerning that branch of music of which we are the interpreters. Chamber music demands more privacy than is obtainable with a numerous audience. It requires a little of the meditation of the sanctuary."

"Yes, gentlemen," said the queen, "this music should be heard as one would hear a strain of celestial harmony, and it is really in a sanctuary that it should—"

"Will, then, your Majesties," said Yvernès, "allow us to transform this room into a sanctuary for an hour, and be heard by your Majesties alone—"

Yvernès had not finished these words when the faces of the two sovereigns brightened.

"Gentlemen," said the king, "you wish—you had thought of this?"

"That is the object of our visit."

"Ah!" said the king, extending his hand to them. "I therein recognize French musicians in whom the heart equals the talent. I thank you in the name of the queen and myself! Nothing—no! nothing could give us greater pleasure."

And while the valet received orders to bring in the instruments and arrange the room for the improvised concert, the king and queen invited their guests to follow them into the garden. There they talked of music as artistes might in the completest intimacy.

The king abandoned himself to his enthusiasm for this art, like a man who felt all its charm, and understood all its beauties. He showed, to the astonishment of his auditors, how well he knew the masters he was to listen to in a few minutes. He talked of the ingenuous and ingenious genius of Haydn. He recalled what a critic had said of Mendelssohn, that unequalled composer of chamber music, who expressed his ideas in the language of Beethoven. Weber, what exquisite sensibility, what a chivalrous spirit, which made him a master different from all the others! Beethoven, that prince of instrumental music. . . . His soul was revealed in his symphonies. The works of his genius yielded neither in grandeur nor in value to the masterpieces of poetry, painting, sculpture, or architecture—that sublime star which finally set in the choir symphony in which the voices of the instruments mingle so closely with human voices.

"And yet he was never able to dance in time."

As may be imagined, it was from Pinchinat that this most inopportune remark emanated.

"Yes," replied the king, smiling, "that shows that the ear is not necessarily an indispensable organ to the musician. It is with the heart, and that alone, that he hears. And has not Beethoven proved that in the incomparable symphony I mentioned, composed when his deafness did not allow him to hear a sound ? "

After Haydn, Weber, Mendelssohn, Beethoven, it was of Mozart that his Majesty spoke with enthusiastic eloquence.

"Ah, gentlemen," he said, "let me give vent to my raptures. It is such a time since I have had an opportunity of saying what I think ! Were you not the first artistes I have been able to understand since my arrival at Floating Island ? Mozart ! Mozart ! One of your dramatic composers, the greatest, in my opinion, of the end of the nineteenth century, has devoted some admirable pages to him ! I have read them, and nothing will ever efface them from my memory ! He tells us with what facility Mozart gave to each word its special emphasis and intonation without affecting the rhythm and character of the musical phrase. He says that to pathetic truthfulness he added the perfection of physical beauty. Was not Mozart the only one who divined with certainty as unfailing, as complete, the musical form of all the sentiments of all the shades of passion and character ; that is all that forms the human drama ? Mozart was not a king —what is a king nowadays ?" added his Majesty, shaking his head ; " I say he was a god, if they will still permit the existence of a god. He was the God of Music ! "

We cannot describe, for it was indescribable, the ardour with which his Majesty manifested his admiration ; and when he and the queen had entered the room, the artistes following him, he took up a pamphlet that lay on the table. This pamphlet, which seemed to have been read and re-read, bore the title, "Mozart's Don Juan." Then he opened it and read these few lines from the pen of the master who most understood and best loved Mozart, the illustrious Gounod: "O Mozart! Divine Mozart! It is little you require to be understood to be adored. Thine is constant truthfulness! Thine is perfect beauty! Thine is inexhaustible charm! Thou art always profound and always clear! Thine are complete humanity and the simplicity of the child! Thou hast felt everything and expressed everything in musical phrase, which has never been surpassed, and never will be surpassed!"

Then Sebastien Zorn and his comrades took their instruments, and in the light of the electric lamp, which shed a gentle radiance through the room, they played the first of the pieces they had chosen for this concert.

It was the second quartette in A minor, op. 13 of Mendelssohn, in which the royal audience took infinite pleasure.

To this quartette succeeded the third in C major, op. 75 of Haydn, that is to say, the Austrian Hymn, executed with incomparable mastery. Never had executants been nearer perfection than in the intimacy of this sanctuary where our artistes had no one to hear them but two deposed sovereigns.

And when they had finished the hymn enriched by the genius of the composer, they played the sixth quartette in B flat op. 18 of Beethoven, the *Malinconia*, of character so sad, and power so penetrating, that the eyes of their Majesties were wet with tears.

Then came the admirable fugue in C minor of Mozart, so perfect, so free from all scholastic research, so natural, that it seemed to flow like limpid water, or pass like the **breeze** through the leaves. Finally, it was one of the most admirable quartettes of the divine composer, the tenth in D major, op. 35, which ended this never-to-be-forgotten evening, of which the nabobs of Milliard City had never had the equal.

And it was not that the Frenchmen were tired of playing these admirable works, or that the king and queen were tired of listening to them ; but it was eleven o'clock, and his Majesty said,—

" We thank you, gentlemen, and our thanks come from the depths of our hearts. Thanks to the perfection of your execution, we have enjoyed artistic delights which nothing will make us forget! It has done us so much good."

" If the king desires it," said Yvernès, " we could still—"

" Thank you, gentlemen, for the last time, thanks. We will not abuse your kindness. It is late, and then—to-night—I am on duty—"

This expression, in the mouth of the king, recalled our artistes to the realities. Before the sovereign who thus spoke they felt somewhat confused—they lowered their eyes.

" Yes, gentlemen," continued the king, playfully, " am I not the astronomer of the observatory of Floating Island, and," added he, with some emotion, " inspector of stars—of falling stars ? "

CHAPTER IV.

DURING the last week of the year, devoted to Christmas joys, numerous invitations were given for dinners, parties, and official receptions ; a banquet given by the Governor to the principal personages of Milliard City, attended by the Starboard and Larboard notables, testified to a certain fusion between the two sections of the town. The Tankerdons and the Coverleys found themselves at the same table. On New Year's Day there was an exchange of cards between the mansion in the Nineteenth Avenue and that in the Fifteenth. Walter Tankerdon even received an invitation for one of Mrs. Coverley's concerts. The welcome with which he was received by the mistress of the house appeared to be of good augury. But it was a long way from that to closer ties, although Calistus Munbar, in his characteristic way, was continually repeating to those who cared to listen to him,—

" It is done, my friends, it is done."

Floating Island continued its peaceful navigation towards the archipelago of Tonga-Tabou. Nothing seemed likely to trouble it, when on the night of the 30th of December there occurred an unexpected meteorologic phenomenon.

Between two and three in the morning distant detonations were heard. The look-outs did not trouble about this more than was necessary. They did not suppose that it meant a naval combat, unless it was between the ships of those South American Republics who are frequently at war. After all, why should they trouble about it on Floating Island, an independent island at peace with the powers of the two worlds ?

Besides, these detonations, which came from the eastern parts of the Pacific, lasted until daylight, and certainly could not be mistaken for the full regular roar of distant artillery.

Commodore Simcoe, informed by one of his officers, went to observe the horizon from the top of the observatory tower. There was no light visible on the surface of the wide segment of sea that lay before his eyes. But the sky had not its usual aspect. Reflections of flames coloured it up to the zenith. The air appeared misty, although the weather was fine and the barometer did not indicate by a sudden fall any perturbation in the atmosphere.

At daybreak the early risers of Milliard City had a strange surprise. Not only did the detonations continue, but the air was full of red and black mist, a kind of impalpable dust, which began to fall like rain. You might call it a shower of fuliginous molecules. In a few moments the streets of the town, the roofs of the houses were covered with a substance in which were combined the colours of carmine, madder, nacarat, and purple with blackish ashes.

The people were all out of doors—except Athanase Dorémus, who never got up before eleven after going to bed at eight. The quartette had, of course, jumped out of bed and gone to the observatory, where the Commodore, his officers, his astronomers, without forgetting the new royal functionary, were endeavouring to discover the cause of the phenomenon.

"It is regrettable," remarked Pinchinat, "that this red matter is not liquid, and that this liquid is not a shower of Pomard or Château Lafitte !"

"Tippler !" said Sebastien Zorn.

But what was the cause of this phenomenon ? There have been many examples of these showers of red dust, composed of silica, alumina, chromic oxide and ferric oxide. At the beginning of the century Calabria and the Abruzzi were inundated with these showers, which the superstitious inhabitants took for drops of blood when, as at Blancen-

berghe, in 1819, they were merely chloride of cobalt.
There have also been clouds of molecules of soot or carbon
borne from distant fires. There have even been showers
of soot at Fernambouc in 1820, yellow showers at Orleans
in 1829, and in the Basses Pyrenees in 1836 showers of
pollen drifted from firs in bloom.

What origin could be attributed to this fall of dust
mingled with scoriæ, with which the air seemed laden and
which fell on Floating Island and the surrounding sea
in thick reddish masses ?

The King of Malecarlie gave it as his opinion that these
substances came from some volcano in the islands to the
west. His colleagues at the observatory agreed with him.
They collected several handfuls of these scoriæ, the temperature of which was above that of the air, and which had
not cooled down in their passage through the atmosphere.
An eruption of great violence would explain the irregular
detonations that had been heard. These regions are strewn
with craters, some in activity, others extinct, but suscep-
tible of revival under subterranean action ; without counting those which geologic upheavals occasionally lift from
the ocean's depths, the force of their projection being often
extraordinary.

And in the midst of this archipelago of Tonga to which
Floating Island was going, had not a few years before the
peak of Tufua been covered with its eruptive matters for
an area of more than a hundred kilometres ? And for
hours had not the detonations of the volcano been heard
two hundred kilometres away ?

Then, in the month of August, 1883, the eruption of
Krakatoa had desolated the parts of the islands of Java
and Sumatra adjoining Sunda Strait, destroying entire
villages, causing earthquakes, covering the soil with com-
pact mud, raising the sea in formidable waves, infecting
the atmosphere with sulphurous vapours, and wrecking
ships. Really, it might be asked if Floating Island were
not threatened with dangers of this kind.

Commodore Simcoe began to be uneasy, for navigation

threatened to become very difficult. He gave orders to slacken speed, and Floating Island began to move with extreme slowness.

A certain amount of alarm seized on the Milliardites. Were the dismal prognostics of Sebastien Zorn regarding the issue of the campaign on the point of realization ?

Towards noon the darkness was profound. The people had left their houses which could not stand if the metal hull were lifted by plutonian forces. There was equal danger in the case of the sea rising and sweeping over the coast.

The governor and the commodore went to Prow Battery, followed by some of the people. Officers were sent to both harbours with orders to remain there. The engineers were at their posts ready to manœuvre the island if it became necessary to retreat in the opposite direction. The misfortune was that the navigation became more difficult as the sky grew darker.

About three o'clock in the afternoon the people could hardly see ten yards in front of them. There was no trace of diffused light, such was the mass of cinders which absorbed the solar rays. It was feared that Floating Island, laden with the weight of the scoria fallen on its surface, would not be able to maintain its water line on the surface of the ocean.

It was not a ship that could be lightened by throwing overboard cargo, or clearing it of its weight. All that could be done was to trust in the strength of the construction.

The evening, or rather the night came, and still the only way to tell the time was by the clock. The darkness was complete. Beneath the shower of scoriæ it was impossible to keep the electric moons aloft, and they were brought down. But the lighting of the streets and houses which had gone on through the day was to be continued as long as the phenomenon lasted.

The night came ; the situation remained unchanged. It seemed, however, that the detonations were less frequent and also less violent. The fury of the eruption was diminishing and the rain of cinder, carried away to the south by rather a strong breeze, began to abate.

The Milliardites, regaining confidence a little, went into their houses, hoping that next day Floating Island would find itself under normal conditions. And then they could proceed to a long and complete clearing up.

No matter! What a miserable New Year's Day for the Pearl of the Pacific, and by how little Milliard City had escaped the fate of Pompeii and Herculaneum. Although it was not situated at the foot of Vesuvius, did not its voyage bring it within range of the volcanoes with which the bed of the Pacific is strewn?

The governor, his assistants, and the council of notables remained in constant attendance at the town hall. The look-outs on the tower watched every change on the horizon or at the zenith. So as to maintain its south westerly direction, Floating Island had not stopped its progress, but its speed was only two or three miles an hour. When day came—or at least when the darkness cleared off —its course would be laid for the Tonga Archipelago. Then doubtless it would be ascertained which of the islands of this part of the ocean had been the theatre of such an eruption.

In any case it was manifest as the night advanced that the phenomenon was passing away.

About three o'clock in the morning there was a fresh incident which caused another outbreak of alarm among the dwellers in Milliard City.

Floating Island received a shock which was felt through all the compartments of its hull. The shock was not sufficient force to cause the destruction of the houses or throw the engines out of work. The screws were not stopped in their propulsive movement. Nevertheless there was no doubt there had been a collision at the fore-end.

What had happened? Had Floating Island grounded on a shoal? No, for it continued to move. Had it then struck against a reef? Amid this profound darkness had it run into some vessel crossing its course, which had not been able to see it lights?

From this collision had there resulted any serious injuries, if not of a nature to imperil its safety, at least sufficient to require important repairs at the next stopping-place?

Cyrus Bikerstaff and Commodore Simcoe made their way not without difficulty through the thick bed of scoriæ and cinders to the Prow Battery.

There the customs' officers informed them that the shock was due to a collision. A ship of large tonnage, a steamer passing from west to east, had been rammed by the prow of Floating Island. The shock had not been serious for the island, but perhaps it had been different for the steamer. They had only sighted her at the moment of the collision. Shouts had been heard, but they had lasted only a few moments. The chief of the station and his men had run to the battery, but had seen nothing and heard nothing. Had the vessel gone down where she was? The hypothesis was unfortunately only too probable.

As to Floating Island, they had found that the collision had not caused it any serious damage. Its mass was such that even at reduced speed it would crumple in any vessel, no matter how strong she might be—even an ironclad of the first class—and sink it there and then. Something of this sort had doubtless happened.

As to the nationality of this ship, the chief of the station thought he had heard orders given in a rough voice—one of those roars peculiar to the commanders of English vessels. He could not, however, say so positively.

This was a serious matter, and might have consequences no less serious. What would the United Kingdom say? An English vessel was a part of England, and we know that Great Britain does not allow amputation with impunity. What claims and responsibilities Floating Island might expect!

Thus the New Year began. At ten o'clock in the morning Commodore Simcoe was still unable to make any observations. The air was still thick with vapours, although the freshening breeze was beginning to blow away the rain of cinders. At length the sun pierced the mists of the horizon.

In what a state were Milliard City, the park, the country, the works, the ports ! What a lot of cleaning had to be done ! After all, that concerned the road officers. It was merely a question of time and money, and neither was wanting.

The most urgent work was started on first. The engineers went to Prow Battery on the side of the coast where the collision had occurred. The damages were insignificant. The solid hull of steel was no more injured than the wedge driven into a piece of wood—the ship, for instance.

On the sea there was no wreckage. From the observatory tower the most powerful glasses could see nothing, although Floating Island had not moved two miles since the collision.

It was only right to prolong the investigations in the name of humanity.

The governor conferred with Commodore Simcoe. Orders were given to the engineers to stop the engines, and to the electric launches of both ports to proceed to sea.

The search, which extended over a range of five or six miles, yielded no result. It seemed only too true that the vessel, rammed below the water line, had sunk without leaving a trace of her disappearance.

Commodore Simcoe then resumed his ordinary speed.

At noon the observation indicated that Floating Island was a hundred and fifty miles south-west of Samoa.

Meanwhile, the look-outs were instructed to watch with extreme care.

About five o'clock in the evening they reported thick smoke in the south-west.

Was this smoke due to the final eruptions of the volcano which had so greatly troubled these regions ? This was hardly likely as the charts showed neither an island nor an islet in the vicinity. Had a new crater arisen from the sea?

No, and it was manifest that the smoke was approaching Floating Island.

An hour afterwards three vessels came in sight together, approaching rapidly.

Half an hour later they were recognized as ships of war. It was the division of the British squadron which, five weeks before, had passed Floating Island.

At nightfall the ships were within four miles of Prow Battery. Were they going to pass in the offing and continue their course? It was not probable, as from their lights they seemed to be remaining stationary.

"These vessels evidently intend to communicate with us," said the commodore to the governor.

"Wait and see," replied Cyrus Bikerstaff.

But in what way would the governor reply to the commander of the division if he had come to make a claim with regard to the recent collision? It was possible, in fact, that such was his intention; perhaps the crew had been picked up, perhaps they had been saved in their boats. It would be time to act when they knew what was the matter.

They knew in the morning very early.

At sunrise, the flag of the rear-admiral floated from the mizen of the leading cruiser, which slowly approached within two miles of Larboard Harbour. A boat was launched, and came towards the port.

A quarter of an hour afterwards Commodore Simcoe received the message,—

"Captain Turner, of Her Britannic Majesty's cruiser *Herald*, desires to be conducted at once to the governor of Floating Island."

Cyrus Bikerstaff, being informed of this, authorized the officer of the port to allow the landing to take place, and replied that he would await Captain Turner at the town hall.

Ten minutes afterwards a car placed at the disposal of the chief of the staff, who was accompanied by a lieutenant, deposited these two personages before the municipal palace.

The governor immediately received them in the room adjoining his office.

The usual salutations were exchanged—very stiffly on both sides.

Then carefully punctuating his words, as if he were reciting some quotations from current literature, Captain Turner expressed himself thus in one long interminable sentence,—

" I have the honour to acquaint his Excellency the Governor of Floating Island, at this moment in a hundred and seventy-seven degrees thirteen minutes east of the meridian of Greenwich, and in sixteen degrees fifty-four minutes south latitude, that during the night of the 31st of December and the 1st of January, the steamer *Glen*, of Glasgow, of three thousand five hundred tons, laden with wheat, indigo, rice, and wine, a cargo of considerable value, was run into by Floating Island, belonging to the Floating Island Company, Limited, whose offices are at Madeleine Bay, Lower California, United States of America, although the steamer was showing the regulation lights, a white at the foremast, green at the starboard side, and red at the port side, and that having got clear after the collision she was met with next morning thirty-five miles from the scene of the disaster, ready to sink on account of a gap in her port side, and that she did sink after fortunately putting her captain, his officers and crew on board the *Herald*, Her Britannic Majesty's cruiser of the first-class under the flag of Rear-Admiral Sir Edward Collinson, who reports the fact to his Excellency Governor Cyrus Bikerstaff, requesting him to acknowledge the responsibility of the Floating Island Company, Limited, under the guarantee of the inhabitants of the said Floating Island, in favour of the owners of the said *Glen*, the value of which in hull, engines, and cargo amounts to the sum of twelve hundred thousand pounds sterling, that is six millions of dollars, which sum should be paid into the hands of the said Admiral Sir Edward Collinson, or in default he will forcibly proceed against the said Floating Island."

One long sentence of about three hundred words, cut up with commas, but without a single full-stop. But it said all and left no way of escape. Yes or no, would the governor decide to admit the claim made by Sir Edward Collinson, and accept the statement as to the responsibility of the Company and the estimated value of twelve hundred thousand pounds attributed to the steamer *Glen*, of Glasgow?

Cyrus Bikerstaff replied by the usual arguments in cases of collision.

The weather was very obscure on account of a volcanic eruption which had happened in the westward. If the *Glen* had her lights going, so had Floating Island. Neither of them could see each other. The matter was beyond the control of either party; and according to the usual practice in such matters, each had to bear his own losses, and there was no question of claim or responsibility.

Captain Turner's reply,—

"His Excellency would doubtless be right in the case of two vessels navigating under ordinary conditions. If the *Glen* fulfilled these conditions, it was manifest that Floating Island did not; it could not be considered a ship; it constituted a constant danger in moving its enormous mass across the maritime routes; it was like an island, an islet, a reef which shifted its position in such a way that it could not be placed on the chart. England had always protested against this obstacle to which it was impossible to give a definite position hydrographically, and Floating Island would always be responsible for accidents of this nature, &c., &c."

It was evident that Captain Turner's arguments were not devoid of a certain logic. In his heart Cyrus Biker-staff felt that they were just. But he could not himself give a decision. The matter would be brought before those who had the right to do so, and all he could do was to acknowledge the receipt of Sir Edward Collinson's claim. Fortunately there had been no loss of life.

"Very fortunately," replied Captain Turner, "but there has been the loss of the ship, and thousands have been swallowed up in the damage done by Floating Island. Will the Governor consent to hand over to Admiral Sir Edward Collinson the estimated value of the *Glen* and her cargo?"

How could the governor consent to this payment? After all, Floating Island offered a sufficient guarantee. It was there to answer for any damage, if the tribunals decided that it was responsible, after investigating the causes of the accident and the value of the loss.

"That is your Excellency's last word?" asked Captain Turner.

"That is my last word," said Cyrus Bikerstaff, "for I am not in a position to admit the Company's responsibility."

Further salutes, stiffer than ever, exchanged between the governor and the English captain. Departure of the latter by the car which took him to Larboard Harbour, and return to the *Herald* by the steam launch.

When Cyrus Bikerstaff's reply was made known to the council of notables, it received their full and entire approbation, as it did that of the whole population of Floating Island.

That being settled, Commodore Simcoe gave orders for Floating Island to resume its voyage at full speed.

But if Admiral Collinson persisted, would it be possible to evade his pursuit? Were not his vessels of much superior speed? And if he enforced his claim with a few melinite shells, would it be possible to resist it? Doubtless the batteries of the island were capable of replying to the Armstrongs with which the cruisers of the division were armed. But the field offered to the English fire was infinitely greater. What would become of the women and children under the impossibility of finding shelter? Every shot would tell, while the batteries of the Prow and Stern would lose about fifty per cent. of her projectiles in aiming at a small and moving target.

It was therefore necessary to wait and see what Admiral Sir Edward Collinson would do.

They had not to wait long.

At nine forty-five a blank cartridge was fired from the central turret of the *Herald*, at the same time as the flag of the United Kingdom ran up to the mast-head.

Under the presidency of the governor and his assistants the council of notables was in session at the town hall. This time Jem Tankerdon and Nat Coverley were of the same opinion. These Americans, being practical men, did not think of attempting a resistance which might endanger the safety of everybody and everything on Floating Island.

A second gun was fired. This time a shell whistled over, aimed in such a way as to fall half a cable's length off in the sea, where it exploded with formidable violence, throwing up enormous masses of water.

By the governor's orders Commodore Simcoe hauled down the flag which had been hoisted in reply to that of the *Herald*. Captain Turner returned to Larboard Harbour. There he received securities signed by Cyrus Bikerstaff, and endorsed by the chief notables, for the sum of twelve hundred thousand pounds.

Three hours later the smoke of the squadron disappeared in the west, and Floating Island continued its course towards the Tonga archipelago.

CHAPTER V.

"And then," said Yvernès, "we shall put in at the principal islands of Tonga-Tabou."

"Yes, my dear fellow," replied Calistus Munbar, "you will have time to make acquaintance with this archipelago, which you can call the archipelago of Hapai, and even the Friendly Islands, as they were called by Captain Cook in acknowledgment of the good welcome he received."

"And we shall probably be better treated than we were at Cook's Islands," said Pinchinat.

"That is probable."

"Shall we visit all the islands of this group?" inquired Frascolin.

"Certainly not, considering that there are about a hundred and fifty of them."

"And afterwards?" asked Yvernès.

"Afterwards, we shall go to the Fijis, then to the New Hebrides, then as soon as we have landed those Malays we shall return to Madeleine Bay, where our campaign will end."

"Will Floating Island stop at many places in the Tonga Islands?"

"At Vavao and at Tonga-Tabou only," replied the superintendent, "and it is not there that you will find the real savages of your dreams, my dear Pinchinat."

"Evidently there are none in the West Pacific," replied his Highness.

"Pardon me, there are a respectable number in the New Hebrides and Solomon Islands. But at Tonga the sub jects of George the First are almost civilized, and I may add the ladies are charming.   I would not, however, advise you to marry one of these delightful Tongans."

"For what reason?"

"Because marriages between foreigners and natives are not usually happy.   There is generally incompatibility of temper."

"Good!" exclaimed Pinchinat, "and yet this old fiddler Zorn was thinking of getting married at Tonga-Tabou!"

"I!" retorted the violoncellist, shrugging his shoulders. "Neither at Tonga-Tabou nor elsewhere, understand, you clumsy joker."

"Evidently our conductor is a wise man," replied Pinchinat.   "You see, my dear Calistus—and even allow me to call you Eucalistus, so much do you inspire me with sympathy—"

"I have no objection, Pinchinat."

"Well, my dear Eucalistus, a man does not scrape the strings of a violoncello for forty years without becoming a philosopher, and philosophy teaches that the only way of being happy in marriage is not to get married."

In the morning of the 6th of January the heights of Vavao appeared on the horizon, the most important island of the northern group.   This group is very different, owing to its volcanic formation, from the two others, Hapai and Tonga-Tabou.   The three lay between seventeen and twenty-two degrees south latitude and a hundred and seventy-six and a hundred and seventy-eight degrees west latitude.   They have an area of two thousand four hundred square kilometres distributed over a hundred and fifty islands, peopled by sixty thousand inhabitants.

The ships of Tasman were there in 1643, and Cook's ships in 1773, during his second voyage of discovery in the Pacific.   After the overthrow of the dynasty of Finare-Finare, and the foundation of a Federal State in 1797, a civil war decimated the population of the archipelago.

Navigation is difficult enough amid this maze of islands and islets planted with cocoanut trees which it is necessary to follow to reach Nu-Ofa, the capital of the Vavao group. Vavao is volcanic, and being such is subject to earthquakes. This is taken into account in building the houses, not one of which has a nail in it. Wattled rushes form the walls with laths of cocoanut wood, and on piles or trunks of trees an oval roof is laid. The whole is very fresh and neat. This more particularly attracted the notice of our artistes posted at Prow Battery, while Floating Island passed along the channels bordered with Kanaka villages. Here and there a few European houses displayed the flags of Germany or England.

But if this part of the archipelago is volcanic, it was not to one of its volcanoes that could be attributed the formidable eruption of scoriæ and cinders that had been spread over these regions. The Tongans had not even been plunged into darkness, the western breezes having driven the clouds of eruptive matter towards the opposite horizon. Probably the crater from which they came belonged to some isolated island in the east, unless it was a volcano of recent formation between Samoa and Tonga.

The stay at Vavao lasted but a week. This island was worth visiting, although a few years before it had been ravaged by a terrible cyclone, which had thrown down the little church of the French Maristes and destroyed a quantity of native dwellings. Nevertheless the country remained very attractive with its numerous villages, enclosed by belts of orange trees, its fertile plains, its fields of sugar-cane and yams, its clumps of banana trees, mulberry trees, bread-fruit trees, and sandalwood trees. The only domestic animals were pigs and poultry. The only birds were thousands of pigeons and noisy parrots of brilliant colours. For reptiles there were only a few harmless serpents and lovely green lizards, which could be mistaken for leaves fallen from the trees.

The superintendent had not exaggerated the beauty of the native type—which is common to the Malay race of the different archipelagoes of the central Pacific. Superb men of tall stature, rather stout, perhaps, but of admirable

build and noble attitude, and a colour as of copper shaded
with olive. The women graceful and well proportioned,
hands and feet of a delicacy of form and a smallness that
must move to envy the Germans and English of the
European colony. The women are employed only in the
making of mats, baskets, and fabrics like those of Tahiti,
and their fingers are not deformed by such manual labour.
And then it is easy to judge of the perfection of Tongan
beauty. Neither the abominable trousers nor the trained
skirt had been adopted in the native fashions. Mere
cotton drawers or a belt for the men, the caraco and short
petticoat with ornaments in fine dried bark for the women,
who are at once distant and coquettish. In both sexes
the headdress is elaborate, the girls raising their hair over
their foreheads and piling it up on a trellis of cocoanut
fibre in the shape of a comb.

But there was nothing in all this to make Sebastien
Zorn recall his resolution. He would not marry either at
Vavao or at Tonga-Tabou or anywhere else in this sub-
lunary world.

It was always a great satisfaction for his comrades and
himself to land on these archipelagoes. They were pleased
enough with Floating Island, but to set foot on firm
ground was none the less pleasing to them. Real mountains, real country, real water-courses were a change from
imitation streams and artificial shores. It required a
Calistus Munbar to assign to his Pearl of the Pacific
a superiority over the works of nature.

Although Vavao is not the usual residence of King
George, he possesses at Nu-ofa a palace, let us say a
pretty cottage, at which he frequently lives. But on this
island of Tonga-Tabou are found the royal palace and the
establishments of the English residents.

Floating Island was to make its last stoppage there
almost at the limit of the Tropic of Capricorn, the
extreme point it would reach in the course of its voyage
across the southern hemisphere.

After leaving Vavao, the voyage of the Milliardites for

two days was one of considerable variety. One island was
not lost sight of until another rose to view ; all of them
presenting the same volcanic character due to the action
of plutonian force. It was with this northern group as
with the central group of Hapai. The hydrographic
charts of these regions are extremely accurate, and allowed
Commodore Simcoe to venture without danger amid the
channels of the labyrinth between Hapai and Tonga-
Tabou. Besides there was no paucity of pilots if he had
wanted their services. A number of vessels were moving
among the islands—for the most part schooners under the
German flag employed in the coasting trade, while the
larger merchant vessels take away the cotton and coprah
and coffee and maize, the principal productions of the
archipelago. Not only would pilots have hastened to
come if Ethel Simcoe had asked them, but also the crews
of their double canoes, united by a platform and able to
carry two hundred men. Yes ! Hundreds of natives
would have come at the first signal, and what a harvest
they would have had if the pilotage dues were calculated
on the tonnage of Floating Island. Two hundred and
fifty-nine million tons ! But Commodore Simcoe, to whom
all these figures were familiar, had no want of their good
offices. He had confidence in himself, and trusted to the
merit of the officers who executed his orders with absolute
precision.

Tonga-Tabou was sighted on the morning of the 9th of
January, when Floating Island was but three or four
miles away from it. Very low, its foundation not being
due to geologic effort, it has not been thrust up from below
like so many other islands that seem to have remained
motionless after coming to the surface of the sea to breathe.
It has been gradually built by infusorians, who have raised
tier upon tier of coral, and what labour ! A hundred
kilometres in circumference, an area of from seven to eight
hundred superficial kilometres on which live twenty
thousand inhabitants.

Commodore Simcoe stopped off the port of Maofuga.

Communications were immediately opened between the sedentary island and the movable island, a sister of the Latona of mythologic memory. What a difference there was between this archipelago and the Marquesas, Paumotu, and the Society Islands! English influence is here predominant, and King George the First was in no hurry to offer a cordial welcome to these Milliardites of American origin.

However, at Maofuga the quartette discovered a small French centre. There resides the Bishop of Oceania, who was then making a pastoral tour among the different groups. There are the Catholic mission, the house of the sisters, the schools for the boys and girls. Needless to say, the Parisians were received with cordiality by their compatriots. As to their excursions, there were only two places of importance for them to go to, Nakualofa, the capital, and the village of Mua, where four hundred inhabitants profess the Catholic religion.

When Tasman discovered Tonga-Tabou he gave it the name of Amsterdam—a name hardly justified by its houses of pandanus leaves at d cocoanut fibres. It is true that European habitations are not wanting; but the native name is more appropriate for this island.

The port of Maofuga is situated on the northern coast. If Floating Island had taken up its position a few miles more to the west of Nakualofa, its royal gardens and its royal palace would have been in sight of it. If, on the contrary, Commodore Simcoe had gone more to the east, he would have found a bay cut deeply into the coast, the head of which is occupied by the village of Mua. He did not do this because the island would have run the risk of being wrecked among the hundreds of islets, the channels between which only give passage to vessels of moderate tonnage. Floating Island had therefore to remain off Maofuga during the whole of the stay.

Though a certain number of Milliardites landed, there were not many who thought of exploring the interior of the island. It is charming nevertheless, and deserves the praises which

Elisée Reclus has showered upon it. Doubtless the heat is very great, the atmosphere stormy, the rains of extreme violence and calculated to calm the ardour of an excursionist, and a man must be touched with the tourist's mania who would venture into the country. Nevertheless this is what Frascolin, Pinchinat, and Yvernès did, for it was impossible to persuade the violoncellist to leave his comfortable room in the casino before the evening, when the sea-breeze refreshed the beach of Maofuga. Even the superintendent begged to be excused for being unable to accompany the enthusiasts.

"I should melt on the road," he told them.

"Well, we could carry you along in a bottle!" replied his Highness.

This engaging prospect did not persuade Calistus Munbar, who preferred to retain his solid state.

Very fortunately for the Milliardites, the sun had been moving northward for three weeks, and Floating Island could keep it at a distance, so as to maintain a normal temperature.

Next morning the three friends left Maofuga at daybreak, and started for the capital of the island. Certainly it was warm; but the warmth was bearable under cover of the cocoanut trees, the leki-lekis, the toui-touis, which are the candle trees, the cocas, whose red and black berries formed bunches of dazzling gems.

It was nearly noon when the capital showed itself in full bloom—an expression which is not inappropriate at this season of the year. The king's palace seemed to rise from a gigantic bouquet of verdure. There was a striking contrast between the native huts covered with flowers and the houses of English aspect which belonged to the Protestant missionaries. The influence of these Wesleyan ministers has been considerable, and after massacring a certain number of them the Tongans have adopted their creed. Observe, however, that they have not entirely renounced the practices of their Kanaka mythology; with them the high priest is superior to the king. In the teach-

ings of their curious cosmogony good and evil geniuses
play an important part. Christianity will not easily up-
root the taboo which is always held in honour, and when
it has been decided to break it, it cannot be done without
expiatory sacrifices in which human life is sometimes
sacrificed.

It should be mentioned that according to the accounts
of explorers—particularly that of Aylie Marin in his
travels in 1882—Nakualofa is still but half-civilized.

Frascolin, Pinchinat, and Yvernès had no desire to pay
their respects at the feet of King George. This is not to
be understood in a metaphoric sense, as the custom is to
kiss the sovereign's feet. And our Parisians congratulated
themselves when, in the square of Nakualofa, they noticed
the " tui " whom they call his Majesty, clothed in a sort of
white shirt, with a little skirt of native stuff tied round his
waist. This kissing of the feet would certainly have
been among the most disagreeable remembrances of the
voyage.

"You can see," said Pinchinat, " that water-courses are
not very abundant in this country."

At Tonga-Tabou, at Vavao, as in the other islands of
the archipelago, the maps show neither stream nor lagoon.
The rain-water is collected in cisterns, and that is all the
natives have, the subjects of George I. being as careful
with it as their sovereign.

During the day the three tourists, greatly fatigued,
returned to the port of Maofuga, and regained their rooms
in the casino with great satisfaction. To the incredulous
Sebastien Zorn they affirmed that their excursion had
been most interesting. But the poetic inducements of
Yvernès could not prevail on the violoncellist to start next
morning for the village of Mua.

The journey promised to be long and very fatiguing.
They might have easily spared themselves this fatigue by
using one of the electric launches that Cyrus Bikerstaff
offered to put at their disposal. But to explore the interior of this curious country was a consideration of some

value, and the tourists started on foot for Mua Bay along the coral shore which bordered the islets, where there seemed to have collected all the cocoanut trees in Oceania.

Their arrival at Mua could not take place before the afternoon. There was a place evidently pointed out for the Frenchmen to stay at. This was the residence of the Catholic missionaries. In welcoming his guests the Superior's delight was most affecting — the welcome recalled the way in which they had been received by the Maristes of Samoa. What an excellent evening! What interesting conversation, in which France was more talked of than the Tongan colony! These good men could not think without regret of their native land so far away.

It was with a certain pride that the Superior showed, to the admiration of his visitors, the establishments of the Mission—the house which was built for nothing by the natives of Mua, and the beautiful church due to the Tongan architects, of which their brethren in France would not be ashamed.

During the evening they took a walk in the environs of the village and visited the ancient tombs of Tui-Tonga, where schist and coral are intermingled with primitive and charming art. They even visited that old plantation of meas, banyans or monstrous fig-trees, with their roots interlaced like serpents, the circumference of which, in places, exceeds sixty metres. Frascolin measured them, and having entered the figures in his note-book, had them certified as correct by the Superior. After that, there could be no doubt as to the existence of such a vegetable phenomenon.

A good supper was followed by a good night in the best rooms of the mission. After that was a good break-fast and hearty farewells from the missionaries, and the return to Floating Island as five o'clock was striking from the belfry of the town hall. This time the three excur-sionists had not to have recourse to metaphorical amplifi-

cation to assure Sebastien Zorn that their journey had
left them with pleasant memories.

Next day Cyrus Bikerstaff received a visit from Captain
Sarol under the following circumstances.

A certain number of Malays—about a hundred—had
been recruited at the New Hebrides and taken to Tonga-
Tabou to work in the clearings—an indispensable importation considering the indifference, or rather idleness, of
the Tongans, who live from day to day. These clearings
had been finished a short time before, and the Malays
were awaiting an opportunity of returning to their country.
Would the Governor allow them to take passage on
Floating Island ? It was this permission which Captain
Sarol had come to ask. In five or six weeks they would
arrive at Erromango, and the carriage of these natives
would not be much expense.

It would not have been generous to refuse these men a
service so easy to render; and so the Governor gave his
permission, for which he was thanked by Captain Sarol,
and also by the Maristes of Tonga-Tabou, for whom these
Malays had been imported.

Who could doubt that Captain Sarol had in this way
increased the number of his accomplices ? that these
New Hebrideans would come to his assistance when he
had need of them, and that he could only congratulate
himself at having met with them at Tonga-Tabou and
introduced them on to Floating Island ?

This was the last day the Milliardites were to spend
in the archipelago, the departure being fixed for the
morning.

During the afternoon they were able to be present at
one of those half-civil, half-religious festivals in which the
natives take part with extraordinary enthusiasm.

The programme of these festivals, to which the Tongans are as partial as their congeners in Samoa and the
Marquesas, comprises several dances. As these were of a
kind to interest our Parisians, they went ashore about
three o'clock.

The superintendent accompanied them, and this time Athanase Dorémus expressed a wish to join them. The presence of a professor of dancing and deportment was surely appropriate at a ceremony of this kind ? Sebastien Zorn decided to follow his comrades, more desirous, doubtless, of hearing the Tongan music than of looking at the choregraphic eccentricities of the population.

When they arrived on the spot, the festival was in full swing. The Kava liquor extracted from the dried root of the pepper plant was circulating in gourds and flowing down the throats of a hundred dancers, men and women, young men and girls, the girls having coquettishly decorated their long hair, which they had to wear in that fashion until their wedding-day.

The orchestra was of the simplest. For instruments, the nasal flute known as the fanghu-fanghu, more than a dozen nafas, as the drums are called, on which they thump vigorously, "and even in time," as Pinchinat remarked.

Evidently the highly superior Athanase Dorémus felt the most perfect contempt for the dances, which did not enter into the category of quadrilles, polkas, mazurkas, and waltzes of the French school. And he did not fail to shrug his shoulders in protest against Yvernès, to whom these dances appeared to be marked with real originality.

First there were seated dances, composed of attitudes, pantomimic gestures, balancings of the body, to a rhythm slow and sad and of strange effect.

To these succeeded standing dances, in which the Tongans abandoned themselves to all the impetuosity of their temperament, representing in pantomime the fury of warriors on the war-path. The quartette looked at this spectacle from an artistic point of view, and wondered what the natives would have done if they had been excited by the fascinating music of a Parisian ball-room.

And then Pinchinat—the idea was characteristic— proposed to his comrades to send for their instruments from the casino, and treat these dancers to the wildest six-eights and most formidable two-fours of Lecoq, Audran, and Offenbach.

The proposal was agreed to, and Calistus Munbar had no doubt that the effect would be prodigious.

Half an hour afterwards the instruments had been brought, and the players began.

Immense surprise of the natives, and also immense delight at listening to this violoncello and these three violins, going at their loudest, and giving off music that was ultra-French.

The natives remained not unaffected, and it was clearly proved that their characteristic dances are instinctive, that they learn without masters—whatever Athanase Dorémus might think. The men and women strove to outdo each other in leaping and swaying when Sebastien Zorn, Yvernès, Frascolin, and Pinchinat attacked the furious rhythms of *Orphée aux Enfers*. The superintendent could not contain himself, and took part in a wild quadrille, while the professor of dancing and deportment veiled his face before such horrors. At the height of this cacophony, in which mingled the nasal flutes and the sonorous drums, the fury of the dancers attained its maximum of intensity, and we know not where it would have stopped, if something had not happened to put an end to this infernal choregraphy.

A Tongan—tall and very strong—wonder-struck at the notes which the violoncellist drew from his instrument, hurled himself on the violoncello, seized it, and rushed away with it, shouting, " Taboo ! taboo ! "

The violoncello was tabooed ! It could not be touched again without sacrilege ! The high priest, King George, the dignitaries of his court, the whole population of the island would rise, if this sacred custom were violated.

Sebastien Zorn did not care about this. He had no idea of parting with this masterpiece of Gand and Benardel. Off he went after the thief. In a moment his comrades were following in pursuit. There was a general stampede

But the Tongan sprang along with such speed that they had to give up their attempt to catch him. In a few minutes he was far away, very far away.

Sebastien Zorn and the others, unable to do more, returned to find Calistus Munbar, out of breath. To say that the violoncellist was in a state of indescribable fury would be insufficient. He foamed, he choked ! Tabooed or not, they would have to give him back his instrument. Even if Floating Island had to declare war against Tonga-Tabou—and had not war broken out for less serious motives ?—the violoncello must be restored to its owner.

Fortunately, the authorities of the island had intervened in the matter. An hour later they had caught the native, and obliged him to bring back the instrument. The restitution was not effected without trouble, and a crisis was only just avoided in which the ultimatum of Cyrus Bikerstaff might, on this question of taboo, have perhaps raised the religious passions of the whole archipelago.

But the breaking of the taboo had to take place in regular form, according to the usual ceremonies. As was customary, a considerable number of pigs had their throats cut, and were cooked in a hole filled with hot stones, and there were sweet potatoes, taros, and macore fruits, which were also afterwards eaten, to the extreme satisfaction of the Tongan stomachs.

The violoncello had its strings let down in the fray, and Sebastien Zorn had to tune it up again, after ascertaining that it had lost none of its qualities by reason of the incantations of the natives.

CHAPTER VI.

IN leaving Tonga-Tabou, Floating Island steered north-west towards the Fiji archipelago, moving away from the tropic in the track of the sun, which was mounting towards the Equator. There was no need for haste. Two hundred leagues only separated it from the Fijian group, and Commodore Simcoe took it along at moderate speed.

The breeze was variable, but what mattered the breeze to this powerful concern? If, now and then, violent storms broke on this twenty-third parallel, the Pearl of the Pacific did not even dream of being anxious. The electricity which saturated the atmosphere was drawn off by the numerous conductors with which its buildings were provided. As to the rain, even in the torrents that the storm-clouds poured down, it was welcome. The park and the country grew verdant under it, rare as it was. Life passed under the most fortunate conditions, amid festivals, concerts, receptions. At this time, friendly communications between the sections were frequent, and it seemed as though nothing would threaten their safety in the future.

Cyrus Bikerstaff had no reason to repent of having given a passage to the New Hebrideans embarked at Captain Sarol's request. These natives endeavoured to make themselves useful. They set to work in the fields, as they had done at Tonga. Sarol and his Malays hardly left them during the day, and at night they returned to the two ports in which the municipality had given them quarters. No complaint was made against them. Perhaps

an opportunity offered for converting them. Up to then they had not adopted Christianity, like a large number of the New Hebrides population, despite the efforts of the Anglican and Catholic missionaries. The clergy of Floating Island had considered this, but the Governor would allow no attempt of such a nature.

These New Hebrideans are between twenty and forty years of age. Darker in hue than the Malays, although they are not so well built as the natives of Tonga or Samoa, they were apparently endowed with more endurance. The little money that they had earned in the service of the Maristes of Tonga-Tabou, they kept with great care, and did not attempt to spend in alcoholic drinks, which would not readily have been sold to them. Being free of all expense, they had probably never been so happy in their savage archipelago.

Thanks to Captain Sarol, these natives would unite with their compatriots, and connive at the work of destruction, the hour of which was approaching. Then all their native ferocity would appear. Were they not the descendants of the murderers who have so formidable a reputation among the people of this part of the Pacific?

Meanwhile, the Milliardites lived in the thought that nothing could compromise an existence which had been so logically provided for and so wisely organized. The quartette continued their successful career. People were never tired of hearing them or applauding them. The works of Mozart, Beethoven, Haydn, Mendelssohn, were run through completely.

Besides the regular concerts at the casino, Mrs. Coverley gave musical evenings, which were largely attended. The king and queen of Malecarlie many times honoured them with their presence. If the Tankerdons had not yet visited the mansion in the Fifteenth Avenue, at least Walter had become assiduous in his attendance at the concerts. It was certain that his marriage with Miss Coverley would come off some day or other. It was talked about openly in the Starboardite and Larboardite drawing-rooms. Even the witnesses to the inevitable marriage were named. The only thing wanting was the announcement from the heads of the families. Would anything happen that would oblige Jem Tankerdon and Nat Coverley to make it?

This circumstance, so impatiently expected, was soon about to take place. But at the cost of what danger, and how greatly the safety of Floating Island was menaced!

In the afternoon of the 16th of January, at about half-way between Tonga and Fiji, a ship was signalled in the south-east. It seemed to be heading for Starboard Harbour, and was apparently a steamer of some eight hundred tons. No flag floated from its peak, and none was hoisted when it was within a mile of the island.

The ship did not attempt to enter one of the harbours, but apparently was passing, and doubtless would soon be out of sight.

The night came, very dark and moonless. The sky was covered with lofty fleecy clouds, which absorbed all the light and reflected none. There was no wind. The calm was absolute in sea and sky. The silence was profound amid the thick darkness.

About eleven o'clock came an atmospheric change. The weather became very stormy. The air was rent by lightning until midnight, and the growls of the thunder continued, without a drop of rain falling.

Perhaps these rumblings, due to some distant storm, prevented the Customs' officers on duty about the Stern Battery from hearing strange hissings and curious roarings, which troubled this part of the coast. These were not the hiss of the lightning or the rumbling of the thunder. The phenomenon, whatever it was, did not occur until between two and three o'clock in the morning.

Next day a new cause of uneasiness spread in the outer quarters of the town. The men engaged in watching the flocks pasturing in the country were seized with a sudden panic and dispersed in all directions, some towards the ports and some towards the gate of Milliard City.

A serious fact was that fifty sheep had been half devoured during the night, and their remains were found in the vicinity of Stern Battery. A few dozen cows, hinds, bucks, in the enclosures of the park, and some twenty horses had met with the same fate.

No doubt these animals had been attacked by wild beasts. What wild beasts? Lions, tigers, leopards, hyænas? Was that improbable? Had any of these formidable carnivores ever appeared on Floating Island? Could it be possible for these animals to arrive by sea? Was the Pearl of the Pacific in the neighbourhood of the Indies, of Africa, of Malaysia, the former of which comprises these varieties of ferocious animals?

No! Floating Island was not near the mouth of the Amazon, or the mouth of the Nile, and yet, about seven o'clock in the morning two women ran into the square of the town hall who had been pursued by an enormous alligator, which had regained the banks of the Serpentine River and disappeared in the water. At the same time the agitation of the plants along the banks indicated that other saurians were struggling there at that very moment.

The effect of this incredible news can be judged. An hour afterwards the look-outs noticed several tigers, lions, and leopards bounding across the country. Several sheep running towards Prow Battery were attacked by two immense tigers. The domestic animals began to run about in all directions, terrified at the roar of the wild beasts. And so did the men whose occupations called them out into the fields in the morning. The first tram for Larboard Harbour had barely time to run into the siding. Three lions had pursued it, and in a hundred yards more would have reached it.

There was no doubt that during the night Floating Island had been invaded by a band of ferocious animals, and so would Milliard City if precautions were not immediately taken.

It was Athanase Dorémus who brought our artístes the
news.   The professor of dancing and deportment had
gone out earlier than usual, and had not dared to return
to his house.   He had taken refuge in the casino, from
which no human power could remove him.

"Come, now!" said Pinchinat.   "Your lions and tigers
and alligators are imaginary."

But he had to yield to the evidence.   The municipality
had given orders to shut the town gates and bar the
entrance to the ports and the custom-house stations along
the coast.   At the same time the service of trams was
suspended, and people were prohibited from venturing
into the park or the country until the dangers of this
inexplicable invasion had been removed.

Then at the moment the gates were being closed at the
extremity of the First Avenue near the square of the
observatory, a couple of tigers had bounded from fifty
yards beyond with eyes aflame and mouths open.   A few
seconds more and these ferocious animals would have been
through the gate.

At the side of the town hall the same precaution had been
taken, and Milliard City had nothing to fear from an attack.

What an incident, what a subject for copy, what varied
reports in the *Starboard Chronicle*, the *New Herald* and
other journals of Floating Island !

Terror was at its height.   Mansions and houses were
barricaded.   The shops closed their shutters.   Not a door
remained open.   At the windows of the upper storeys
affrighted faces appeared.   The only people in the streets
were the detachments of militia under the orders of
Colonel Stewart and the police under the command of
their officers.

Cyrus Bikerstaff and his assistants, Barthélemy Ruge
and Hubley Harcourt, who had met at the earliest
moment, remained on duty at the town hall.   By the
telegraph from the two ports, the batteries and the posts
along the shore, the municipality received the most
disquieting news.   There were wild beasts almost every-

where, hundreds at least, said the telegrams, to which perhaps fear had added a cipher too many. It was undoubtedly the case that a number of lions, tigers, panthers, and caymans were at large in the island.

What, then, had happened ? Had a menagerie broken out of its cages and taken refuge on Floating Island ? But whence had this menagerie come ? What ship had brought it ? Was it the steamer that had been seen the evening before ? If so, where had this steamer come from ? Had she communicated with the shore during the night ? Had the animals swum ashore and landed on the low part of the coast near the mouth of Serpentine River ? Had the ship sunk immediately afterwards ? And yet, as far as the look-outs could see, as far as Commodore Simcoe's glasses could carry, there was not a fragment of wreckage on the surface of the sea, and Floating Island had hardly moved during the night ! Besides, if this ship had foundered, why had not the crew taken refuge on the island as the carnivores had done ?

The telephone from the town hall questioned the different posts on this subject, and the posts replied that there had been neither collision nor shipwreck. There could be no mistake in this matter, although the darkness had been profound. Evidently, of all the hypotheses this was the least likely.

" Mystery ! mystery !" Yvernes continued to repeat.

He and his comrades were gathered at the casino, where Athanase Dorémus was sharing their early breakfast, which would be followed by their luncheon and their dinner at six o'clock.

" My word !" said Pinchinat, munching his chocolate journal, which he had soaked in the smoking basin. " I give up these dogs or wild beasts. Anyhow, let us eat Mormein, Dorémus, until we are eaten."

" Who knows ?" replied Zorn. " Perhaps by lions, or tigers, or cannibals."

" I would rather have cannibals !" replied his Highness " Every one to his taste, eh ?"

He laughed, this indefatigable joker, but the professor of dancing and deportment did not laugh, and Milliard City, a prey to terror, had no cause for laughter.

At eight o'clock in the morning, the council of notables, convoked at the town hall, had all attended the Governor's summons. There was nobody in the avenues nor in the streets except the squads of militia and police going to the positions assigned to them.

The council, at which Cyrus Bikerstaff presided, immediately began its deliberations.

"Gentlemen," said the Governor, "you are acquainted with the cause of this well-justified panic which has seized on the people of Floating Island. During the night our island has been invaded by a band of carnivores and saurians. It is urgent that we proceed to the destruction of these animals, and we shall certainly do so. But the people must conform to the measures we decide upon. If traffic is still authorized in Milliard City, the gates of which are shut, it cannot be permitted in the park and in the country. Hence, until fresh orders, communications are forbidden between the town, the two ports and the batteries."

These measures being approved, the council passed to the discussion of the means which would permit of the destruction of the formidable animals which infested Floating Island.

"Our militia and our sailors," continued the Governor, "are organizing expeditions to the different points of the island. Those of you who are sportsmen we would like to join us, to direct their movements so as to prevent any possible catastrophe."

"Years ago," said Jem Tankerdon, "I had some shooting in India and in America, and it will not be my first attempt. I am ready, and my eldest son will accompany me."

"We thank the honourable Jem Tankerdon," replied Cyrus Bikerstaff, "and for my part I will follow his example. At the same time as Colonel Stewart's militia, a squad of sailors will be in the field, under Commodore Simcoe's orders, and their ranks are open to you, gentlemen."

Nat Coverley made a similar proposition to that of Jem Tankerdon, and finally all the notables whose age allowed, offered their services. Magazine rifles of long range were not wanting at Milliard City. There was little doubt that, thanks to everyone's devotion and courage, Floating Island would soon be cleared of this formidable band. But, as Cyrus Bikerstaff repeated, the main point was not to have to regret anyone's death.

" These wild beasts, of which we cannot estimate the number," he added, " must be destroyed as quickly as possible. To leave them time to acclimatize themselves, to multiply, would be to endanger the safety of our island."

" It is not likely," said one of the notables, " that there are many of these animals."

" Quite so. It could only come from some ship which was carrying a menagerie," replied the Governor, " some ship from India, from the Philippines, or the Sunda Islands, on account of some Hamburg house, which is noted for its trade in these animals. The animals may have escaped or been thrown overboard owing to their becoming unmanageable."

The principal market for wild beasts is at Hamburg, the current prices being two thousand francs for elephants, twenty-seven thousand for giraffes, twenty-five thousand for hippopotamuses, five thousand for lions, four thousand for tigers, two thousand for jaguars—good prices, as will be seen, which have a tendency to rise, while those for snakes are going down.

A member of the council having observed that the menagerie in question might have some representatives of the ophidians, the Governor replied that no ophidians had as yet been reported. Besides if lions, tigers, and alligators had been able to swim ashore, that would not have been possible with snakes.

Cyrus Bikerstaff remarked,—

" I think we have nothing to fear from the presence of boas, coral-snakes, rattle-snakes, najas, vipers, and other examples of that kind. Nevertheless, we will do all that is necessary to reassure the people on this subject. But we must not lose time, gentlemen, and before inquiring into the cause of this invasion of wild beasts, let us destroy them. They are here, and they must not remain here."

Nothing could be more sensible, and it could not have een better put.

CHAPTER VII.

THE total destruction of the animals which had invaded Floating Island must be proceeded with. Not a single pair of these formidable beasts must escape, as the future safety of the island was in danger. This pair would multiply, and the people might just as well live in the forests of India or Africa.

And at the outset, contrary to what had been asked by certain families under their influence of terror, there was no reason why the population should take refuge on the steamers at the two ports, and escape from Floating Island. Besides, the ships were not large enough.

The Milliardites set to work without losing a moment. A few had not hesitated to propose extreme methods; amongst others that of introducing the sea on to the island, of burning down the trees in the parks so as to drown or burn all this vermin. But in any case the means would not be efficacious as regards the amphibians, and it would be better to proceed by means of well-organized shooting parties.

This is what was done.

Captain Sarol, the Malays, and the New Hebrideans had offered their services, which had been eagerly accepted by the Governor. These gallant fellows were desirous of showing their gratitude to the Governor. In reality Captain Sarol was afraid that this incident would interrupt his plans, that the Milliardites and their families would abandon Floating Island. That would oblige the management to go back direct to Madeleine Bay, and thus foil his intentions.

The quartette showed themselves equal to the circumstances and worthy of their nationality. It would not be
said that four Frenchmen had not risked their lives when
danger was to be incurred. They put themselves under
the direction of Calistus Munbar, who, according to his
account, had been in a worse plight before, and shrugged
his shoulders in sign of contempt for lions, tigers, panthers,
and other inoffensive beasts! Perhaps he had been a
tamer, this grandson of Barnum, or at least a manager of
a travelling menagerie?

The hunt began that morning, and opened well.

During the first hour two crocodiles had the imprudence
to venture out of Serpentine River, and as we know
saurians, though formidable in their liquid element, are
much less so on land owing to the difficulty they have in
turning, Captain Sarol and his Malays attacked them
with courage, and not without one receiving a wound,
cleared the park.

Meanwhile twelve more were observed, which doubtless
constituted the band. These were animals of large size,
measuring from four to five metres, and consequently very
dangerous. As they had taken refuge under the water,
the sailors stood ready to send them a few of their
explosive bullets, which would shatter the hardest cara-
paces.

On the other hand the detachments of hunters went out
over the country. One of the lions was killed by Jem
Tankerdon, who had reason to say that this was not his
first attempt, and who recovered his coolness and skill as
an old hunter in the Far West. The beast was superb—
one of those worth from five to six thousand francs. A
steel slug had passed through its heart at the moment it
bounded on the quartette, and Pinchinat affirmed that he
felt the wind of its tail as it went by!

In the afternoon, during an attack in which one of the
militia was bitten in the shoulder, the Governor brought
down a lioness of remarkable beauty.

The day did not end before a couple of tigers had fallen

under the bullets of Commodore Simcoe, at the head of a detachment of sailors, one of whom, seriously wounded by a claw, had to be taken to Starboard Harbour. According to report, these terrible felines appeared to be the most numerous of the carnivores landed on Floating Island.

At the fall of night, the wild beasts on being resolutely pursued had retired under the trees at Prow Battery, whence it was proposed to dislodge them at break of day.

From the evening to the morning frightful growls spread terror among the female and infant population of Milliard City.

At daybreak the hunt commenced as on the day before. At the Governor's orders, conformably to the advice of Commodore Simcoe, Colonel Stewart brought up his artillery against the carnivores so as to sweep their hiding-places. Two cannons from Starboard Harbour, working on the Hotchkiss system in firing charges of bullets. were brought into the vicinity of Prow Battery.

At this place the clumps of nettle-trees were traversed by the tramway which branched towards the observatory. It was under the shelter of these trees that a certain number of the wild beasts had passed the night. A few heads of lions and tigers with gleaming eyes appeared among the lower branches. The sailors, the militia, the hunters, led by Jem and Walter Tankerdon, Nat Coverley, and Hubley Harcourt, took up their position on the left of this clump, waiting for the rush of wild beasts which the discharge from the cannon did not kill on the spot.

At Commodore Simcoe's signal the two pieces of cannon were fired simultaneously. Formidable growls were heard in reply. There was no doubt many of the carnivores had been hit. The others (about twenty) rushed out, and passing near the quartette, were saluted with a fusillade, which struck two mortally. At this moment an enormous tiger jumped on to the group, and Frascolin was struck by so terrible a leap that he rolled for ten paces.

His comrades rushed to his help. They raised him,

almost unconscious.   But he almost immediately recovered. He had only received a shock. Ah ! what a
shock !

Meanwhile the caymans were being pursued under the
waters of the Serpentine River, but how could they be got
rid of with certainty?   Fortunately, Hubley Harcourt
thought of raising the sluices of the river, and it was
possible to attack the saurians under the best conditions,
not without success.

The only victim to be regretted was a magnificent dog
belonging to Nat Coverley. Seized by an alligator, the
poor animal was cut in two by a bite. But a dozen of
these saurians had succumbed under the bullets of the
militia, and it was possible that Floating Island was
definitely delivered from these redoubtable reptiles.

On the whole it had been a good day. Six lions, eight
tigers, five jaguars, nine panthers, male and female, were
among the beasts slain.

The evening came, and the quartette, including Frascolin, recovered from his shock, had just sat down at the
table in the restaurant.

" I should like to believe that we are at the end of our
troubles," said Yvernès.

"Unless this steamer, like a second Noah's Ark, contained all the animals in creation," said Pinchinat.

This was not probable, and Athanase Dorémus felt
himself sufficiently reassured to return to his house in the
Twenty-fifth Avenue. There in the barricaded house he
found his old servant in despair at the thought that
nothing was left of her old master but a few shapeless
fragments.

This night was tranquil enough. Only a few distant
roars had been heard on the Larboard Harbour side. It
was to be hoped that next day, by proceeding to a general
hunt across the country, the destruction of these wild beasts
would be complete.

The group of hunters met in the early morning. During
the twenty-four hours, it need scarcely be said that

Floating Island had remained stationary, all the machinery staff being engaged with the rest.

The squads, each comprising twenty men with magazine rifles, had orders to advance through the island. Colonel Stewart did not consider it advisable to use cannon against the wild beasts, now they had dispersed. Thirteen tracked to the vicinity of Stern Battery fell to his gun. But he had to rescue, not without difficulty, two customs officers from the neighbouring post, who had been knocked down by a tiger and a panther, and had received serious wounds.

This last attack brought up to fifty-three the number of animals killed since the beginning of the day before.

It was four o'clock in the morning. Cyrus Bikerstaff and Commodore Simcoe, Jem Tankerdon and his son, Nat Coverley and the two assistants, escorted by a detachment of militia, were proceeding towards the town hall, where the council were awaiting the reports from the two ports and the two batteries.

At their approach, when they were within a hundred yards of the hall, loud shouts arose. A number of people, women and children, seized with a sudden panic, were running along First Avenue.

Immediately the Governor, Commodore Simcoe, and their companions rushed towards the square, the gate of which ought to have been shut. But by some inexplicable negligence this gate was open, and there could be no doubt that one of the wild beasts—the last perhaps—had entered by it.

Nat Coverley and Walter Tankerdon were the first to run into the square.

Suddenly, while he was within three yards of Nat Coverley, Walter Tankerdon was knocked down by an enormous tiger.

Nat Coverley, having no time to slip a cartridge into his gun, drew the hunting knife at his belt, and jumped to the rescue of Walter at the moment the animal's claws struck the young man's shoulder.

Walter was saved, but the tiger turned and attacked Nat Coverley.

He stabbed the animal with his knife without reaching the heart, and fell under.

The tiger recoiled, his throat roaring, his jaws open, his tongue bleeding—

There was the report of a gun.

It was Jem Tankerdon who had fired.

There was a second report.

It was the bullet which had exploded in the tiger's body.

They raised Walter, his shoulder wounded.

As to Nat Coverley, if he was not hurt, he had at least been close to death.

He rose, and advancing towards Jem Tankerdon, said in a solemn voice :

" You have saved me—thanks ! "

" You have saved my son—thanks ! " replied Jem Tankerdon.

And they shook hands in token of a reconciliation which might end in a sincere friendship.

Walter was immediately taken to the mansion in Nineteenth Avenue, where his family had taken refuge ; while Nat Coverley regained his house on the arm of Cyrus Bikerstaff.

We need not be astonished if next morning Mrs. Tankerdon visited Mrs. Coverley to express her thanks for the service rendered to Walter, and if Mrs. Coverley visited Mrs. Tankerdon to express her thanks for the service rendered Nat Coverley. Let us even say that Miss Coverley accompanied her mother, and was it not natural that both should ask how the young man was progressing ?

In fact everything was for the best, and, rid of its formidable visitors, Floating Island could safely resume its voyage towards the Fijis.

CHAPTER VIII.

" How many did you say ? " asked Pinchinat.

" Two hundred and fifty-five, my friends," replied **Fras-colin.** " Yes, there are two hundred and fifty-five islands and islets in the Fiji Archipelago."

"And how does that interest us," replied Pinchinat, " if the Pearl of the Pacific does not make two hundred and fifty-five stoppages ? "

"You will never learn geography !" proclaimed **Fras-colin.**

"And you—you know too much," replied his Highness.

And that was always the sort of welcome the second violin received when he tried to instruct his recalcitrant comrades.

However, Sebastien Zorn, who listened more willingly, allowed himself to be taken before the map at the casino, on which the position was marked each day. It was easy to follow the itinerary of Floating Island since its departure from Madeleine Bay. This itinerary formed a sort of large S, of which the lower loop curved up to the Fiji group.

Frascolin showed the violoncellist this collection of islands, discovered by Tasman in 1643—an archipelago comprised between the sixteenth and twentieth parallels of south latitude, and between the hundred and seventy-fourth and hundred and seventy-ninth meridians of east longitudes.

" So we are going to take our cumbrous machine among

those hundreds of pebbles scattered on the road?" observed Sebastien Zorn.

"Yes, my old string-fellow," replied Frascolin, "and if you look with attention—"

"And shut your mouth," added Pinchinat.

"Why?"

"Because the proverb says that the fly cannot enter a closed mouth!"

"Of what fly are you speaking?"

"The one that stings you whenever you want to break out against Floating Island!"

Sebastien Zorn shrugged his shoulders disdainfully, and turned to Frascolin.

"You were saying?"

"I was saying that to reach the two large islands of Viti-Levu and Vanua-Levu, there are three passages which cross the eastern group, those of Nanuku, La-kemba, and Oneata."

"To say nothing of the passage where you are smashed into a thousand pieces!" exclaimed Sebastien Zorn. "That will be the end of it! Is it possible to navigate such seas with such a town, and a large population in that town? No, it is contrary to the laws of nature!"

"The fly!" retorted Pinchinat. "That is Zorn's fly; see it!"

In fact, the obstinate violoncellist was always full of these dismal prognostics, and made no attempt to control them.

In this part of the Pacific the first group of the Fijis forms quite a barrier to ships arriving from the East. But there were passages wide enough for Commodore Simcoe to venture to bring Floating Island through them besides those pointed out by Frascolin. Among these islands the most important are the two Levus, situated in the west, and Ono, Ngaloa, Kandavu, &c.

A sea is enclosed within their summits emerged from the depths of the ocean, the Koro Sea, and if this archipelago, discovered by Cook, visited by Bligh in 1789, by Wilson in 1792, is so minutely known, it is because the remarkable voyages of Dumont D'Urville in 1828 and in 1833, of the American Wilkes in 1839, of the English Erskine in 1853, and the *Herald* expedition, under Captain Durham of the British Navy, have enabled them to be charted with a precision that does honour to the hydrographers.

Hence there was no hesitation on the part of Commodore Simcoe. Coming from the south-east, he entered the Voulanga passage, leaving to port the island of that name, in shape like a cut cake served on a coral dish. Next morning Floating Island entered the interior sea, which is protected against the ocean surges by substantial submarine chains.

It need hardly be said that all fears had not been allayed regarding the wild beasts. The Milliardites remained constantly on the alert. Constant expeditions were organized through the woods, fields and waters. No trace of wild beasts was discovered. No growling was heard by day or night.

The most positive result was the complete reconciliation that had been effected between the two sections of the town. After the Coverley-Tankerdon affair, the Starboardite and Larboardite families visited each other, invited each other, received each other. Every evening there was a ball and concert at one of the chief notables', particularly at the mansion in Nineteenth Avenue and the mansion in the Fifteenth. The Quartette Party had more than they could do; the enthusiasm they provoked did not diminish ; on the contrary it increased.

At last the great news came one morning while Floating Island was beating with its powerful screws the tranquil surface of this Koro Sea. Jem Tankerdon had gone officially to the house of Nat Coverley, and demanded the hand of Miss Di Coverley for his son Walter. And Nat Coverley had given Miss Coverley's hand to Walter Tankerdon, the son of Jem Tankerdon. The question of dowry had led to no difficulty. It would be two hundred millions for each of the young couple.

" They should have enough to live on—even in Europe," remarked Pinchinat, judiciously.

Felicitations reached both families from all parts. The Governor, Cyrus Bikerstaff, made no attempt to hide his extreme satisfaction. Thanks to this marriage, there would disappear all those causes of rivalry which had menaced the future of Floating Island. The king and queen of Malecarlie were among the first to send their compliments and good wishes. Visiting cards, printed in gold on aluminium, rained into the boxes at the mansions. The journals had paragraph after paragraph regarding the splendours in preparation—such as had never been seen at Milliard City, nor anywhere else on the globe. Cablegrams were sent to Paris with regard to the trousseau. The linendrapers' shops, the establishments of the great dressmakers, the jewellers, received the most extraordinary orders. A special steamer, starting from Marseilles, would come by Suez and the Indian Ocean, bringing these marvels of French industry. The wedding day was to be five weeks from then, on the 27th of February. The tradesmen of Milliard City had their share of profit in the affair. They had · to furnish their contingent to this wedding outfit, and fortunes were to be made out of the orders they received from the nabobs of Floating Island.

There could be no doubt who would organize the entertainments. Calistus Munbar was evidently the man. His state of mind was indescribable when the marriage of Walter Tankerdon and Miss Coverley was publicly announced. We know how he desired it, how he would have done everything to bring it about. It was the realization of his dream, and as the municipality intended to give him a free hand, rest assured that he would be at the height of his powers in organizing an ultra-marvellous festival.

At the date chosen for the nuptial ceremony, Commodore Simcoe announced in a note to the newspapers that Floating Island would be in that part of the sea between

Fiji and the New Hebrides. Before then it would stop at Viti-Levu, where the stay would last twelve days—the only one it was proposed to make amid this vast archipelago.

The voyage was delightful. Many whales played on the surface of the sea. With the thousand jets of water from their blowholes, it seemed like an immense basin of Neptune, in comparison with which that of Versailles was but a child's toy, as Yvernès said. But also in hundreds appeared enormous sharks, escorting Floating Island as if they were following a ship under way.

This portion of the Pacific is the boundary of Polynesia, which here is bordered by Melanesia, in which the group of the New Hebrides is situated.[1] It is cut by the hundred and eightieth degree of longitude—the conventional line which forms the boundary between the two parts of this immense ocean. When they reach this meridian, sailors coming from the east omit a day from their calendar, and, inversely, those coming from the west add one. Without this precaution there would be no concordance of dates. The preceding year Floating Island had not had to make this change, for it had not advanced to the westward beyond this meridian. But this time it had to conform to the rule, and as it came from the east, the 22nd of January had to become the 23rd.

Of the two hundred and fifty-five islands of which the archipelago of Fiji is composed, only a hundred are inhabited. The total population does not exceed a hundred and twenty-eight thousand inhabitants—a very slight density for an extent of twenty-one thousand square kilometres.

Of these islets, mere fragments of atolls, or summits of submarine mountains, fringed with coral, there are none that measure more than a hundred and fifty superficial

---

[1] These positions are according to the French charts, the zero meridian of which passes through Paris—a meridian which was generally adopted at this period.

kilometres. This political domain England has annexed to her colonial empire. If the Fijians have at length decided to submit to a British Protectorate, it is because they were in 1859 threatened with a Tongan invasion, which was checked by the United Kingdom. The archipelago is divided into seventeen districts, administered by the native chiefs, more or less related to the royal family of the last king, Thakumbau.

"Is it the consequence of the English system," asked Commodore Simcoe, who was talking on this subject with Frascolin, "that the Fijis will be like Tasmania? I do not know, but it is certain that the natives are disappearing. The colony does not prosper, nor does the population increase, as is shown by the numerical inferiority of the women compared to the men."

"That is a sign of the approaching extinction of a race," said Frascolin; "and in Europe there are already a few States which this inferiority menaces."

"Here," said the commodore, "the natives are really but serfs, like the natives of the neighbouring islands, recruited by the planters for the work of clearing the ground. Diseases decimate them, and in 1875 small-pox swept off more than thirty thousand. But it is an admirable country, as you can see. If the temperature is high in the interior of the islands, it is at least moderate on the shore. The country is very fertile in fruits and vegetables, in trees —cocoanut trees, bananas, etc. There is little more than the trouble of gathering the yams and taros, and the nourishing sap of the palm which produces sago."

"Sago!" exclaimed Frascolin, "what a remembrance of our 'Swiss Family Robinson'!"

"As to the pigs and the fowls," said the commodore, "these animals have multiplied since their importation with extraordinary prolificness. They furnish all the means of subsistence. Unfortunately, the natives are inclined to indolence, although they are intelligent and witty."

"And as they have high spirits—" said Frascolin.

"The children amuse themselves," replied Commodore Simcoe.

In fact, all these natives, Polynesians, Melanesians, and others, are nothing but children.

In approaching Viti-Levu, Floating Island sighted many intermediate islands, such as Vanua-Vatu, Moala, Ngau, without stopping at them.

From all parts came scudding along the coast flotillas of those long out-rigger canoes with intersecting bamboos, which serve to maintain the equilibrium of the vessel and carry the cargo. They were gracefully handled, but did not seek to enter Starboard Harbour or Larboard Harbour. Probably they would not have been allowed to on account of the evil reputation of these Fijians. These natives have embraced Christianity, it is true. Since the European missionaries established themselves at Lecumba, in 1835, they have nearly all become Wesleyans, mingled with a few thousand Catholics. But previously they were so addicted to the practice of cannibalism that perhaps they have not yet quite lost the taste for human flesh. Besides, it is a matter of religion. Their gods love blood. Kindness is regarded among these people as weakness, and even sin. To eat an enemy is to do him honour. They cook the man they despise, but they do not eat him. Children furnished the principal joints at their festivities, and the time is not so distant when King Thakumbau delighted to sit under a tree, from every branch of which hung a human limb reserved for the royal table. Sometimes a tribe—as happened to the Nulocas in Viti-Levu near Namosi—was devoured completely except a few females, one of whom died in 1880

Decidedly if Pinchinat did not meet on one of these islands the grandchildren of cannibals retaining the customs of their ancestors, he would have to give up asking for local colour in these archipelagoes of the Pacific.

The western group of the Fijis comprises two large islands, Viti-Levu and Vanua-Levu, and two smaller islands, Kandavu and Taviuni. More to the north-west lie the Wassava Islands and the Ronde Passage, by which Commodore Simcoe would make his way out towards the New Hebrides.

On the afternoon of the 25th of January the heights of Viti-Levu appeared on the horizon. This mountainous island is the largest of the archipelago, being a third larger than Corsica. Its peaks run from twelve to fifteen hundred metres above the level of the sea. These are volcanoes, extinct, or rather dormant, and apt to be disagreeable when they wake up. Viti-Levu has an area of six thousand four hundred and seventy-five square kilometres, and is connected with Vanua-Levu, its neighbour to the north, by a submarine barrier of reefs, which were doubtless above water when the land was formed. Above this barrier Floating Island could venture without danger. To the north of Viti-Levu the depths are estimated at from four to five hundred metres, and to the south from five hundred metres to two thousand.

Formerly the capital of the archipelago was Levuka, in the island of Ovalau, to the east of Viti-Levu. Perhaps the offices founded by English houses are still more important than those of Suva, the present capital, in the island of Viti-Levu. But the harbour of the latter has many advantages, being situated at the south-east extremity of the island, between two deltas. The port of call used by steamers in the Fijis occupies the head of Ngalao Bay, at the south of the island of Kandavu, the position of which is the nearest to New Zealand, Australia, and the French islands of New Caledonia and the Loyalties.

Floating Island stopped at the mouth of Suva harbour. The formalities were completed the same day and free pratique was accorded. As the visit would be a source of profit to both colonists and natives, the Milliardites were sure of an excellent welcome, in which there was probably more interest than sympathy.

Next day, the 26th of January, the tradesmen of Floating Island who had purchases to make or sales to effect went ashore early in the morning. The tourists, and among

them our Parisians, were almost as early. Although
Pinchinat and Yvernès made fun of Frascolin—the distinguished pupil of Commodore Simcoe—concerning his
ethno-geographical studies, they none the less availed
themselves of his knowledge. To the questions of his
comrades on the inhabitants of Viti-Levu, their customs,
their practices, the replies of the second violin were always
instructive. Sebastien Zorn did not disdain to refer to
him occasionally, and when Pinchinat learnt that these
regions were not long ago the principal theatre of
cannibalism, he could not restrain a sigh as he said :

"Yes—but we shall arrive too late, and you will see
that these Fijians, enervated by civilization, have come
down to fricasseed fowl and pigs' feet à la Sainte Mene-
hould !"

"Cannibal!" exclaimed Frascolin, "you deserve to
have figured on the table of King Thakumbau. Ah! ah!
Entrecote de Pinchinat à la Bordelaise."

"Come," said Sebastien Zorn, "if we are to waste our
time in these useless recriminations—"

"We shall make no progress by a forward movement,"
said Pinchinat. "That is the sort of phrase you like,
isn't it, my old Violoncelluloidist? Well, forward,
march !"

The town of Suva, built on the right of a little bay, has
its buildings scattered on the back of a green hill. It has
quays for mooring ships, roads furnished with plank side-
ways, like the beaches of our large bathing places. The
wooden houses have but one floor ; a few of them have
two floors, but all are cheerful and fresh-looking. In the
suburbs the native huts display their gable-ends raised
into horns and ornamented with shells. The roofs are
substantial, to resist the winter rains from May to October,
which fall in torrents. In fact in March, 1871, according
to Frascolin, who was very strong on statistics, Mbua,
situated in the east of the island, had a rainfall in one day
of thirty-eight centimetres.

Viti-Levu, like the other islands of the archipelago, is

subject to great differences in climate, and the vegetation differs on each shore. On the side exposed to the south-east trades the atmosphere is humid, and magnificent forests cover the soil. On the other side are immense savannahs suitable for cultivation. But it is noticeable that certain trees tend to disappear, among others the sandal-wood, almost entirely exhausted, and also the dakua, a pine peculiar to Fiji.

However, in their promenades, the quartette discovered that the flora of the island is of tropical luxuriance. Everywhere are forests of cocoanut trees and palms, their trunks covered with parasitic orchids, clumps of casuarinas, pandanus, acacias, tree ferns, and in the marshy parts numbers of mangrove trees with roots winding out of the ground. But the cultivation of cotton and tea has not given the results the climate had led people to expect. The soil of Viti-Levu, as in the rest of the group, is clayey and yellowish in colour, formed of volcanic cinders to which decomposition has given the productive qualities.

The fauna is not more varied than in other parts of the Pacific ; some forty species of birds, acclimatized parrots and canaries, bats, rats in legions, reptiles of non-venomous species, much appreciated by the natives from a com-missariat point of view, lizards, and horrible cockroaches of cannibalistic voracity. But of wild beasts there were none which provoked this sally from Pinchinat.

"Our Governor, Cyrus Bikerstaff, should have kept a few lions, tigers, panthers, crocodiles, and landed these useful carnivores in the Fijis. It would be a curious ex-periment in acclimatisation."

The natives, of mixed Polynesian and Melanesian race, still yield some fine examples, less remarkable, however, than those of Samoa and the Marquesas. The men are copper-coloured, almost black, their heads covered with a thick mass of hair, among them being a number of half-breeds, and they are tall and strong. Their clothing is rudimentary enough, oftenest being but mere cotton drawers made of the native fabric called "masi," produced by a species of mulberry tree, which also produces paper. In its first stage this fabric is quite white, but the Fijians know how to dye it and stripe it, and it is in demand in all the archipelagoes of the Eastern Pacific. It must be added that the men do not disdain to clothe themselves, when opportunity offers, in old European garments sent out from the old clothes stores of the United Kingdom or Germany. A fine field for joking was thus offered to a Parisian, when he saw these Fijians clad in worn-out trousers, a great-coat the worse for age, and even a black coat, which, after many phases of decadence, had come to end its days on the back of a native of Viti-Levu.

" You might make a romance out of one of those coats !" observed Yvernès.

" A romance that might end in a waistcoat !" replied Pinchinat.

The women have the short petticoat and masi jacket, which they wear in a fashion more or less decent. They are well-built, and with the attractions of youth some of them might pass for pretty. But what a detestable habit they have—as have also the men—in plastering their hair with lime so as to form a sort of calcareous hat to preserve themselves against sunstroke. And then they smoke as much as their husbands and brothers the tobacco of the country, which has the odour of burning hay, and when the cigarette is not between their teeth it is stuck into the lobe of their ears in the place where in Europe you have the pendants of diamonds and pearls.

In general these women are reduced to the condition of slaves, doing the hardest of household work, and the time is not distant when, after toiling to encourage the indolence of their husband, they were strangled on his tomb.

On many occasions, during the three days they devoted to their excursions round Suva, our tourists endeavoured to visit the native huts. They were repulsed, not by the inhospitality of their owners, but by the abominable odour that was given forth. All these natives, rubbed over with cocoa-nut oil, live in promiscuity with the pigs, the fowls,

the dogs, the cats, in evil-smelling huts, the choking light
being obtained by burning the resinous gum of the
dammana. No! They could not stop there. And if they
had taken their places at the Fijian fireside, would they
not, at the risk of failing in politeness, have had to steep
their lips in the bowl of kava, the special Fijian drink?
Though extracted from the dried bark of the pepper plant,
this pimentoed kava is unpleasing to European palates
owing to the way in which it is prepared. Is it not
enough to provoke the most insurmountable repugnance?
They do not grind their pepper, they chew it, they triturate
it through their teeth, then they spit it out into the water
in a vase, and offer it you with a savage insistence that
will hardly bear refusal. And nothing remains but to
thank them by pronouncing these words, which are current
in the archipelago, *E mana ndina*, otherwise *amen*.

Do not let us forget the cockroaches which swarm in
the huts, the white ants which devastate them, and
mosquitoes—mosquitoes in thousands—that can be seen
on the walls, on the ground, on the clothes in innumerable
bands.

CHAPTER IX.

WHILE our artistes were passing their time in walking about, and taking note of the customs of the archipelago, a few notables of Floating Island had not disdained to enter into communication with the native authorities of the archipelago. The "papalangis," as strangers are called in these islands, had no fear of being badly received.

During the stay the Tankerdon and Coverley families organized excursions in the neighbourhood of Suva, and in the forests which clothe its heights up to their topmost peaks.

And with regard to this, the superintendent made a very just observation to his friends the quartette.

"If our Milliardites are so fond of these excursions into high altitudes, it shows that Floating Island is not sufficiently undulating. It is too flat, too uniform. But I hope that some day we shall have an artificial mountain, rivalling the loftiest summits of the Pacific. Meanwhile, every time they have an opportunity our citizens are eager to ascend a few hundred feet, and breathe the pure and refreshing air of space. It meets a want of human nature."

"Very well," said Pinchinat. "But a suggestion, my dear Eucalistus! When you build your mountain in sheet steel or aluminium, do not forget to put a nice volcano inside it—a volcano with plenty of fireworks."

"And why, Mr. Facetious?" replied Calistus Munbar.

"And why not?" replied his Highness.

As a matter of course Walter Tankerdon and Miss
Coverley took part in these excursions arm-in-arm.

The curiosities of the capital of Viti-Levu were visited,
their "mbure-kalou," the temples of the spirits, and also
the place used for the political assemblies. These constructions, raised on a base of dry stones, are composed of
plaited bamboos, of beams covered with a sort of vegetable lace-work, of laths ingeniously arranged to support
the thatch of the roofs. The tourists went to see the
hospital, the botanic garden, laid out like an amphitheatre, behind the town. These walks often lasted until
late, and the tourists returned, lantern in hand, as in the
good old times.

And Captain Sarol and his Malays and the New Hebrideans embarked at Samoa. What were they doing
during this stay? Nothing out of their usual way. They
did not go ashore, knowing Viti-Levu and its neighbours,
some by having frequented these parts during their
coasting cruises, others by having worked there for the
planters. They very much preferred to remain on
Floating Island, exploring it in every part—town, harbours, park, country, and batteries. A few weeks more,
and thanks to the kindness of the company, thanks to
Governor Cyrus Bikerstaff these fellows would land in
their own country, after a sojourn of five months on
Floating Island.

Occasionally our artistes talked to Sarol, who was very
intelligent, and spoke English fluently. Sarol spoke to
them enthusiastically of the New Hebrides, of the natives
of the group, of their way of living, their cooking—which
interested his Highness particularly. The secret ambition
of Pinchinat was to discover some new dish, the recipe for
which he could communicate to the gastronomic societies
of Old Europe.

On the 30th of January, Sebastien Zorn and his comrades, at whose disposal the Governor put one of the
electric launches of Starboard Harbour, went away with
the intention of ascending the course of the Rewa, one of

the principal rivers of the island. The captain of the
launch, an engineer, and two sailors were on board, with
a Fijian pilot. In vain had Athanase Dorémus been
asked to join the excursionists ; the feeling of curiosity
was extinct in the professor of dancing and deportment.
And then, during his absence, a pupil might apply, and he
would therefore rather not leave the dancing-room.

At six o'clock in the morning, well armed, and furnished with a few provisions, for they would not return
until the evening, the launch left the Bay of Suva, and
ran along the coast to the bay of the Rewa.

Not only reefs, but sharks showed themselves in great
numbers in these parts, and as much care had to be taken
of one as of the other.

"Phew !" said Pinchinat. "Your sharks are only salt-
water cannibals ! I'll undertake to say that those fellows
have lost the taste for human flesh."

"Do not trust them," replied the pilot, "any more than
you would trust the Fijians of the interior."

Pinchinat contented himself with shrugging his shoulders.
He was getting weary of these pretended cannibals, who
did not even become cannibalistic on festival days !

The pilot was thoroughly acquainted with the bay and
the course of the Rewa. Up this important river, called
also the Wai-Levu, the tide is apparent for a distance
of forty-five kilometres, and vessels can go up as far as
eighty.

The width of the Rewa exceeds two hundred yards at
its mouth. It runs between sandy banks, low on the left,
steep on the right, from which the banana and cocoa-nut
trees rise luxuriantly from a wide stretch of verdure. Its
name is Rewa-Rewa, conformably to that duplication of
the word which is almost general among the people of
the Pacific. And, as Yvernès remarked, is this not an
imitation of the childish pronunciation one finds in such
words as papa, dada, bonbon, etc. ? In fact, these natives
have barely emerged from childhood.

The true Rewa is formed by the Wai-Levu (the great

water) and the Wai-Manu, and its principal mouth bears the name of Wai-Ni-Ki.

After the circuit of the delta, the launch ran past the village of Kamba, half hidden in its basket of flowers. It did not stop here, so as to lose nothing of the flood-tide, nor did it stop at the village of Naitasiri. Besides, at this epoch the village had been declared "taboo," with its houses, its trees, its inhabitants, up to the waters of the Rewa which bathed its beach. The natives would permit no one to set foot in it.

As the excursionists ran along in front of Naitasiri, the pilot pointed out a tall tree, a tavala, which rose in an angle of the bank.

"And what is there remarkable about that tree?" asked Frascolin.

"Nothing," replied the pilot, "except that its bark is gashed from its roots to the fork. These indicate the number of human bodies that were cooked there and then eaten."

"Like the notches of a baker on his sticks," observed Pinchinat, shrugging his shoulders as a sign of incredulity.

But he was wrong. The Fiji Islands are pre-eminently the country of cannibalism, and, it is necessary to repeat it, these practices are not entirely extinct. The love of good living will keep them alive for a long time yet among the tribes of the interior. Yes, the love of good living! for, in the opinion of the Fijians, nothing is comparable in taste and delicacy to human flesh, which is much superior to beef. If the pilot were to be believed, there was a certain chief, Ra-Undrenudu, who set up stones on his estate, and when he died these stones numbered eight hundred and twenty-two.

"And do you know what these stones indicated?"

"It is impossible for us to guess," said Yvernès, "even if we apply all our intelligence as instrumentalists!"

"They showed the number of human bodies this chief had devoured."

"By himself?"

"By himself."

"He was a large eater!" replied Pinchinat, whose opinion was made up regarding these "Fijian fairy-tales."

About eleven o'clock a bell rang on the right bank. The village of Naililii, composed of a few straw huts, appeared among the foliage, under the shade of cocoa-nut trees and banana trees. A Catholic mission is established in this village. Could the tourists stop an hour and shake hands with the missionary, a compatriot? The pilot saw no reason why they should not, and the launch was moored to the root of a tree.

Sebastien Zorn and his comrades landed, and they had not walked for two minutes before they met with the Superior of the mission.

He was a man of about fifty, of pleasant face and energetic figure. Happy to be able to welcome Frenchmen, he took them to his hut in the village, which comprises about a hundred Fijians. He insisted that his guests must accept some of the refreshments of the country. He assured them that this did not mean the repugnant kava, but a sort of drink, or rather soup, of agreeable flavour, obtained by cooking the cyrenæ, molluscs very abundant on the beaches of the Rewa.

This missionary admitted that it was a hard task to withdraw his faithful from the lord of "bukalo," that is to say, human flesh. "And as you are going towards the interior, my dear guests," added he, "be prudent, and keep on your guard."

"Do you hear that, Pinchinat?" said Sebastien Zorn.

They left a little before the noonday angelus sounded from the bell of the little church. As they proceeded the launch met several canoes laden with bananas. This is the local currency in which the natives pay their taxes. The river banks continued to be bordered with laurels, acacias, citron trees, and cactus with blood-red flowers. Over them the banana and cocoa-nut trees raise their lofty branches laden with bunches, and all this verdure stretches back to the mountains dominated by the peak of Mbugge-Levu.

Among these masses of foliage are one or two European factories, little in keeping with the savage nature of the country. These are sugar factories, fitted up with the best modern machinery, and their products, as a traveller, M. Verschnur, says, "can advantageously bear comparison with the sugars of the Antilles and other colonies."

About one o'clock the launch reached the end of its voyage on the Rewa. In two hours the ebb would begin, and it was as well to take advantage of it for the return journey. The run down would not take long, as the tide ebbs quickly. The excursionists ought to be back on Floating Island before ten o'clock in the evening.

A little time could be spent here, and it could not be better employed than in visiting the village of Tampoo, the first huts of which were visible about half a mile away.

It was arranged that the engineer and two sailors should remain in charge of the launch, while the pilot piloted his passengers to the village, where the ancient customs were preserved in all their Fijian purity. In this part of the island the missionaries have wasted their trouble and their sermons. There still reign the sorcerers; there still are worked the sorceries, particularly those bearing the complicated name of "Vaka-Ndran-in-Kan-Tacka," that is to say, "incantation by leaves." Here the people worship the Katvavous, the gods whose existence had no beginning, and will have no end, and who do not disdain special sacrifices that the governor-general is powerless to prevent, and even to punish.

Perhaps it would have been more prudent not to venture among these suspicious tribes. But our artistes, quite Parisian in their curiosity, insisted on it, and the pilot consented to accompany them, advising them not to get far away from each other.

On entering Tampoo, which consisted of a hundred straw huts, they met some women, real savages, wearing but cotton drawers knotted round their waist : they betrayed no surprise at the sight of the strangers. They were occupied in the preparation of curcuma, made of roots preserved in trenches previously lined with grasses and banana leaves. These roots were taken out, grilled, scraped, pressed into baskets lined with ferns, and the juice which ran out was poured into bamboos. This juice serves as food and pomatum, and in both respects is very widely used.

The party entered the village. There was no welcome on the part of the natives, who were in no hurry to greet the visitors, or to offer them hospitality. The exterior of the huts was not attractive. Considering the odour that issued from them in which that of rancid cocoa-nut oil prevailed, the quartette congratulated themselves that the laws of hospitality were not much honoured here.

However, when they arrived before the habitation of the chief—a Fijian of tall stature, and stern and ferocious look—he advanced towards them amid an escort of natives. His woolly hair was white with lime. He had assumed his ceremonial garb, a striped shirt, a belt round his body, an old carpet slipper on his left foot, and—how did Pinchinat restrain a burst of laughter ?—an old blue coat with gold buttons, patched in many places, and its unequal tails flapping against his calves. As he advanced towards the papalangis, the chief stumbled against a stump, lost his equilibrium, and fell to the ground.

Immediately, conformably to the etiquette of the "bale muri," the whole of the escort fell down flat " in order to take their share in the absurdity of this fall."

This was explained by the pilot, and Pinchinat approved of the formality as being no more ridiculous than many others in use in European courts—at least in his opinion.

When the natives had got up, the chief and the pilot exchanged a few sentences in Fijian, of which the quartette did not understand a word. These sentences, translated by the pilot, were merely asking why the strangers had come to the village of Tampoo. The reply being that they wished to visit the village and take a walk round the neighbourhood, permission was given, after an exchange of several questions and replies.

The chief, however, manifested neither pleasure nor displeasure at this arrival of tourists in Tampoo, and at a sign from him the natives returned to their huts.

"After all," said Pinchinat, "they do not seem to be so very bad."

"That is no reason for our not being careful," replied Frascolin.

For an hour our artistes walked about the village without being interfered with by the natives. The chief in his blue coat had gone into his hut, and it was obvious that the visit was treated as a matter of indifference.

After moving about Tampoo without any hut being opened to welcome them, Sebastien Zorn, Yvernès, Pinchinat, Frascolin, and the pilot strolled towards the ruins of some temples, like abandoned huts, which were not far from the dwelling of one of the sorcerers of the place.

This sorcerer, who was seated at his door, gave them anything but an encouraging look, and his gestures appeared to indicate that he certainly was not giving them a blessing.

Frascolin tried to enter into conversation with him through the pilot; but he assumed so repulsive a look, and so threatening an attitude, that they had to abandon any hope of a word from this Fijian porcupine.

Meanwhile, in spite of the advice which had been given him, Pinchinat had strolled off through a thick clump of bananas on the side of a hill.

When Sebastien Zorn, Yvernès and Frascolin had been rebuffed by the sorcerer's surliness, and were preparing to leave Tampoo, their comrade was out of sight.

The time had come for them to get back to the launch. The tide had begun to ebb, and there were none too many hours for them to run down the Rewa.

Frascolin, uneasy at not seeing Pinchinat, hailed him in a loud voice.

There was no reply.

"Where is he, then?" asked Sebastien Zorn.

"I do not know," replied Yvernès.

"Did any of you see him go away?" asked the pilot.

No one had seen him.

"Probably he has gone back to the launch by the foot-path from the village," said Frascolin.

"Then he was wrong," said the pilot. "But let us lose no time, and rejoin him."

They left, not without considerable anxiety. As they went through Tampoo the pilot remarked that not a Fijian was visible. All the doors of the huts were shut. There was no gathering in front of the chief's house. The women who were occupied in the preparation of curcuma had disappeared. It seemed that the village had been abandoned for some time.

The party hurried along. Frequently they shouted for the absent one, and the absent one did not reply. Had he not, then, got back to the shore where the launch was moored? Or was the launch no longer then in charge of the engineer and two sailors?

There remained but a few hundred yards to traverse. They hurried along, and as soon as they were through the trees saw the launch and the three men at their posts.

"Our comrade?" shouted Frascolin.

"Is he not with you?" replied the engineer.

"No—not for the last half-hour."

"Has he not come back?" asked Yvernès.

"No."

What had become of him? The pilot did not conceal his extreme uneasiness.

"We must return to the village," said Sebastien Zorn. "We cannot abandon Pinchinat."

The launch was left in charge of one of the sailors, although it was dangerous to do so. But it was better to return to Tampoo in force and well armed this time. If they had to search all the huts, they would not leave the village, they would not return to Floating Island until they had found Pinchinat.

They went back along the road to Tampoo. The same solitude in the village and its surroundings. Where had the population gone? Not a sound was heard in the streets, and the huts were empty.

There could be no doubt as to what had happened. Pinchinat had ventured into the banana wood; he had been seized and dragged away—where? As to the fate reserved for him by these cannibals whom he derided, it was only too easy to imagine it! A search in the environs of Tampoo produced no result. How could you find a track through this forest region, which is known only to the Fijians? Besides, was it not to be feared that they would try to capture the launch, guarded only by a single sailor? If that misfortune happened, all hope of rescuing Pinchinat was at an end, the safety of his companions would be endangered.

The despair of Frascolin, Yvernès, and Sebastien Zorn was indescribable. What could be done? The pilot and the engineer did not know what to do.

Frascolin, who had preserved his coolness, said,—

"We must return to Floating Island."

"Without our comrade?" asked Yvernès.

"Do you think so?" added Sebastien Zorn.

"I do not see what else to do," replied Frascolin. "The governor of Floating Island should be informed; the authorities of Viti-Levu should be communicated with and asked to take action—"

"Yes; let us go!" said the pilot, "and if we are to take advantage of the tide, we have not a minute to lose."

"It is the only way of saving Pinchinat," said Frascolin, "if it is not too late."

The only way, in fact.

They left Tampoo, fearing that they might not find the launch at her post. In vain the name of Pinchinat was shouted by all! And if they had been less excited they might have seen among the bushes a few savage Fijians watching their departure.

The launch had not been interfered with. The sailor had seen no one prowling on the banks of the Rewa.

It was with inexpressible sadness that Sebastien Zorn, Frascolin and Yvernès decided to take their places in the boat. They hesitated; they shouted again. But they had to go, as Frascolin said, and they were right in doing so.

The engineer set the dynamos going, and the launch with the tide under her flew down the Rewa at prodigious speed.

At six o'clock the western point of the delta was rounded, and half an hour afterwards they were alongside the pier at Starboard Harbour.

In a quarter of an hour Frascolin and his two comrades had by means of the tram reached Milliard City, and were at the town hall.

As soon as he had heard what had occurred, Cyrus Bikerstaff started for Suva, and there he asked for an interview with the governor-general of the archipelago, which was granted him.

When this official learned what had passed at Tampoo, he admitted that it was a very serious matter. This Frenchman was in the hands of one of the tribes of the interior who evaded all authority.

"Unfortunately," he added, "we cannot do anything before to-morrow. Our boats cannot get up to Tampoo against the tide. Besides, it is indispensable for us to go in force, and the best way would be to go through the bush."

"Quite so," replied Cyrus Bikerstaff; "but it is not to-morrow, but to-day—this very moment—that we should start."

"I have not the necessary men at my disposal," said the governor.

"We have them, sir," replied Cyrus Bikerstaff. "Under the orders of one of your officers who know the country—"

"Very well, sir, you can start at once."

Half an hour afterwards, a hundred men, sailors and militia, landed at Suva, under the orders of Commodore Simcoe, who had asked to take the command of the expedition. The superintendent, Sebastien Zorn, Yvernès, Frascolin, were at his side. A detachment of the Viti-Levu police went with them.

The expedition started into the bush under the guidance of the pilot, who knew these difficult regions of the interior. They went the shortest way, and at a rapid rate, so as to reach Tampoo as quickly as possible.

It was not necessary to go as far as the village. About an hour after midnight orders were given for the column to halt.

In the deepest part of an almost impenetrable thicket the glare of a fire was noticed. Doubtless the natives of Tampoo were gathered here, the village being within half an hour's march to the east.

Commodore Simcoe, the pilot, Calistus Munbar, the three Parisians, went on in front.

They had not gone a hundred yards before they stopped.

In the light of the fire, surrounded by a tumultuous crowd of men and women, Pinchinat, half naked, was tied to a tree, and the Fijian chief was advancing towards him axe in hand.

"Forward! Forward!" shouted Commodore Simcoe to his sailors and militia.

Sudden surprise and well-grounded terror on the part of the natives, on whom the detachment spared neither fire nor steel. In a moment the place was deserted, and the whole band had dispersed under the trees.

Pinchinat, detached from the tree, fell into the arms of his friend Frascolin.

How can we describe the joy of these artistes, these brothers—in which were mingled a few tears, and also well-merited reproaches.

"But, you wretch," said the violoncellist, "what possessed you to go away from us?"

"Wretch as much as you like, my old Sebastien," replied Pinchinat, "but do not sit upon an alto as poorly clothed as I am at this moment. Pass me my clothes, so that I can present myself before the authorities in a more suitable fashion."

His clothes were found at the foot of a tree, and he put them on with the greatest coolness imaginable. Then when he was "presentable" he went to shake hands with the commodore and superintendent.

"Well," said Calistus Munbar, "do you now believe in the cannibalism of the Fijians?"

CHAPTER X.

THE departure of Floating Island was fixed for the 2nd of February. The day before the excursions ended, the different tourists returned to Milliard City. The Pinchinat affair created a great sensation. All the Pearl of the Pacific was interested in his Highness, for the Concert Party were held in universal esteem. The council of notables accorded its entire approbation to the energetic conduct of the governor, Cyrus Bikerstaff. The newspapers warmly congratulated him. Pinchinat became the celebrity of the day. Could you have an alto terminating his artistic career in the stomach of a Fijian? It was cheerfully admitted that the natives of Viti-Levu had not absolutely renounced their cannibalistic tastes. After all, human flesh was so good, according to them, and this fellow, Pinchinat, was so appetizing!

Floating Island started at daybreak and moved off towards the New Hebrides. This would take it about twelve degrees or two hundred leagues out of the way; but it could not be avoided if Captain Sarol and his companions were to be landed in the New Hebrides. No one regretted it, however. Everybody was glad to be of service to these brave fellows who had shown so much courage in the proceedings against the wild beasts. And they appeared to be so satisfied at being taken home in this way after such a long absence! Added to which it would be an opportunity of visiting a group with which the Milliardites were not yet acquainted.

The voyage proceeded with intentional slowness. It was in these regions between the Fijis and the New

Hebrides in one hundred and seventy degrees thirty-five minutes of east longitude, and nineteen degrees thirteen minutes south latitude, that the steamer from Marseilles chartered by the Tankerdon and Coverley families was to meet Floating Island.

The marriage of Walter and Miss Coverley was more than ever the subject of general interest. How could anything else be thought of? Calistus Munbar had not a minute to himself. He was preparing and organizing the different elements of a festival that would make its mark in the annals of Floating Island. That he grew thin over the task need surprise nobody.

Floating Island did not move more than from twenty to twenty-five kilometres a day. It came within sight of Viti, whose superb banks are bordered with luxuriant forests of sombre verdure. It took three days traversing the tranquil waters from Wanara to Ronde. The passage to which this name is given on the charts afforded a wide road for the Pearl of the Pacific. A number of terrified whales collided with the steel hull, which trembled at the blows. But the plates of the compartments held firm and there were no damages.

At length in the afternoon of the sixth, the last summits of Fiji disappeared below the horizon. At this moment Commodore Simcoe left the Polynesian for the Melanesian region of the Pacific.

During the three next days, Floating Island continued to drift towards the west, after reaching the nineteenth degree of south latitude. On the 10th of February it was in the locality where it had been arranged for the steamer from Europe to meet it. The point marked on the charts displayed in Milliard City was known to all. The look-outs at the observatory were on the alert. The horizon was swept by hundreds of telescopes, and as soon as the ship was signalled—all the population were expectant— was not this as it were the prologue of the drama the people were so eager for, the marriage of Walter Tankerdon and Miss Coverley?

Floating Island had only to remain stationary, to keep in position against the currents of these seas shut in by archipelagoes. Commodore Simcoe gave his orders accordingly, and his officers saw that they were carried out.

"The position is decidedly most interesting!" said Yvernès.

This was during the two hours' rest that he and his comrades habitually allowed themselves after luncheon.

" Yes," replied Frascolin, "and we shall have no reason to regret this campaign on Floating Island—whatever friend Zorn may think."

"Wait until it is over," said the violoncellist, " and when we have pocketed the fourth instalment of the salary we have earned."

"Well," said Yvernès, " the company has paid us three since our departure, and I very much approve of what Frascolin, our worthy accountant, has done in sending this large sum to the bank at New York."

In fact the worthy accountant had deemed it wise to pay the money through the bankers of Milliard City into one of the best banks in the Union. This was not out of any distrust, but because a bank on shore seemed to offer more security than one floating over five or six thousand metres of Pacific water.

It was during this conversation, amid the scented wreaths of smoke from pipes and cigars, that Yvernès was led to make the following observation,—

" The marriage festivities promise to be splendid, my friends. Our superintendent is sparing neither imagination nor pains. He will have showers of dollars, and the fountains of Milliard City will flow with generous wine, I have no doubt. But do you know what is wanting about this ceremony ? "

"A cataract of liquid gold flowing from rocks of diamonds," exclaimed Pinchinat.

" No," replied Yvernès, " a cantata."

"A cantata ? " asked Frascolin.

" Undoubtedly," said Yvernès; " there will be music,

we shall play our most favourite pieces, appropriate to the
circumstances, but if there is no cantata, no nuptial song,
no epithalamium in honour of the young couple—"

"Why not?" said Frascolin. "If you, Yvernès, will
throw together a few lines of unequal length with a rhyme
here and there, Sebastien Zorn, who has had experience as
a composer, can easily set your words to music."

"Excellent idea!" said Pinchinat.

"That will suit you, old growler! Something matri-
monial, you know, with plenty of *spiccatos* and *allegros* and
molto agitatos and a delirious *coda*—at five dollars a note."

"No ; for nothing this time," said Frascolin.

"It shall be the Quartette Party's offering to the nabobs
of Floating Island."

It was agreed upon, and the violoncellist declared
himself ready to implore the inspiration of the God of
Music if the God of Poetry would pass his inspiration
into the heart of Yvernès.

And it was from this noble collaboration that there
originated the Cantata of Cantatas, in imitation of the
Song of Songs, in honour of the union of the Tankerdons
and the Coverleys.

During the afternoon of the 10th, a report got about that
a large steamer was in sight, coming from the north-east.
Its nationality was unknown, as it was still ten miles off
when the shades of twilight sank upon the sea.

The steamer seemed to be coming at full speed, and
there was no doubt it was making for Floating Island.
Probably it would not come alongside until sunrise.

The news produced an indescribable effect. All the
feminine imaginations were excited at the thought of the
marvels of jewellery and fashion brought by this ship,
which had been transformed into a huge wedding basket,
of five or six hundred horse power.

There was no mistake as to the steamer being bound
for Floating Island. Early in the morning she had
rounded the jetty of Starboard Harbour, and displayed the
flag of the Floating Island Company.

Suddenly another item of news came through the telephones to Milliard City. The flag of this vessel was
awaft.

What then had happened? An accident—a death on
board? That would be a sorry omen for the marriage
that was to assure the future of Floating Island.

But there was something else. The steamer in question
was not the one expected, and it did not come from
Europe. It came from America, from Madeleine Bay.
Besides, the steamer laden with the nuptial treasures was
not behind time. The wedding was fixed for the 27th,
and it was now only the 11th.

What, then, did this ship mean? What news did it
bring? Why was its flag awaft? Why had the Company
sent it off to the New Hebrides, where they knew it would
fall in with Floating Island?

Had they to communicate any message of exceptional
gravity to the Milliardites?

Yes, and this was soon to be known.

The steamer had hardly come alongside than a passenger
landed.

He was one of the superior officers of the Company, who
declined to reply to the questions of the numerous and
impatient crowd that had assembled on the pier of Starboard Harbour.

A tram was ready to start, and without losing a moment,
the man jumped into one of the cars.

Ten minutes later he had reached the town hall, and demanded an audience of the Governor "on urgent business"
—an audience which was immediately granted.

Cyrus Bikerstaff received the visitor in his office, the
door of which was closed.

A quarter of an hour had not elapsed before each of the
members of the council of thirty notables was summoned
telephonically to a meeting of urgency in the assembly room.

Meanwhile, imagination ran riot in the harbour and the
town, and apprehension, following on curiosity, was at its
height.

At twenty minutes to eight the council had assembled under the presidency of the Governor. The visitor then made the following declaration :—

" On the 23rd of January, the Floating Island Company, Limited, stopped payment, and William T. Pomering was appointed liquidator, with full powers to do his best for the interests of the said Company."

William T. Pomering, on whom these functions had devolved, was the new arrival.

The news spread, and, in truth, did not provoke as much excitement as it had produced in Europe. Why should it ? Floating Island, as Pinchinat said, was a detached piece of the United States of America. There was nothing in a failure to astonish Americans, still less to overwhelm them. Was it not one of the phases natural to business, an incident acceptable and accepted? The Milliardites looked at the matter with their habitual coolness. The Company had gone under. Well ? That might happen to the most respectable financial companies. Were its liabilities considerable ? Very considerable ; for, according to the liquidator, they amounted to five hundred million dollars. And what had caused this failure ? Speculations —insane, if you please, as they had turned out badly— but which might have succeeded—an immense undertaking for founding a new town on land in Arkansas, which had been swallowed up in a geological depression that no one could have foreseen. After all, it was not the Company's fault, and if the land came up again, the shareholders might come up again at the same time. Solid as Europe appeared, it might go down some day in a similar way. But there was nothing of that sort to be feared with regard to Floating Island, and did not that triumphantly show its superiority over estates on the continents or terrestrial islands !

The pressing point was to act. The assets of the Company consisted of the value of Floating Island, hull, works, hotels, houses, country, flotilla—in a word, all that was borne by the floating apparatus designed by William

Tersen, all that was connected with it, and the establishments at Madeleine Bay into the bargain. Was it advisable for a new company to be formed to take over the assets by arrangement? Yes. There was no hesitation on this point, and the proceeds of the sale would be applied to the liquidation of the Company's debts. But in forming this new company, would it be necessary to apply to outside sources? Were not the Milliardites rich enough to pay for Floating Island out of their own pockets? From mere tenants would it not be preferable to become owners of this Pearl of the Pacific?

That there were millions in the pocket-books of the members of the council of notables we know. And so they were of opinion that it was advisable to buy Floating Island, and without delay. Had the liquidator power to treat? He had. If the Company could realize without delay the sum required for its liquidation, the money must come from the notables of Milliard City, among whom were some of the largest shareholders. Now that the rivalry had ceased between the two principal families and the two sections of the town, the matter could be easily managed. Among the Anglo-Saxons of the United States there is no delay in business matters. The money was at once forthcoming. In the opinion of the notables there was no need to appeal to the public. Jem Tankerdon, Nat Coverley, and a few others offered four hundred million dollars. There was no discussion as to the price. It could be taken or left—and the liquidator took it.

The council met at thirteen minutes past eight in the room at the town hall. When it separated at forty-seven minutes past nine, the ownership of Floating Island had passed into the hands of the two richest Milliardites and a few of their friends under the name of Jem Tankerdon, Nat Coverley & Co.

Just as the news of the Company's failure had caused no emotion among the population of Floating Island, neither did the news of its acquisition by the chief notables. It seemed only natural, and if it had been necessary to raise a more considerable sum, the money would have been there in a moment. It was a great satisfaction to the Milliardites to feel that they were at home, or at least that they were no longer dependent on an outside company. And so the Pearl of the Pacific, as represented by all classes, conveyed its thanks to the two heads of the families who had so well understood the general feeling.

That very day a meeting was held in the park, and a motion to this effect carried amid a triple round of cheers. Delegates were nominated, and a deputation sent to the Coverley and Tankerdon mansions.

The deputation was graciously received, and departed with the assurance that nothing would be changed with regard to the regulations, usages, and customs of Floating Island. The administration would remain as it was. All the functionaries would be retained in their functions, and all the employés in their employ.

And how could it be otherwise?

Hence it resulted that Commodore Ethel Simcoe remained in charge of the navigating branch, having the chief direction of the movements of Floating Island, conformably to the itineraries decided on by the council of notables. The same as regards Colonel Stewart and the command of the militia. There was no change in the observatory, and the King of Malecarlie continued to be astronomer. Nobody was discharged from the place he occupied at the ports, at the works, or in the municipal administration. Athanase Dorémus was not even relieved of his useless functions, although pupils obstinately declined to attend the classes in dancing and deportment.

There was no change in the arrangements with the Quartette Party, who, to the end of the voyage, would continue to draw the unheard-of salary that had been promised at their engagement.

"These people are extraordinary," said Frascolin, when he learnt that matters had been arranged to the general satisfaction.

"That is because they have plenty of money," said Pinchinat.

"Perhaps we might take advantage of this change of proprietors to withdraw from our engagement," observed Sebastien Zorn, who could not shake off his absurd prejudice against Floating Island.

"Withdraw!" exclaimed his Highness. "Let me see you try!"

And with his left hand, opening and closing his fingers as if he were stopping the fourth string, he threatened to give the violoncellist one of those blows of the fist which attain a speed of eight metres and a half in a second.

But a change had to take place in the position of the Governor. Cyrus Bikerstaff, being the direct representative of the *Floating Island Company*, considered that he ought to resign, and under the circumstances the determination appeared reasonable. His resignation was accepted, but in terms most flattering to the Governor. His two assistants, Barthélemy Ruge and Hubley Harcourt, half ruined by the failure of the company, in which they were large shareholders, intended to leave Floating Island by one of the next steamers.

At the same time Cyrus Bikerstaff agreed to remain at the head of the municipal administration until the end of the voyage.

Thus was accomplished without noise, without discussion, without trouble, without rivalry, this important financial transformation, and the business was so wisely, so quickly completed, that that very day the liquidator was able to re-embark, taking with him the signatures of the principal purchasers and the guarantee of the council of notables.

As to the personage of such prodigious consideration known as Calistus Munbar, superintendent of the fine arts and amusements of the incomparable Pearl of the Pacific, he was simply confirmed in his office and emoluments, and, really, could a successor have been found to this irreplaceable man?

"Come!" said Frascolin, "everything is for the best, the future of Floating Island is assured; there is nothing more to fear."

"We shall see!" murmured the obstinate violoncellist.

Under these conditions, then, the marriage of Walter Tankerdon and Miss Coverley would take place. The two families would be united by pecuniary interests, which in America, as elsewhere, form the strongest social ties. What assurance of prosperity for the citizens of Floating Island! Now it belonged to the Milliardites, it would seem more independent than ever, more mistress of its destinies. Before, a cable had attached it to Madeleine Bay, in the United States—now the cable was broken!

At present everything was flourishing.

Is it necessary to insist on the happiness of the parties in question, to express the inexpressible, to depict the happiness that radiated around them? What appeared but a marriage of policy was really a love match. Both Walter and Di loved each other with an affection into which interest in no way entered. They both had the qualities which would assure them the happiest of lives. This Walter had a soul of gold, and Miss Di's was of the same metal—figuratively speaking, be it understood, and not in the sense that their millions might justify. They were made for one another, and never was this somewhat hackneyed phrase more strictly true. They counted the days, they counted the hours, which separated them from this longed-for date of the 27th of February. They regretted one thing, that Floating Island did not move towards the hundred and eightieth meridian, when, coming from the west, it would have to eliminate twenty-four hours from its calendar. Their happiness might be advanced a day. No! It was in sight of the New Hebrides that the ceremony was to take place, and all they could do was to resign themselves to it.

But the ship laden with all the marvels of Europe had not yet arrived. Here was a wealth of things with which they would willingly have dispensed. What need had they of these quasi-regal magnificences? They mutually gave each other their love—what more could they give?

But the families and the friends and the people of Floating Island desired that this ceremony should be surrounded with extraordinary brilliancy. And so glasses were obstinately levelled at the eastern horizon. Jem Tankerdon and Nat Coverley even offered a handsome prize to whoever first sighted this steamer, whose propeller could never propel fast enough for the public impatience.

Meanwhile the programme of the festivities was carefully elaborated. It comprised games, receptions, the double ceremony at the Protestant temple and the Catholic cathedral, the gala evening at the town hall, the festival in the park. Calistus Munbar had an eye for everything, he was everywhere, he was indefatigable, it might even be said he was ruining his health. What would you have? His temperament drove him ahead, and you could no more stop him than you could stop an express train.

The cantata was ready. Yvernès, the poet, and Sebastien Zorn, the musician, proved worthy of each other. This cantata would be sung by the choral masses of an orpheonic society founded expressly for the purpose. The effect would be very grand when it was heard in the square of the observatory, electrically lighted, at the fall of night. Then would come the appearance of the young couple before the officer of the civil power, and the religious marriage would be celebrated at midnight amid the fairy surroundings of Milliard City.

At last the expected ship was signalled in the offing. It was one of the look-outs at Starboard Harbour who won the prize, which was worth a respectable number of dollars.

It was nine o'clock in the morning of the 19th of February when the steamer came into harbour, and the landing at once began.

Useless to give in detail the names of the articles, jewels, dresses, objects of art, which composed this nuptial cargo. Suffice it to know that they were on view in the vast saloons of the Coverley mansion, and the show was an unprecedented success. The whole population of Milliard City wanted to inspect these marvels. That numbers of people extraordinarily rich might obtain such magnificent products at a price may be true; but we must also take into account the taste and artistic feeling which had presided at their selection, and that could not be sufficiently admired. If any one is anxious to see a list of the said articles, he will find them in the *Starboard Chronicle* and *New Herald* of the 21st and 22nd of February. If they are not satisfied at that, it is because absolute satisfaction does not exist in this world.

"Fichtre!" said Yvernès, when he came away from the saloons in Fifteenth Avenue in company with his three comrades.

"Fichtre!" said Pinchinat, "appears to me to be the correct expression. It intimates that you would like to marry Miss Coverley without her dowry—for herself alone."

As to the two young people, the truth is that they took but little notice of this stock of masterpieces of art and fashion.

After the steamer's arrival, Floating Island resumed its westerly course so as to reach the New Hebrides. If one of the islands was sighted before the 27th, Captain Sarol would be landed with his companions, and Floating Island would begin its return journey.

The Malay captain was very familiar with these regions of the Western Pacific, and this made the task of navigating an easy one. By request of Commodore Simcoe, who had secured his services, he remained on duty at the observatory tower. As soon as the first heights appeared nothing would be easier than to approach the island of Erromango, one of the most easterly of the group—which would enable them to avoid the numerous reefs of the New Hebrides.

Was it chance, or was it that Captain Sarol, desirous of being present at the marriage festivities, took the Island along so slowly that the first islands were not signalled until the morning of the 27th of February—the very day fixed for the wedding.

It mattered little, however. The marriage of Walter Tankerdon and Di Coverley would be none the less happy for having been celebrated in view of the New Hebrides, and it gave so much pleasure to these brave Malays—and they made no secret of it—who would be free to take part in the festivities on Floating Island.

Several islets were first sighted and passed according to the very precise indications of Captain Sarol, and Floating Island then steered for Erromango, leaving to the south the heights of Tanna.

In these regions Sebastien Zorn, Frascolin, Pinchinat, and Yvernès were not far—three hundred miles at the outside—from the French possessions in this part of the Pacific, the Loyalty Islands and New Caledonia, that penitentiary situated at the antipodes of France.

Erromango is much wooded in the interior, undulated with many hills, at the foot of which extend wide cultivable plateaux. Commodore Simcoe stopped within a mile of Cook Bay, on the eastern coast. It was not prudent to approach nearer, as the coral reefs ran half a mile out to sea at the water level. The Governor's intention was not to remain stationary off this island, nor to stay at any other island in the Archipelago. After the festivities the Malays would land, and Floating Island would steer towards the Equator, on the way to Madeleine Bay.

It was one o'clock in the afternoon when Floating Island remained stationary.

By order of the authorities every one had a holiday, even the sailors and militiamen, with the exception of the customs officers on duty along the coast.

Needless to say the weather was magnificent, and the sea-breeze refreshing. According to the usual expression, " The sun shone on them."

" Positively," said Pinchinat, " this haughty disc appears

to be at the orders of the shareholders! They will ask
him, as Joshua did, to make the day longer, and he will
obey them! O power of gold!"

We need not enlarge on the different items of the sensational programme that had been drawn up by the superintendent. At three o'clock all the inhabitants, those of
the country as well as those of the town and the forts,
flocked into the park along the banks of the Serpentine.
The notables mixed familiarly with the populace. The
sports were carried on with an enthusiasm which might
perhaps be accounted for by the value of the prizes.
Dances were organized in the open air. The most brilliant
was given in one of the large halls of the casino, in which
the young people danced with much grace and animation.
Yvernès and Pinchinat took part in these dances, and
yielded to none in their duties as partners to the prettiest
of the Milliardites. Never had his Highness been so
amiable, never had he shown so much wit, never had he
such a success. All the Tankerdons and Coverleys were
there, and the graceful sisters of the bride seemed to be
very happy at her happiness. Miss Coverley walked
about on Walter's arm, in which there was nothing strange
considering that they were citizens by birth of free
America. They were applauded, they were offered
flowers, compliments were bestowed on t.iem, which they
received with perfect affability.

And during the hours that followed refreshments were
served in profusion, so that nothing should interfere with
the people's good humour.

When night came, the park was resplendent with the
electric fires that the aluminium moons poured down in
torrents. The sun had wisely disappeared below the
horizon. Would he not have been humiliated by these
artificial effluences which made the night as bright as the
day!

The cantata was sung between nine and ten o'clock,
with such success as neither poet nor musician had ever
hoped for. Perhaps, at this moment, the violoncellist felt

inclined to withdraw his unjust prejudices against the Pearl of the Pacific.

Eleven o'clock struck, and a long procession advanced towards the town hall. Walter Tankerdon and Miss Coverley were walking in the midst of their relatives. The whole population accompanied them along First Avenue.

Governor Cyrus Bikerstaff was waiting in the grand saloon of the town hall. The finest of all the marriages it had been given him to celebrate during his administrative career, was about to be accomplished.

Suddenly shouts were heard towards the outer quarter of the Larboard section.

The procession stopped in the middle of the avenue.

Almost immediately with these shouts, which increased, detonations were heard.

A moment afterwards some customs officers—many of them wounded—ran into the square opposite the town hall.

Anxiety was at its height. Through the crowd ran that unreasoning fear which precedes an unknown danger.

Cyrus Bikerstaff appeared on the steps of the town hall, followed by Commodore Simcoe, Colonel Stewart, and the notables, who had just joined them.

To the questions put to them, the customs officers replied that Floating Island had just been invaded by a band of New Hebrideans—three or four thousand of them —and that Captain Sarol was at their head.

CHAPTER XI.

SUCH was the outbreak of the abominable conspiracy prepared by Captain Sarol with the concurrence of the Malays rescued with him by Floating Island, the New Hebrideans embarked at Samoa, and the natives of Erromango and the neighbouring islands. What would it end in? No one could say, considering the conditions under which this sudden and terrible attack was made.

The New Hebridean group comprises at least a hundred and fifty islands, which, under the protection of England, forms a geographical dependency of Australia. Nevertheless, here, as at the Solomon Islands, situated in the north-west of the same regions, this question of protectorate is an apple of discord between France and the United Kingdom. And again, the United States do not look favourably on the establishment of European colonies in an ocean of which they dream of claiming the exclusive enjoyment.

The population of the New Hebrides is composed of negroes and Malays of Kanaka origin. But the character of these natives, their temperament, their instincts, differ according as they belong to the northern or southern islands—which permits of the archipelago being divided into two groups.

In the northern group at Santo Island at Saint Philip Bay, the natives are of a higher type, their colour not so dark' and their hair not so woolly. The men, short and strong, gentle and peaceful, rarely attack the business establishments or European ships. The same may be said regarding Vaté or Sandwich Island, in which most of the villages are flourishing, among others, Port Vila, the capital of the archipelago—which also bears the name of Franceville—where our colonists avail themselves of the riches of an admirable soil, luxuriant pasturages, fields adapted for cultivation, land suitable for plantation of coffee, bananas, cocoanuts, and the lucrative industry of coprah-making. In this group the customs of the natives have completely changed since the arrival of the Europeans. Their moral and intellectual level has been raised. Thanks to the efforts of the missionaries, the scenes of cannibalism, so frequent formerly, have ceased to exist. Unfortunately the Kanaka race is disappearing, and it is only too evident that it will finish by becoming extinct, to the detriment of this northern group, in which it has been transformed by the contact of European civilization.

But these regrets would be misplaced with regard to the southern islands of the archipelago. And it was not without reason that Captain Sarol had chosen this group for his criminal attempt on Floating Island. On these islands the natives remain veritable Papuans, and may be relegated to the lowest scale of humanity, at Tanna as at Erromango. Concerning this last, an old sandal-wood dealer remarked to Doctor Hayers, "If this island could speak, it would tell things that would make the hair stand on your head."

In fact, the race of these Kanakas of inferior origin has not been improved by Polynesian blood, as in the northern islands. At Erromango, of ten thousand five hundred inhabitants, the English missionaries, five of whom have been massacred since 1839, have converted only half. The other half remains Pagan. Besides, converted or not, they all still represent those savage natives, who deserve their evil reputation, although they are of shorter stature and less robust constitution than those of Santo Island and Sandwich Island. And hence the serious dangers against which it is necessary to warn tourists venturing into the southerly group.

We may mention a few examples. Fifty years ago the brig *Aurore* was piratically attacked, and there were severe repressive measures in consequence on the part of France. In 1869 the missionary Gordon was killed by tomahawks. In 1875 the crew of an English ship was treacherously attacked and massacred, and then eaten by cannibals. In 1894, in the neighbouring Louisiade Archipelago, at Rossel Island, a French merchant and his workmen, and the captain of a Chinese ship and his crew, perished under the blows of cannibals. Finally the English cruiser *Royalist* was forced to undertake a campaign to punish these savage people for having massacred a great number of Europeans. And as Pinchinat was being told this story, he, who had recently escaped from the terrible molars of the Fijians, forbore to shrug his shoulders.

Such were the people among whom Captain Sarol had recruited his accomplices. He had promised them the pillage of this opulent Pearl of the Pacific, not an inhabitant of which was to be spared. Of these savages, who were awaiting his appearance at the approaches to Erromango, some had come from the neighbouring islands, separated by narrow arms of the sea ; principally from Tanna, which is within thirty-five miles to the south. From here had come the sturdy natives of the district of Wanissi, savage worshippers of the god Teapolo, and whose nudity is almost complete, the natives of Plage Noire, of Sangalli, the most formidable and the most dreaded of the archipelago.

But although the northern group is relatively less savage, it does not follow that no contingent from there had placed itself under Captain Sarol. To the north of Sandwich Island there is the island of Api, with its eighteen thousand inhabitants, where they eat their prisoners, the body of which is reserved for the young people, the arms and thighs for the full-grown men, the intestines for the dogs and pigs. There is the island of Paama with its ferocious tribes, who yield in nothing to the natives of Api. There is the island of Mallicolo, with its cannibal Kanakas.

There is finally Aurora Island, one of the worst of the archipelago, in which no white man lives, and in which, a few years before, had been massacred the crew of the French coaster. It was from these different islands that reinforcements had come to Captain Sarol.

As soon as Floating Island appeared, as soon as it was within a few cables' lengths of Erromango, Captain Sarol had given the signal expected by the natives.

In a few minutes the rocks at the water level had given passage to three or four thousand savages.

The danger was most serious, for these New Hebrideans let loose on Milliard City would recoil from no attempt, from no violence. They had the advantage of surprise, and were armed not only with long javelins tipped with bone, which make very dangerous wounds, and with arrows poisoned with a sort of vegetable venom, but with Snider rifles, the use of which has greatly spread in the archipelago.

At the beginning of this affair, which had been a long time in preparation—for it was Sarol who was marching at the head of the assailants—the militia, the sailors, the functionaries, every man in a fit state to fight, was called upon.

Cyrus Bikerstaff, Commodore Simcoe, and Colonel Stewart were quite equal to the occasion. The King of Malecarlie had offered his services. Although he was no longer in the vigour of youth, he at least had courage. The natives were still at Larboard Harbour, where the officer of the port was trying to organize resistance. But no doubt the bands would not delay to precipitate themselves on the town.

To begin with, orders were given to shut the gates of the enclosure round Milliard City, in which almost the whole population had assembled for the marriage festivities.

That the country and park would be ravaged was to be expected. That the two harbours and the electrical works would be devastated was to be feared. That the batteries at the Prow and Stern would be destroyed, there was nothing to prevent. The greatest misfortune would be that the artillery of Floating Island would be turned against the town, and it was not impossible that the Malays knew how to use it.

First of all, at the King of Malecarlie's proposal, most of the women and children were sent to the town hall. This vast municipal hotel was plunged in profound obscurity, as was the entire island, for the electrical apparatus had ceased working, owing to the engineers having to escape from the assailants.

However, by Commodore Simcoe's efforts, the arms deposited at the town hall were distributed to the militia and the sailors, and there was no scarcity of ammunition. Leaving Di with Mrs. Tankerdon and Mrs. Coverley, Walter came to join the group, which now included Jem Tankerdon, Nat Coverley, Calistus Munbar, Pinchinat, Yvernès, Frascolin, and Sebastien Zorn.

"Well," murmured the violoncellist, "it seems as though this was to be the end of it."

"But it is not the end of it!" exclaimed the Superintendent. "No! it is not the end; and it is not our dear Floating Island which will succumb to a handful of Kanakas!"

Well spoken, Calistus Munbar! We can understand what rage devoured you at the thought of these rascally New Hebrideans interrupting so well-organized a festival! Yes! he must hope to repulse them. Unfortunately they were not superior in number, and they had not the advantage of the offensive.

The reports of guns were heard in the distance, in the direction of both harbours. Captain Sarol had begun by interfering with the working of the screws, without which Floating Island could not get away from Erromango, which was his basis of operations.

The Governor, the King of Malecarlie, Commodore Simcoe, Colonel Stewart, united in a committee of defence, had at first thought of making a sortie. No, that would be to sacrifice a number of the defenders of whom they had such want. There was no mercy to be hoped from these savages, who, like the wild beasts a fortnight before, had invaded Floating Island. Besides, would they not attempt to wreck it on the rocks of Erromango, and then hand it over to pillage ?

An hour afterwards the assailants arrived before the gates of Milliard City. They tried to break them in in vain. They tried to climb them, but were driven back by firearms.

As Milliard City had not been taken by surprise, it had become difficult to force an entry in the darkness. And so Captain Sarol drew off his savages towards the park and country, and there waited for daylight.

Between four and five o'clock the first hues of the morning appeared on the eastern horizon. The militia and sailors under Commodore Simcoe and Captain Stewart, leaving half their forces at the town hall, marched to the observatory square, expecting that Captain Sarol would endeavour to force the gates on that side ; for as no help could come from without, it was necessary, at all costs, to prevent the savages from penetrating into the town.

The quartette followed the defenders, whose officers led them towards the end of First Avenue.

"To have escaped from the cannibals of Fiji," said Pinchinat, "to be obliged to defend one's cutlets from the cannibals of the New Hebrides ! "

"They will not eat the whole of us ! " said Yvernès.

"And I will resist to my last fragment ! " added Yvernès.

Sebastien Zorn remained silent. We know that what he thought of the adventure would not prevent him from doing his duty.

As soon as the light came, shots began to be interchanged through the gates of the square. There was a courageous defence in the enclosure of the observatory. There were victims on both sides. Among the Milliardites, Jem Tankerdon was wounded in the shoulder slightly, but he would not abandon his post. Nat Coverley and Walter were conspicuous in the fight. The King of Malecarlie endeavoured to bring down Captain Sarol, who did not spare himself among the savages.

In truth, the assailants were too many. All that Erromango, Tanna, and the neighbouring islands could furnish were in this attack on Milliard City. There was one fortunate circumstance, however, and Commodore Simcoe noticed it: Floating Island, instead of drifting on to Erromango, was being gently carried by a slight current towards the northern group, although it would have been better if it had been moving out to sea.

Nevertheless time went on, the savages redoubled their efforts, and in spite of their courageous resistance, the defenders could not keep them back. About ten o'clock the gates were forced. Before the howling crowd that swarmed into the square Commodore Simcoe had to retreat towards the town hall, which could be defended like a fortress.

In their retreat, the militia and sailors gave way foot by foot. Perhaps now they had entered the town, the New Hebrideans, carried away by their instincts of pillage, might disperse through the different quarters, and thus give the Milliardites some advantage.

Vain hope! Captain Sarol would not allow his men to leave First Avenue. By it they would reach the town hall, where they would overcome the last efforts of the besieged. When Captain Sarol was master of that, the victory would be complete. The hour of pillage and massacre would sound.

"Decidedly there are too many of them," said Frascolin, whose arm was grazed by a javelin.

And the arrows rained, and the bullets too, as the retreat became quicker.

About two o'clock the defenders had been driven back to the town hall square. Of dead there were already fifty—of wounded about twice or thrice as many. Before the town hall was reached by the savages, its doors were closed; the women and children were moved into the interior apartments, where they would be sheltered from the projectiles.　Then Cyrus Bikerstaff, the King of Male-carlie, Commodore Simcoe, Colonel Stewart, Jem Tankerdon, Nat Coverley, their friends, the militiamen and the sailors, posted themselves at the windows, and the firing recommenced with fresh violence.

"We must hold this," said the Governor.　"This is our last chance, and it will require a miracle to save us."

The assault was immediately ordered by Captain Sarol, who felt sure of success, although the task was a serious one.　In fact, the doors were strong, and it would be difficult to break them in without artillery.　The savages attacked them with tomahawks, under the fire from the windows, which made them lose heavily.　But that did not matter to their chief; though if he could be killed, his death might change the face of matters.

Two hours elapsed.　The town hall still held out.　If the bullets decimated the assailants, their masses were renewed unceasingly.　In vain the most skilful marksmen, Jem Tankerdon, Colonel Stewart, endeavoured to hit Captain Sarol.　While numbers of his people fell around him, he seemed invulnerable.

And it was not Sarol, amid a more furious fusillade than ever, whom a Snider bullet had hit on the central balcony.　It was Cyrus Bikerstaff, shot full in the chest. He fell—he could only utter a few stifled words, the blood mounted to his throat.　He was carried into the room behind, where he soon yielded his last breath.　Thus died the first governor of Floating Island, an able administrator, an honest and great man.

The assault was pursued with redoubled fury.　The doors were yielding to the axes of the savages.　How could the last fortress of Floating Island be saved? How could they save the women, the children, all those within from a general massacre?

The King of Malecarlie, Ethel Simcoe, and Colonel

Stewart, were discussing whether it would be better to retreat by the rear of the town hall. But where would they go ? To the battery at the Stern ? But could they reach it ? To one of the harbours ? But were not the savages in possession of them ? And the wounded, already numerous, how could they resolve to abandon them ?

At this moment a fortunate thing happened, which would probably change the state of affairs.

The King of Malecarlie stepped out on to the balcony, without heeding the bullets and arrows which rained around him. He brought up his rifle and aimed at Captain Sarol, just as one of the doors was about to give passage to the assailants.

Captain Sarol fell dead.

The Malays drew back, carrying the body of their chief, and began to retreat towards the gates of the square.

Almost immediately shouts were heard at the top of First Avenue, where a fusillade broke out with renewed intensity.

What had happened ? Had the defenders of the ports and batteries been successful ? Had they advanced on the town ? Had they attempted to take the natives in the rear, notwithstanding their small numbers ?

" The firing is increasing near the observatory," said Colonel Stewart.

" The scoundrels have had a reinforcement," said Commodore Simcoe.

" I do not think so," observed the King of Malecarlie. " This firing cannot be explained—"

" Yes ! There it is again," said Pinchinat, " and again to our advantage."

" Look ! look !" said Calistus Munbar ; " the beggars are beginning to run."

" Come, my friends," said the King of Malecarlie, " let us chase these rascals out of the town. Forward ! "

Officers, militiamen, sailors, ran downstairs and out of the principal doorway.

The square was abandoned by the crowd of savages, who fled, some down First Avenue, others along the neighbouring streets.

What was the cause of this rapid and unexpected change? Was it to be attributed to the disappearance of Captain Sarol—to the absence of leadership which had followed? Was it possible that the assailants, so superior in force, had been discouraged by the death of their chief at the very moment the town hall was about to be carried?

Led by Commodore Simcoe and Colonel Stewart, about two hundred men of the sailors and militia, with them Jem and Walter Tankerdon, Nat Coverley, Frascolin and his comrades, advanced down First Avenue, chasing the fugitives, who did not even turn to give them a bullet or an arrow, and threw away Sniders, bows, and javelins.

"Forward! Forward!" shouted Commodore Simcoe, in a voice of thunder.

Round the observatory the firing grew fiercer. It was evident that a terrible fight was going on.

Help, then, had arrived on Floating Island! But what help? Where had it come from?

Anyhow, the assailants were retreating on all sides, a prey to an incomprehensible panic. Had they been attacked by reinforcements from Larboard Harbour?

Yes. A thousand New Hebrideans had invaded Standard Island, under the leadership of the French colonists of Sandwich Island. We need not be astonished at the quartette being greeted in their national language, when they met their brave compatriots.

It was under these circumstances that this unexpected, or it might be said quasi-miraculous intervention had taken place.

During the preceding night and since daybreak Floating Island had continued to drift towards Sandwich Island, where, it will be remembered, there resided a prosperous French colony. As soon as the colonists got wind of the attack devised by Captain Sarol, they resolved, with the aid of a thousand natives devoted to them, to go to the help of Floating Island. But to transport them the vessels of Sandwich Island were not sufficient.

Judge of the joy of these gallant colonists when, during the morning, Floating Island came drifting up on the current. Immediately they threw themselves into fishing-boats, followed by the natives, most of them swimming, and landed at Larboard Harbour.

In a moment the men in the Prow and Stern batteries, and those in the port, joined them. Across the country, across the park they ran, towards Milliard City, and owing to this diversion the town hall did not fall into the hands of the assailants, already shaken by the death of Captain Sarol.

Two hours afterwards, the New Hebridean bands, pursued on all sides, had to seek safety by plunging into the sea, so as to reach Sandwich Island, while the greater number of them fell under the bullets of the militia.

And now Floating Island had no more to fear ; it was saved from pillage, massacre, and annihilation.

It might seem that the issue of this terrible affair would have evoked manifestations of public joy. No! Oh! these Americans are always astonishing! They said that there was nothing surprising in the result—that they had foreseen it. And yet how nearly had the attempt of Captain Sarol ended in a terrible catastrophe!

However, we may be allowed to think that the chief proprietors of Floating Island congratulated themselves in private at having been able to retain their property, and that at the moment when the marriage of Walter Tankerdon and Miss Coverley would make the future secure.

It should be said that when the lovers met again, they fell into each other's arms. And no one thought of seeing in that any breach of the proprieties. Should they not have been married a day ago ?

There was no need to seek for any ultra-American reserve in the welcome our Parisian artistes gave to the French colonists of Sandwich Island. What an exchange of grips of the hand! What felicitations did the Quartette Party receive from their compatriots! If the bullets had spared them, they had none the less done their duty, these two violins, this alto, and this violoncello! As to the excellent Athanase Dorémus, he had been quietly waiting in his room at the casino, ready for the pupil who never came—and who could reproach him?

An exception must be made with regard to the Superintendent. Ultra-Yankee as he was, his joy was delirious. But what would you have? In his veins flowed the blood of the illustrious Barnum, and it will be cheerfully admitted that the descendant of such an ancestor would hardly be as sane as his fellow-citizens of North America.

After the affair was over, the King of Malecarlie, accompanied by the Queen, returned to his house in Thirty-seventh Avenue, where the council of notables conveyed to him the thanks which his courage and devotion to the common cause deserved.

Thus Floating Island was safe and sound. Its safety had cost it dear.

Cyrus Bikerstaff, killed at the height of the battle, sixty militiamen and sailors hit by bullets or arrows, and almost as many among the government servants and tradesmen, who had fought so bravely.

In the public mourning the people all joined, and the Pearl of the Pacific would never forget it.

With the rapidity of execution characteristic of them, these Milliardites promptly set to work to repair damages.

After a stay of a few days at Sandwich Island all trace of the sanguinary strife would disappear.

Meantime, there was complete accord with regard to the question of the military powers, which were left in the hands of Commodore Simcoe. On this head there was no difficulty, no competition. Neither Jem Tankerdon nor Nat Coverley had any ambition on this head. Later, an election would settle the important question as to the new governor of Floating Island.

The day after, an imposing ceremony summoned the population to the quays of Starboard Harbour. The corpses of the Malays and the natives were thrown into the sea; but it was not so with those of the citizens who had died in defence of Floating Island. Their bodies were taken to the temple and the cathedral to receive the honours due to them; from Governor Cyrus Bikerstaff to the humblest amongst them, all were the object of the same prayer and the same sorrow.

Then this funeral cargo was confided to one of the swift steamers of Floating Island, and the ship departed for Madeleine Bay, carrying these honoured corpses to a Christian land.

CHAPTER XII.

FLOATING ISLAND left the neighbourhood of Sandwich Island on the 3rd of March. Before its departure, the French colony and their native allies were the object of cordial gratitude on the part of the Milliardites. These were friends whom they would see again; they were brothers whom Sebastien Zorn and his comrades left on this island of the New Hebrides group, who would for the future appear in the annual itinerary.

Under Commodore Simcoe's direction, the repairs were quickly made. The damages were not extensive. The electrical machinery was uninjured. With what remained of the stock of petroleum, the working of the dynamos was assured for many weeks. Besides, Floating Island would soon be back in that part of the Pacific where its submarine cables would allow of its communicating with Madeleine Bay. There was, consequently, the certainty of the campaign ending without disaster. Within four months Floating Island would be on the American coast.

"Let us hope so," said Sebastien Zorn, when the Superintendent was as usual enlarging on the future of this marvellous maritime invention.

"But," observed Calistus Munbar, "what a lesson we have received! These Malays, so obliging, this Captain Sarol, no one would have suspected them. This is the last time Floating Island will give shelter to strangers."

"Not even if a shipwreck throws them in the way?" asked Pinchinat.

"I do not believe any more in shipwrecks or shipwrecked crews!"

But though Commodore Simcoe had charge as before of the navigation of Floating Island, it did not follow that the civil powers were in his hands. Since the death of Cyrus Bikerstaff Milliard City had had no mayor, and, as we know, the assistants had resigned their positions. Consequently it would be necessary to nominate a new governor of Floating Island.

As there was no official of the civil power they could not proceed to the marriage of Walter Tankerdon and Di Coverley. Here was a difficulty which would not have arisen had it not been for the machinations of that scoundrel Sarol! And not only the couple themselves, but all the notables of Milliard City, and all the population, were anxious that this marriage should be definitely settled. In it was one of the safest guarantees of the future. That there might be no delay, Walter Tankerdon was already talking of embarking on one of the Starboard Harbour steamers with the two families to the nearest archipelago, where a mayor could proceed with the nuptial ceremony. There were mayors at Samoa, at Tonga, at the Marquesas, and in less than a week, if they went full steam—

The wiser minds argued with the impatient young man. The people were busy getting ready for the election. In a few days the new governor would be nominated. The first act of his administration would be to celebrate with great pomp the marriage so ardently expected. The programme of the festivities would be resumed. A mayor! a mayor! That was the cry in every mouth.

"Let us hope that these elections may not revive the rivalries that may not be entirely extinct!" said Frascolin.

No, and Calistus Munbar had resolved to do his best to bring matters to an end.

"Besides," he exclaimed, "have we not our lovers? You will, I think, agree with me that self-esteem has no chance against love?"

Floating Island continued its course to the north-east, towards the point where the twelfth degree of south

latitude crosses the hundred and seventy-fifth of west
longitude.

It was in these parts that the last cablegrams sent before
the stay at the New Hebrides had communicated with the
supply ships loading at Madeleine Bay. Commodore
Simcoe was not at all anxious regarding provisions. The
reserves were enough for more than a month, and there
could be no trouble on this point. It is true that foreign
news was running short. The political chronicle was
meagre. The *Starboard Chronicle* complained, the *New
Herald* was in despair. But what mattered it ? Was not
Floating Island a little world in itself, and what had it to do
with what happened on the rest of the terrestrial spheroid ?
Did it want politics ? Well, there would soon be politics
enough for it—perhaps too much.

In fact the electoral contest began. The council of
notables, in which the Larboardites equalled the Starboardites, was busy. It was certain that the choice of a
new governor would give rise to discussions, for Jem
Tankerdon and Nat Coverley would be on opposite sides.

A few days were spent in preliminary meetings. From
the outset it was evident that the parties would not agree.
Secret agitation arose in the town and ports. The agents
of the two sections tried to provoke a popular movement to
bring pressure on the notables. As time went on, it did not
seem as though an agreement could be brought about. It
began to be feared that Jem Tankerdon and the principal
Larboardites would now endeavour to carry out their
ideas, so objected to by the Starboardites, and make
Floating Island an industrial and commercial island.
Never would the other section consent to that ! The
more the Coverley party grew angry, the more the
Tankerdon party persisted. Hence offensive recriminations, bitterness between the two camps, manifest coolness
between the two families—a coolness which Walter and
Di did not care to notice. What had all this rubbish about
politics to do with them ?

There was a very simple way of arranging these matters,

at least from an administrative point of view ; that was to resolve that the two competitors should take it in turn to be governor, six months one and six months the other, even a year apiece if that seemed preferable. Then there would be no rivalry, and the arrangement would satisfy both parties. But good sense has never a chance of being adopted in this world, and though it was independent of the terrestrial continents, Floating Island was none the less subject to all the passions of sub-lunary humanity.

"There," said Frascolin one day to his companions. "There you have the difficulties I feared."

"And what do these dissensions matter to us ? " replied Pinchinat. "How can they damage us ? In a few months we shall be at Madeleine Bay, and our engagement will be at an end, and we can set foot on firm ground, with a little million in our pockets."

"If some catastrophe does not take place ? " added the intractable Sebastien Zorn. "Is such a floating machine ever sure of a future ? After the collision with the English ship, the invasion of the wild beasts ; after the wild beasts the invasion of the New Hebrideans ; after the savages the—"

"Silence, bird of ill augury ! " exclaimed Yvernès. "Silence, we will put a padlock on your beak ! "

Nevertheless, it was greatly to be regretted that the marriage had not been celebrated at the date fixed. The families being united by a new tie, the problem would be less difficult of solution. The newly married couple might intervene in a more efficacious fashion. After all, the agitation would not last, as the election would take place on the 15th of March.

Commodore Simcoe tried to bring about an understanding between the two sections of the town. He was asked not to interfere in what did not concern him. He had to navigate the island, let him navigate it. He had reefs to avoid, let him avoid them. Politics were not his business.

Commodore Simcoe did as he was told.

Religious passions began to enter into the debate, and
the clergy—in which they were perhaps wrong—interfered
more than was desirable. They had been living in such
accord, the temple and the cathedral, the pastor and the
bishop.

The newspapers, of course, descended into the arena.
The New Herald fought for the Tankerdons, *The Starboard Chronicle* for the Coverleys. Ink flowed in deluges,
and it was to be feared that the ink would be mingled
with blood! Great Heaven! Had it not already been
too much sprinkled, this virgin soil of Floating Island,
during the struggle with the savages of the New
Hebrides!

The bulk of the population were chiefly interested in
the two young people, whose romance had been interrupted at the first chapter. But what could they do to
make them happy? Already communications had ceased
between the two sections of Milliard city. No more receptions, invitations, musical evenings. If this sort of thing
lasted, the instruments of the Quartette Party might go
mouldy in their cases, and our artistes earn their enormous
salaries with their hands in their pockets.

The Superintendent, although he would not admit it, was
in an agony of anxiety. He was in a false position, for
his whole mind was occupied in displeasing nobody—a
sure means of displeasing everybody.

On the 12th of March, Floating Island was approaching
the Equator, although it had not reached the latitude in
which it would meet the ships sent from Madeleine Bay.
It would not be long before they did so, but apparently
the elections would take place beforehand, as they were
fixed for the 15th.

Meanwhile the Starboardites and Larboardites took to
forecasting the result. Always the same promise of
equality. No majority was possible, unless some voters
would change sides. And the voters remained as firm as
the teeth in a tiger's jaw.

Then arose a genial idea. It seemed to have occurred at the same moment to the minds of all. This idea was simple, it was an honourable one, it would put an end to the rivalry. The candidates themselves would doubtless bow to this just solution.

Why not offer the government of Floating Island to the King of Malecarlie ? The ex-sovereign was a wise man, of firm and liberal mind. His toleration and his philosophy would be the best guarantee against the surprises of the future. He knew men from having lived amongst them. He knew that he had to reckon with their weaknesses and their ingratitude. Ambition was not his failing, and never would the thought occur to him to substitute the personal power for the democratic institutions which existed on Floating Island. He would never be more than the president of the council of administration of the new company, *Tankerdon, Coverley & Co.*

An important group of merchants and functionaries of Milliard City, with whom were a certain number of the officers and sailors at the ports, decided to convey this proposal to their royal fellow-citizen.

It was in the room on the ground floor of the house in Thirty-ninth Avenue that their Majesties received the deputation. They listened with friendliness, and answered with a decided refusal. The deposed sovereigns remembered the past, and under this impression the King replied,—

"I thank you, gentlemen. We are not insensible to your request, but we are happy at present, and we hope that nothing will trouble our future. Believe me, we have finished with the illusions that are inherent to any sovereignty whatever. I am now only an astronomer at the observatory of Floating Island, and I do not wish to be anything else."

There was no opportunity to persist, after so formal a reply, and the deputation retired.

During the few days preceding the election the excitement increased. It was impossible to arrive at an understanding. The partisans of Jem Tankerdon and Nat Coverley avoided meeting each other, even in the streets. People no longer went from one section to the other. Neither the Starboardites nor the Larboardites crossed First Avenue. Milliard City was now formed into two hostile camps. The only personage who went from one to the other, agitated, crushed, knocked up, perspiring water and blood, exhausting himself in good advice, repulsed to the right, repulsed to the left, was the despairing Superintendent, Calistus Munbar. And three or four times a day he ran aground, like a rudderless ship, in the rooms of the casino, where the quartette overwhelmed him with vain consolations.

Commodore Simcoe confined himself to his special duties. He navigated Floating Island according to the itinerary. Having a holy horror of politics, he would accept whatever governor was given him. His officers, like those of Colonel Stewart, were quite as little interested in the question which had set so many heads on the boil. It was not in Floating Island that pronunciamentos were to be feared.

However, the council of notables, in permanent session at the town hall, discussed and disputed. They were taking to personalities. The police were compelled to take certain precautions, for the crowd thronged from morning to night in front of the town hall, and raised seditious cries.

On the other hand, deplorable news got abroad. Walter Tankerdon had called at the Coverley mansion, and not been admitted. The two young people were forbidden to see one another, and as the marriage had not been celebrated before the attack of the New Hebridean bands, who dared say if it ever would be accomplished?

At last the 15th of March arrived. The election was to take place in the principal room of the town-hall. A noisy crowd blocked the square, as the Roman populace formerly did before the palace of the Quirinal, when the conclave proceeded to the elevation of a Pope to the throne of Saint Peter.

What would come out of this supreme deliberation? The forecast showed that there would be an equality of votes. If the Starboardites remained faithful to Nat Coverley and the Larboardites to Jem Tankerdon, what would happen?

The great day arrived. Between one and three o'clock the ordinary life seemed to be suspended on Floating Island. From five to six thousand people stood excited beneath the windows of the municipal edifice. They awaited the result of the voting of the notables—a result which would be immediately communicated by telephone to the two sections and the two ports.

A first scrutiny took place at thirty-five minutes past one.

The candidates had obtained the same number of suffrages.

An hour afterwards there was a second scrutiny.

It in no way modified the figures of the first.

At thirty-five minutes past three there was the third and last scrutiny.

This time neither had a vote in excess of the other.

The council then separated, and it was best to do so. If it had remained sitting, the members would have become so exasperated that they would have taken to blows. As they crossed the square on their way, some of them to the Tankerdon mansion, and some to the Coverley mansion, the crowd greeted them with the most disagreeable murmurs.

But it was necessary to put an end to this state of affairs, which was most damaging to the interests of Floating Island.

"Between ourselves," said Pinchinat, when they had heard from the Superintendent the result of the three scrutinies, "it seems that there is a very simple way of settling the question."

"And what is that?" asked Calistus Munbar, lifting his arms in despair to heaven. "What?"

"Cut the island in half; divide it into two equal parts, like a cake ; let the two halves go on as they please, each with a governor of its own ! "

"Cut our island in half!" gasped the Superintendent, as if Pinchinat had proposed to cut off a limb.

"With a cold chisel, a mallet, and a screw-wrench, the question would be solved, and there would be two moving islands instead of one on the surface of the Pacific Ocean."

Pinchinat could never be serious, even when circumstances were of such gravity.

His advice was not accepted—at least in a material sense ; but if there were no mallet and screw-wrench, if no division was made down the middle of First Avenue from Prow Battery to Stern Battery, the separation was none the less accomplished from a political point of view. The Larboardites and Starboardites had become as much strangers to each other as if a hundred leagues of sea separated them. In fact, the thirty notables had decided to vote separately in default of an understanding. On one side, Jem Tankerdon was a pointed governor of his section, and he could govern it as he pleased. On the other, Nat Coverley was appointed governor of his section, and he could govern it as he pleased. Each of them would keep his port, his ships, his officers, his sailors, his militiamen, his functionaries, his tradesmen, his electrical works, his engines, his motors, his engineers, his stokers.

This was very well, but what would Commodore Simcoe do when he wanted to turn, and how could Calistus Munbar perform his duties to the common satisfaction?

As regards the latter, it is true, it was not of much importance. His place had become a sinecure. There could be no question as to amusements and festivities when Floating Island was menaced by civil war—for a reconciliation was not possible.

This was evident from a single indication. On the 17th of March the newspapers announced that the marriage between Walter Tankerdon and Miss Coverley was definitely broken off.

Yes! Broken off—in spite of their prayers, in spite of their supplications; and yet Calistus Munbar had once said that love was the strongest! Well, no! Walter and Di would not separate. They would abandon their relatives; they would marry in some foreign country; they would find a corner in the world where they could be happy without so many millions hanging round their hearts!

After the nomination of Jem Tankerdon and Nat Coverley, nothing had been changed with regard to the course of Floating Island. Commodore Simcoe continued to steer north-east. Once they reached Madeleine Bay, it was probable, if the present state of things continued, that several of the Milliardites would seek on the Continent the quiet which was no longer offered them by the Pearl of the Pacific. Perhaps even Floating Island would be abandoned. And then they would liquidate it; they would put it up to auction; they would sell it at so much a pound, like old and useless iron, and it would be melted down!

But the five thousand miles it had to travel would take another five months to accomplish. During the voyage would the direction be interfered with by the obstinacy of the two chiefs? The spirit of revolt had begun to show itself among the people. Would the Larboardites and Starboardites come to blows, and take to firing on each other, and bathing with blood the steel sidewalks of Milliard City?

No! The parties would not, apparently, go to these extremities. There would not be another secession war between north and south, or rather between the Larboard and Starboard sections of Floating Island. But the inevitable happened, at the risk of provoking a catastrophe.

In the morning of the 19th of March, Commodore Simcoe was in his office at the observatory, waiting for the first observation of altitude to be communicated to him. In his opinion Floating Island could not be far from the spot where it would meet with the supply ships. Look-outs on the tower surveyed the vast circuit of sea, so as to signal the steamers as soon as they appeared on the horizon. With the Commodore were the King of Malecarlie, Colonel Stewart, Sebastien Zorn, Pinchinat, Frascolin, Yvernès, and a few officers and functionaries— who might all be classed as neutrals, for they had not yet taken part in the intestine dissensions. The essential point for them was to arrive as soon as possible at Madeleine Bay, where this deplorable state of things would end.

At this moment two bells sounded, and two orders were transmitted to the Commodore by telephone. They came from the town hall, where Jem Tankerdon and Nat Coverley, with their respective supporters, were in different wings. Here they administered Floating Island, and we need not be astonished at the orders being contradictory.

This very morning the two governors had resolved to disagree regarding the course hitherto followed by Ethel Simcoe. Nat Coverley had decided that Floating Island should go north-east, so as to touch at the Gilbert Islands. Jem Tankerdon, with the object of opening up commercial relations, decided to go south-west, towards Australia.

Thus had the rivals committed themselves, and their friends had sworn to support them.

When he received the two orders sent simultaneously to the observatory, the Commodore remarked,—

" This is what I feared."

" And which must not last, in the public interest," said the King of Malecarlie.

" What do you decide ? " asked Frascolin.

" I am curious to see how you will manœuvre," said Pinchinat.

" Inform Jem Tankerdon and Nat Coverley," said the Commodore, " that we cannot execute their orders, as they contradict each other. Besides, it is better for Floating Island to remain where it is, and wait for the ships which are to meet it here."

This very wise reply was immediately telephoned to the town hall.

An hour passed without the observatory receiving any other orders. Probably the two governors had given up their intentions.

Suddenly Floating Island began to move in a strange manner. What did this movement indicate? That Jem Tankerdon and Nat Coverley had persisted in their obstinacy to the furthest limits.

All the persons present looked at each other interrogatively.

"What is the matter? What is the matter?"

"What is the matter?" answered the Commodore, shrugging his shoulders; "Jem Tankerdon has sent his orders direct to Watson, the engineer at Larboard Harbour, and Nat Coverley has sent contradictory orders to Somwah, the engineer at Starboard Harbour. One has given orders to go north-east, the other to go southwest. The result is that Floating Island is swinging round on its centre, and the gyration will last as long as the caprice of these two obstinate personages."

"Well!" said Pinchinat. "This ought to end in a waltz! Athanase Dorémus might as well resign. The Milliardites do not want his lessons!"

This absurd situation—comic from one point of view—probably caused a laugh. Unfortunately the double manœuvre was extremely dangerous, as the Commodore observed. Driven round and round by six million horsepower, Floating Island was in danger of being shaken to pieces.

In fact, the engines were going full speed, the screws working at their maximum power, and the steel subsoil was all of a tremble. The motion became more noticeable. Floating Island pirouetted on its centre. The park, the country described concentric circles, and the places on the shore swung round at from ten to twelve miles an hour.

To argue with the engineers was not to be thought of. Commodore Simcoe had no authority over them. They were subject to the same passions as the Starboardites and Larboardites. Faithful servants of their chiefs, Watson and Somwah would drive on to the bitter end, engine for engine, dynamo for dynamo.

Then occurred a phenomenon, the unpleasantness of which should have calmed the heads by softening the hearts.

On account of the rotation of Floating Island, a number of Milliardites, especially the women, began to feel strangely unwell. Within the houses there were attacks of sickening nausea, principally in those which, being farthest from the centre, were most affected by this waltzing motion.

At this farcical result, Yvernès, Pinchinat, and Frascolin burst out into peals of laughter, although matters were getting most serious.

Under the influence of this continuous whirling, Sebastien Zorn became pale, very pale. He "struck his colours," as Pinchinat said, and his heart mounted to his lips. Was this ill-timed joke never to finish? To be a prisoner on this immense turning table, which did not even have the gift of revealing the secrets of the future.

For a whole week Floating Island continued to spin round on its centre, which was Milliard City. In vain the King of Malecarlie, Commodore Simcoe, and Colonel Stewart attempted to intervene between the two powers which shared the municipal palace. Neither would lower his flag! Cyrus Bikerstaff himself, if he could have come to life again, would have found his efforts fail against such ultra-American tenacity.

Then, to add to the misfortune, the sky had been so constantly covered with clouds during this week, that it was not possible to take an altitude. Commodore Simcoe did not know where Floating Island was. Driven round by its powerful screws, it trembled in every wall of its compartments. No one thought of staying indoors. The park was crowded with people camping in the open air. On either side were heard cries of " Hurrah for Tankerdon ! " and " Hurrah for Coverley ! " Eyes flashed lightnings, fists were clenched threateningly. Was civil war going to break out, with its worst excesses, now that the people had reached a paroxysm of madness ?

Neither one side nor the other would see anything of the approaching danger. They would not give in, even if the Pearl of the Pacific were to break into a thousand fragments, and it would continue to spin until the dynamos ceased to drive the screws.

Amid this general irritation, in which he took no part, Walter Tankerdon was a prey to the keenest anguish. He feared not for himself, but for Miss Coverley, that some sudden breaking up would annihilate Milliard City. For eight days he had not seen her. Twenty times he had begged his father to have done with this deplorable manœuvre ; but all was in vain.

Then on the night of the 27th of March, taking advantage of the darkness, he endeavoured to see Miss Coverley. He wished to be near her when the catastrophe occurred. Gliding through the crowd which blocked First Avenue, he penetrated into the hostile section, so as to reach the Coverleys' house.

A little before daybreak a terrific explosion shook the air. Driven beyond the pressure they would bear, the boilers of the Larboard section blew up with the buildings and machinery. And as the source of electrical energy suddenly gave out on this side, half Floating Island was plunged into profound darkness.

CHAPTER XIII.

IF the engines of Larboard Harbour were now useless, on account of the bursting of the boilers, those of Starboard Harbour were uninjured. But it was as if Floating Island had lost all power of locomotion. Reduced to its starboard screws, all it could do was to turn round and round on itself, for it could not go ahead.

This accident consequently made matters worse. While Floating Island had two sets of engines, capable of acting together, it was only necessary for an understanding to be arrived at between the Tankerdon and Coverley parties for this state of things to be put an end to. The motors would then resume their customary task of working together, and the island, after its delay of a few days, could have resumed its course to Madeleine Bay.

Now this was impossible, and Commodore Simcoe had not the propelling force necessary to enable him to leave his present position.

If Floating Island had remained stationary during the last week, if the steamers came up it might still be possible to regain the northern hemisphere.

But it was not, for an astronomic observation taken this day showed that Floating Island had drifted to the south during its prolonged gyration. It had drifted from the twelfth parallel to the seventeenth.

In fact, between the New Hebrides group and the Fiji group there are certain currents, due to the proximity of the two archipelagoes to each other, which flow to the south-east. While the engines worked together Floating Island could easily make headway against the current.

But as soon as it became afflicted with vertigo it had been irresistibly drawn towards the tropic of Capricorn.

When this was recognized, Commodore Simcoe did not hide from those we have called neutrals the gravity of the circumstances.

"We have drifted," he said, "five degrees south. What a sailor can do with a steamer when her engines break down I cannot do with Floating Island. An island has no sails, and we are at the mercy of the currents. Where will they take us? I do not know. As to the steamers despatched from Madeleine Bay, they will seek us in vain in the place agreed upon, and it is towards the least frequented portion of the Pacific that we are drifting, at the rate of from eight to ten miles an hour."

In these few sentences Ethel Simcoe stated the position, which it was impossible to modify. Floating Island was like an immense wreck delivered over to the caprices of the currents. If they ran towards the north, it would go north; if they ran towards the south, it would go south— perhaps to the extreme limits of the Antarctic Ocean. And then

This state of things soon became known to the people at Milliard City, as at both harbours. A feeling of great fear arose. Hence—which was very human—a certain softening of asperities under the fear of this new peril. They no longer dreamt of coming to blows in a fratricidal strife, and if hatreds continued, they would not at least lead to violence. Gradually every one returned to his section, his quarter, his house. Jem Tankerdon and Nat Coverley gave up their dispute for first place. At the proposal of the two governors, the council of notables came to the only reasonable decision dictated by the circumstances, and transferred its powers to the hands of Commodore Simcoe, the only chief to whom the safety of Floating Island was henceforth entrusted.

Ethel Simcoe accepted the task without hesitation. He reckoned on the devotion of his friends, his officers, his staff. But what could he do with this vast floating apparatus, with an area of twenty-seven square kilometres, become unmanageable, now that it had no longer its two sets of engines?

And was there not some foundation for saying that this was the condemnation of Floating Island, up to then regarded as the masterpiece of marine construction, inasmuch as such accidents would render it the sport of the winds and waves?

It is true that this accident was not due to the forces of nature, over which the Pearl of the Pacific had triumphed since its foundation. It was the fault of these intestine dissensions, these rivalries of the Milliardites, this unreasonable obstinacy of some to go south and others to go north. It was their immeasurable madness that had brought about the explosion of the Larboard boilers.

But what was the good of recriminations? What was necessary was to inquire into the damages at Larboard Harbour. Commodore Simcoe assembled his officers and his engineers. The King of Malecarlie went with them. It was assuredly not this royal philosopher who was surprised at human passions bringing about such a catastrophe.

The commission went to the Larboard engine works. The explosion of the over-driven boilers had caused the deaths of two engineers and six stokers. The ravages were no less complete in the workshops where the electricity was produced for the different services of this half of Floating Island. Fortunately, the starboard dynamos continued to work, and as Pinchinat observed,—

"We have got off with the loss of one eye."

"That may be," replied Frascolin, "but we have also lost a limb, and the one that is left is of little use to us."

To be blind and lame was too much.

The result of the inquiry was that the damages could not be repaired, and that it would be impossible to arrest the movement towards the south. Hence the need of waiting until Floating Island got out of the current which was taking it below the tropic.

This being ascertained, the next thing was to examine the state of the compartments of the hull. Had they not suffered from the gyratory movement which had so violently shaken them? Were the plates strained, the rivets started?

If leaks had opened, what means were there of stopping them?

The engineers proceeded to this second inquiry. Their reports, communicated to Commodore Simcoe, were anything but comforting. In many places the shaking had cracked the plates and broken the ties. Thousands of rivets had been started, and there had been a good deal of breakage. Certain compartments had already been invaded by the sea. But as the line of flotation had not been lowered, the strength of the hull had not been seriously affected, and the new proprietors of Floating Island had nothing to fear for their property. It was near the Stern Battery that the cracks were most numerous. At Larboard Harbour one of the piers had dropped off into the sea when the explosion occurred. But Starboard Harbour was all right, and its docks afforded every safety for vessels against the waves of the sea.

Orders were given to repair all that was repairable. It was important that the population should be tranquillized. It was enough, it was too much, that without its larboard screws Floating Island could not make for the nearest land. For that there was no remedy.

There remained the serious question of hunger and thirst. Would the reserves be sufficient for a month, for two months?

These particulars were furnished to Commodore Simcoe.

With regard to the water there was nothing to fear. One of the distilling apparatus had been destroyed by the explosion, but the other, which continued at work, could furnish all requirements.

With regard to provisions, the state of affairs was not so promising. Taking everything into account, their duration would not exceed a fortnight, unless these ten thousand

people were placed on short rations. The fruits and
vegetables came, as we know, from the outside. And
outside—where was that? Where was the nearest land,
and how could it be reached?

Then, whatever might be the effect, Commodore Simcoe
had to make instant arrangements as to putting the people
on rations. That evening the telephones and telautographs spread this melancholy news.

Whereupon general dismay in Milliard City and the
two ports, and a presentiment of worse catastrophes.
Would not the spectre of famine, to adopt a familiar image,
soon appear on the horizon, as there existed no means of
replenishing the stock of provisions? In fact, Commodore
Simcoe had not a single ship to send to the American
continent. Fate had so willed it that the last had been
sent away three weeks before with the mortal remains of
Cyrus Bikerstaff and the defenders in the battle at
Erromango. It was to be feared that matters of mere
self-esteem would put Floating Island in a worse position
than when it was invaded by the New Hebrideans.

What is the use of possessing millions, of being as rich
as Rothschilds, Mackays, Astors, Vanderbilts, Goulds,
when no riches can keep away famine? Doubtless, these
nabobs had the greater part of their fortunes safely placed
in the banks of the new and old continents. But who
knew if the day were not approaching when a million
would not procure a pound of meat or a pound of bread!

After all, the fault was in their absurd dissensions, their
stupid rivalries, their desire to seize upon power! The
culprits were the Tankerdons and the Coverleys, who had
caused all the trouble. Let them take care of reprisals, of
the rage of the officers, and functionaries, and employees,
and tradesmen, of the whole of the population they had
brought into such danger! To what excesses might not
these betake themselves when they were suffering the
tortures of hunger.

Let us say, that no reproaches were levelled against
Walter Tankerdon nor Miss Coverley, who shared none

of the blame deserved by their families. No! The young man and the girl were not responsible! They were the bond that might have assured the future of both sections, and it was not they who had broken it!

For two days, owing to the state of the sky, no observation could be taken, and the position of Floating Island could not be ascertained with any certainty.

On the 31st of March the zenith at dawn was clear enough, and the mists in the offing soon died away. There was reason to hope that an altitude could be taken under good conditions.

The observation was awaited with feverish impatience. Many hundreds of the inhabitants went out to Prow Battery. Walter Tankerdon joined them. But neither his father, nor Nat Coverley, nor any of the notables, who could be justly accused of having brought about this state of affairs, left their houses, where they were kept indoors by public indignation.

A little before noon the observers prepared to catch the solar disc at the instant of its culmination. Two sextants, one in the hands of the King of Malecarlie, the other in the hands of Commodore Simcoe, were directed towards the horizon.

As soon as the altitude was taken, the calculations began, with the needful corrections, and the result gave 29° 17' latitude south. About two o'clock a second observation, made under the same favourable conditions, indicated 179° 32' longitude east.

And so, since Floating Island had been a prey to this gyratory folly, the currents had carried it about a thousand miles to the south-east.

When the position was marked on the map, this was what appeared.

The nearest islands—a hundred miles distant at least—were the Kermadecs, barren rocks, hardly inhabited, without resources; and, besides, how could they be reached? Three hundred miles to the south was New Zealand, and how could that be reached if the currents took them along the open sea ? To the west, fifteen hundred miles, was Australia—to the east, several thousand miles, was South America, in the neighbourhood of Chili. Beyond New Zealand was the Antarctic Ocean. Was it there, on the lands of the Pole, that Floating Island was to be wrecked ? Was it there that navigators would one day find a whole population dead of misery and hunger ?

Commodore Simcoe proceeded to study the currents of these seas with the greatest care. But what would happen if they did not change, if they did not meet opposing currents, if one of those formidable tempests broke out which are so frequent in the circumpolar regions ?

The news was well calculated to provoke alarm. Feeling rose higher and higher against the authors of the trouble —these mischievous nabobs of Milliard City, who were responsible for this state of affairs. It required all the influenze of the King of Malecarlie, all the energy of Commodore Simcoe and Colonel Stewart, all the devotion of their officers, all their authority over the sailors and soldiers of the militia to prevent an insurrection.

The day passed without change. All had to submit to be rationed, and to restrict themselves to the absolutely necessary as regards food—the wealthiest as well as those who were not so wealthy.

Meanwhile a service of look-outs was carefully arranged, and the horizon strictly watched. If a ship appeared, they would signal it, and perhaps it would be possible to enter into communication with it. Unfortunately Floating Island had drifted out of the maritime routes, there being few vessels which traverse these regions bordering on the Antarctic Ocean. And beyond to the south, there arose before the affrighted imagination the spectre of the Pole lighted by the volcanic gleams of Erebus and Terror.

A fortunate circumstance occurred in the night of the 3rd of April. The north wind, which had been violent for some hours, fell suddenly. A dead calm succeeded, and the breeze went suddenly round to the south-east, in one of those atmospheric caprices so frequent at the periods of the equinox.

Commodore Simcoe began to hope. Floatiı g Island need only be forced a hundred miles to the westward for the counter-current to take it near Australia or New Zealand. Anyhow, its progress towards the Polar Sea would be checked, and it was possible that ships might be met with in the vicinity of the large islands of Australasia.

As the sun rose, the breeze freshened from the south-east. Floating Island was plainly enough affected by it. Its high buildings, the observatory, the town hall, the temple, the cathedral, offered a certain resistance to the wind. They acted as sails for this enormous vessel of four hundred and thirty-two million tons.

Although the sky was swept by swift clouds, the solar disc appeared at intervals, and a good observation would probably be taken. In fact, on two occasions the sun was caught between the clouds, and the calculation showed that since the day before, Floating Island had mounted two degrees towards the north-west.

It was difficult to admit that this was entirely due to the influence of the wind. The conclusion was that the Island had drifted into one of the eddies which divide the great currents of the Pacific; that it had had the good fortune to enter one that was taking it to the north-west, and that its chances of safety were considerable. But there must be no delay, for it was necessary to further reduce the rations. The reserves were diminishing at a rate which caused anxiety in the presence of ten thousand inhabitants to feed.

When the last astronomical observation was communicated to the ports and the town it somewhat allayed the excitement. We know how suddenly a crowd will pass from one sentiment to another, from despair to hope. That is what happened. These people, very different to the miserable masses of the great continental cities, ought to be and were less subject to panic, more reflective, more

patient. But with a threatened famine was not everything
to be feared ?

During the morning the wind showed a tendency to
freshen. The barometer fell slowly. The sea rose in
long, powerful waves, proving that it was subject to great
agitation in the south-east. Floating Island, hitherto
impassible, was no longer insensible to these enormous
disturbances of level. Some of the houses shook from top
to bottom, and the things in them began to shift, as if
there were an earthquake. The phenomenon was new to
the Milliardites, and gave rise to considerable uneasiness.

Commodore Simcoe and his staff remained constantly
on duty at the observatory, where the whole administration
was concentrated. The shocks began to affect the observatory, and the extreme seriousness of the matter was
recognized.

" It is too evident," said the Commodore, " that Floating
Island has been injured below. Its compartments have
opened. Its hull has no longer the rigidity which rendered it so solid."

" It is to be hoped," said the King of Malecarlie, " that it
will not have to stand a violent storm, for it is no longer
strong enough to resist it."

Yes ! And now the people began to lose confidence in
the artificial soil. They felt that their foothold was about
to fail them. Better a hundred times be smashed on the
rocks of the Antarctic lands. To fear every moment that
Floating Island would open and be swallowed up in the
depths of the Pacific, which had never yet been sounded,
was enough to make the bravest hearts fail as they thought
of it.

It was impossible to doubt that fresh injuries had
cocurred in some of the compartments. Partitions had
given way, and the rivets of the plates must have been
torn out. In the park, along the Serpentine, on the surface of the outer streets of the town, there were strange
undulations resulting in dislocations of the soil. Already
some of the buildings had begun to lean, and if they fell,

they would break in the substructure on which their foundation rested. That the sea had made its way into the subsoil was unmistakable, for the water line had altered. Nearly all round, at the two ports as at the batteries, the line had sunk a foot, and if it sunk more the waves would come over the coast. Floating Island was in danger; its foundering was only a question of a few hours.

Commodore Simcoe would have kept this quiet, for it would probably cause a panic and worse perhaps. To what excesses might not the people be led against those responsible for this disaster? They could not seek safety in flight like the passengers of a ship, throw themselves into boats, or construct a raft, as a crew does, in the hope of being saved from the sea. No! The raft was Floating Island itself; and it was going down.

From hour to hour during the day Commodore Simcoe noted the changes in the water line. Floating Island continued to settle down. Hence infiltration must be taking place in the compartments, slow, but incessant and irresistible.

At the same time the weather was getting worse. The sky was covered with red, coppery hues. The barometer was falling more quickly. The atmosphere had every sign of an approaching storm. Behind the accumulated vapours the horizon became so restricted that it seemed to be limited to the shore of Floating Island.

As the evening came on, terrible gusts of wind arose. In the fury of the surge the compartments burst, the cross-bars broke, the plates were torn away. Everywhere was a sound of the cracking of metal. The avenues of the town, the lawns of the park, threatened to gape open. As night approached, Milliard City was abandoned for the country, which, less laden with heavy buildings, seemed to be safer. The whole population lay scattered between the ports and the batteries.

About nine o'clock a violent shock shook Floating Island to its foundations. The works at Starboard Harbour, which furnished the electric light, fell into the sea. The darkness was so profound that neither sky nor sea was visible.

Immediately more quakings of the ground took place, and the houses began to fall as if they were built of cards. In a few hours nothing would be left of the superstructure of Floating Island.

"Gentlemen," said Commodore Simcoe, "we can no longer remain at the observatory, which is in danger of being a heap of ruins. Let us get into the country, and wait until the storm is over."

"It is a cyclone," replied the King of Malecarlie, showing the barometer, fallen to 713 millimetres.

Floating Island had been caught in one of those cyclonic movements which act like powerful condensers. These eddying tempests formed by a mass of water, whose gyration takes place round an almost vertical axis, move from east to west along the north of the southern hemisphere. A cyclone is the atmospheric phenomenon most fraught with disasters, and to escape from it, its comparatively calm centre must be reached, or at least the right side of its trajectory, the workable semicircle which is free from the fury of the waves. But this manœuvre was impossible for want of motors. This time it was not human stupidity nor the imbecile obstinacy of its leaders which was ruining Floating Island, but a formidable atmospheric disturbance which would end by annihilating it.

The King of Malecarlie, Commodore Simcoe, Colonel Stewart, Sebastien Zorn and his comrades, the astronomers, and the officers, abandoned the observatory, where they were no longer safe. It was time. Scarcely had they gone a hundred yards, before the lofty tower collapsed with a horrible noise, fell through the ground, and disappeared into the abyss.

A moment afterwards the entire edifice was a mass of ruins.

Nevertheless the quartette thought of going up First Avenue and running to the casino, where their instruments were, which they wished to save if possible. The casino was still standing. They reached it, they mounted to their rooms, they carried off the two violins, the alto, and the violoncello to the park, in which they sought refuge.

There were gathered several thousand persons of both sections. The Tankerdon and Coverley families were there, and perhaps it was fortunate for them that amid the darkness they could not see each other, could not recognize each other.

Walter had, however, been fortunate enough to meet with Di. He would try and save her at the moment of the supreme catastrophe. He would cling with her to some piece of wreckage.

The girl divined that the young man was near her, and this cry escaped her,—

" Ah ! Walter ! "

" Di, dear Di ! I am here ! I will not leave you any more."

As to our Parisians, they would not leave each other. They would remain together. Frascolin had lost nothing of his coolness. Yvernès was very nervous. Pinchinat was ironically resigned. Sebastien Zorn said to Athanase Dorémus, who had at last decided to join his compatriots,—

" I told them it would end badly ! I predicted it ! "

"Enough of your tremolos in a minor key, old Isaiah," said his Highness ; "start on your penitential psalms."

Towards midnight the force of the cyclone increased. The converging winds raised monstrous waves and hurled them against Floating Island. Where would this strife of the elements take them ? To be sheltered on some reef ? To be rent asunder in mid-ocean ?

The hull was now rent in a thousand places. The joints were cracking everywhere. St. Mary's church, the temple, the town hall, had fallen through the gaping fissures through which the sea came leaping up. Of these magnificent edifices not a vestige remained. What riches, what treasures, pictures, statues, objects of art had vanished

for ever! The people would see no more of this superb
Milliard City when daylight came, if ever the daylight came
for them.

The sea began to spread over the country, over the park.
The island sank lower and lower in the water. The
surface of Floating Island was at the level of the sea, and
the cyclone was driving the waves over on to it.

No shelter now anywhere. Prow Battery, which was
then to windward, afforded no protection against the waves
or the squalls which swept on to it. The compartments
opened, and the dislocation continued, with a noise that
was heard above the most violent rolls of thunder. The
supreme catastrophe was approaching.

About three in the morning the park cracked along a
length of two kilometres in the bed of Serpentine
River, and through this the sea flowed. Instant flight
was inevitable, and the people dispersed into the country.
Some ran towards the ports, others towards the batteries.
Families were separated; mothers in vain sought for their
children; while the sea rolled over Floating Island as if
in an enormous tidal wave.

Walter Tankerdon, who had not left Di, tried to lead
her towards Starboard Harbour. She had not strength to
follow him. He lifted her, almost inanimate; he carried
her in his arms; and in this way he went through the
terror-stricken crowd, amid this horrible darkness.

At five o'clock in the morning, more cracking and rend.
ing of metal were heard in the east.

A piece about half a square mile in area had been
detached from Floating Island.

It was Starboard Harbour, with its works, its engines, its
warehouses, that had drifted off.

Beneath the redoubled blows of the cyclone, then at the
height of its violence, Floating Island was thrown about
like a wreck. Its hull became broken up. The compartments divided; and some, as the waves leapt over
them, disappeared in the depths of the ocean.

•　　　•　　　•　　　•　　　•

"After the burst-up of the company," said Pinchinat, "the burst-up of Floating Island."

That was the summing-up of the situation.

Of the marvellous Floating Island there now remained but a few scattered pieces, like the sporadic fragments of a shattered comet, floating not in space, but on the surface of the wide Pacific.

CHAPTER XIV.

WHEN the day broke, a spectator from a height of a few hundred feet would have seen three fragments of Floating Island, measuring two or three hectares each, floating on the sea, and about a dozen of smaller size at a short distance from one another.

The cyclone began to die away with the first appearance of daylight. With the rapidity peculiar to these great atmospheric disturbances, its centre moved thirty miles towards the east. But the sea, so terribly lashed, continued tremendous, and the wrecks large and small rolled and pitched like vessels on an ocean in fury.

The part of Floating Island which had suffered most was that which had formed the base of Milliard City. It had sunk beneath the weight of its edifices. In vain would you search for any vestige of its monuments, of the houses which bordered the main avenues of both sections. Never had the separation between Larboardites and Starboardites been more complete, and never assuredly had they dreamt of such.

Was the number of victims considerable? It was to be feared so, although the people had taken refuge in time in the centre of the country, where the ground offered more resistance to dismemberment.

Well! Were they satisfied, these Coverleys and Tankerdons, of the result due to their culpable rivalry? It was not one of them who would govern, to the exclusion of the other. Swallowed up was Milliard City, and with it the enormous price they had paid for it. But do not pity their fate! There remained to them millions enough in the coffers of the American and European banks to assure them of their daily bread in their old age.

The largest fragment comprised that portion of the country which extended between the observatory and Prow Battery. Its area was about three acres, and on it the shipwrecked people—if we can so describe them—were gathered to the number of three thousand.

On the next largest portion were some of the buildings in the neighbourhood of Larboard Harbour, the port, with some of the storehouses of provisions and one of the tanks of fresh water. The electric works, the buildings in which were the machinery and boilers, had disappeared at the time of the explosion. On this second fragment two thousand people had taken refuge.

With regard to Starboard Harbour, it will not have been forgotten that this part of Floating Island had been violently forced off at three o'clock in the morning. It had doubtless sunk, for as far as the eye could reach, nothing could be seen of it.

With the first two fragments floated a third, of an area of from four to five hectares, comprising that portion of the country about Stern Battery, on which were about four thousand people. And there were twelve more pieces, measuring a few hundred square metres each, on which the rest of the people saved from the disaster had taken refuge.

That was all that was left of the Pearl of the Pacific.

There must, therefore, have been many hundred victims of the catastrophe; and the survivors might be thankful that Floating Island had not been swallowed up entirely in the waters of the Pacific.

But if they were far from land, how were these fragments to reach a coast? Were the people to perish by famine? And would there survive a single witness of this disaster, unequalled in maritime necrology?

No, there was no need to despair. These drifting fragments bore energetic men, and all that was possible to do for the common safety would be done.

It was on the fragment around Prow Battery that were
gathered Commodore Ethel Simcoe, the King and Queen
of Malecarlie, the staff of the observatory, Colonel Stewart,
some of the officers, a certain number of the notables of
Milliard City, the clergy—in fact, an important part of the
population.

There also were the Coverley and Tankerdon families,
overwhelmed by the frightful responsibility which rested
on their chiefs. And were they not also smitten in their
dearest affections, for Walter and Di had disappeared!
Were they on one of the other fragments? Couɪd they
ever hope to see them again?

The Quartette Party with their precious instruments
were complete. To use a well-known formula, "death
alone would separate them." Frascolin was still taking
matters coolly, and had not lost all hope. Yvernès, who
was accustomed to look at things on their extraordinary
side, remarked:

" It would be difficult to imagine a grander finish."

Sebastien Zorn was nearly crazy. To have been the
prophet predicting the misfortunes of Floating Island, as
Jeremiah did the misfortunes of Sion, did not console him.
He was hungry, he was cold, he was continually coughing.

And Calistus Munbar? Well, the superintendent was
simply sublime—yes, sublime! He would not despair of
the safety of the people, or the safety of Floating Island.
Floating Island could be repaired. The fragments were
sound, and it could not be said that the elements had
triumphed over this masterpiece of naval architecture.

It was certain that danger was no longer imminent.
All that could sink during the cyclone had sunk with
Milliard City—its hotels, its houses, the works, the batteries,
all the heavy superstructure. The fragments now were in
good condition. They were floating higher than before,
and the waves were not sweeping over their surface.

Here was a respite, a tangible amelioration, and as the
fear of immediate sinking was removed, the people's spirits
had improved. They were much calmer. Only the

women and children, incapable of reasoning, had failed to overcome their terror.

And what had happened to Athanase Dorémus? At the commencement of the breaking up, the professor of dancing and deportment had been carried away with his old servant on one of the fragments. But a current had brought him towards the piece on which were his compatriots of the quartette.

Commodore Simcoe, like the captain of a disabled ship, aided by his devoted staff, had set to work. In the first place, would it be possible to join up the pieces that were floating separately? If it were impossible, could they establish communications between them? This last question was easily answered in the affirmative, for several boats had remained uninjured in Larboard Harbour. By sending them from one fragment to another, Commodore Simcoe could ascertain what resources were left, what amount of fresh water and provisions.

But was he able to find out the longitude and latitude of this flotilla of wreckage?

No! For want of instruments to take an altitude, the position could not be determined, and hence they could not know if they were near any island or continent.

About nine o'clock in the morning, Commodore Simcoe embarked with two of his officers in a boat which had come from Larboard Harbour to fetch him. In this boat he visited the different fragments, and this was what he ascertained in the course of the inquiry.

The distilling apparatus at Larboard Harbour had been destroyed, but the tank contained enough drinking water for a fortnight, if the consumption were reduced to what was strictly necessary. The reserves in the store-houses were sufficient for the food of the people for nearly as long.

It was therefore necessary that in two weeks at the outside a landing should be effected on some point in the Pacific.

This information was in a certain measure reassuring.

But Commodore Simcoe could not help discovering that there had been many hundred victims of this terrible night. The grief of the Tankerdon and Coverley families was inexpressible. Neither Walter nor Di had been found on any of the fragments visited by the boat. At the moment of the catastrophe the young man, carrying his betrothed, was going towards Starboard Harbour, and of this part of Floating Island nothing remained on the surface of the Pacific.

In the afternoon the wind abated from hour to hour, the sea fell, and the fragments were barely affected by the undulations of the surge. By means of the boats from Larboard Harbour, Commodore Simcoe provided for the food of the people, sending them what was necessary to save them from dying of hunger.

Communications became easier and more rapid. The different pieces, obedient to the laws of attraction, like fragments of cork on the surface of a basin of water, approached one another. And was not that of good augury to the confident Calistus Munbar, who saw in it the reconstitution of the Pearl of the Pacific?

The night went by in darkness. The time had gone when the avenues of Milliard City, the streets of the commercial quarters, the lawns in the park, the fields and prairies were bright with electric lights, when the aluminium moons poured in profusion a dazzling effulgence over the surface of Floating Island!

Amid the darkness there were a few collisions between the fragments. These shocks could not be avoided, but fortunately they were not violent enough to cause serious damage.

At daybreak it was seen that the pieces were all very near together, and floating on a tranquil sea. In a few strokes of the oar it was easy to pass from one to the other. Commodore Simcoe had every facility for regulating the consumption of food and fresh water. That was the important point, and the people understood it and were resigned.

The boats took several families about. They went in search of those they had not yet found. What happiness among these who were met with again, who gave no thought to the dangers with which they were still threatened. What sorrow for those who vainly sought for the absent?

It was evidently a fortunate circumstance that the sea had calmed down. But it was perhaps regrettable that the wind had not continued blowing from the south-east. It would have helped the current which in this part of the Pacific runs towards the Australian coast.

By order of Commodore Simcoe, look-outs were posted to watch every point of the horizon. If a ship appeared, they would make signals. But ships are few in these distant regions at this period of the year when the equinoctial storms prevail.

There was, therefore, a very poor chance of noticing either smoke or masts and sails along the line of sky and water. And yet about two in the afternoon Commodore Simcoe received the following communication from one of the look-outs:

"In the north-east there is something on the move, and although the hull cannot be distinguished, it is certain that a vessel is passing in the offing."

This news caused extraordinary excitement. The King of Malecarlie, Commodore Simcoe, the officers and engineers, all went to the side where the vessel had been signalled from. Orders were given to attract attention by hoisting flags at the end of spars and by simultaneous discharges of the firearms they had left. If the night came before these signals were noticed, a fire would be lighted, and during the night, as it would be visible at a great distance, it was impossible that it could escape being perceived.

It was not necessary to wait until the evening. The mass in question visibly approached. Clouds of smoke rolled overhead, and there could be no doubt it was making for the fragments of Floating Island.

The glasses kept it in view, although its hull was very

little above the sea, and it possessed neither masts nor sails.

" My friends," Commodore Simcoe soon exclaimed, "I am not mistaken ! It is a piece of our island ! It is Starboard Harbour which was carried away by the currents. Doubtless Mr. Somwah has repaired his engines, and is coming to us."

Demonstrations verging on madness welcomed the news. It seemed that the safety of all was now assured. It was as it were a vital part of Floating Island which came back with this piece of Starboard Harbour.

Matters had, in fact, happened as Commodore Simcoe supposed. After the breaking off, Starboard Harbour, seized by a counter-current, had drifted off to the northeast. When day came Mr. Somwah had repaired the slight damages to his engines, and returned to the scene of the wreck, bringing with him several hundred more survivors.

Three hours afterwards, Starboard Harbour was not more than a cable's length from the flotilla. And what transports of joy, what shouts of enthusiasm welcomed its arrival. Walter Tankerdon and Di Coverley, who had taken refuge there before the catastrophe, were there side by side.

With the arrival of Starboard Harbour, with its reserves of provisions and water, there was some chance of safety. The stores contained enough oil to drive the engines and dynamos and work the screws for some days. Its five million horse-power would enable it to reach the nearest land. This land, according to the observations made by the officer of the port, was New Zealand.

But the difficulty was that these thousands of people could not take passage on Starboard Harbour, its area being only from six to seven thousand square metres. Would it have to be sent fifty miles away in search of help?

No ! The voyage would require considerable time, and there were not many hours to spare. There was not a day to lose if the people were to be preserved from the horrors of famine.

"We can do better than that," said the King of Male-carlie. "The fragments of Starboard Harbour and the batteries can carry all the survivors of Floating Island. Fasten these three fragments together by strong chains, and tow them one behind the other as if they were barges. Then, with Starboard Harbour at the head, its five million horse-power can take us to New Zealand."

The advice was excellent, it was practicable, it had every chance of success, now that Starboard Harbour possessed such enormous locomotive power. Confidence returned to the people as if they were already in sight of port.

The rest of the day was employed in the work necessitated by the fixing of the chains which were furnished by the stores of Starboard Harbour. Commodore Simcoe estimated that in this way a speed of from eight to ten miles a day could be obtained. In five days they would, if assisted by the current, accomplish the fifty miles which separated them from New Zealand. There was no doubt that the provisions would last until then. But to provide against delays, the rations were prudently maintained as before.

The preparations being complete, Starboard Harbour took the head of the procession about seven o'clock in the evening. Under the propulsion of its screws the two other fragments were slowly towed over the calm sea.

Next morning at daylight the look-outs had lost sight of the fragments left behind.

Nothing of importance occurred during the 4th, 5th, 6th, 7th, and 8th of April. The weather was favourable, the motion of the sea was hardly perceptible, and the voyage continued under excellent conditions.

About eight o'clock on the morning of the 9th of April, the land was sighted on the port bow—a high land that could be seen from a considerable distance.

Observations being taken with the instruments at Starboard Harbour, there was no doubt as to the identity of this land.   It was the northern island of New Zealand.

A day and a night passed, and on the 10th of April, in the morning, Starboard Harbour ran aground about a cable length from the shore in Ravaraki Bay.

What satisfaction, what security the people experienced when they felt the real ground beneath their feet, and not the artificial soil of Floating Island.   And yet how long might not this substantial maritime apparatus have lasted, if human passions, stronger than the winds and the sea, had not driven it to destruction.

The shipwrecked people were very hospitably received by the New Zealanders, who gave everybody food who required it.

As soon as they arrived at Auckland, the marriage of Walter Tankerdon with Di Coverley was at last celebrated with all the pomp the circumstances deserved. Let us add that the Quartette Party were heard for the last time at this ceremony, at which all the Milliardites were present.   It would be a happy union—would it had taken place sooner, in the interest of all! Doubtless the young couple only possessed a poor million each—

"But," as Pinchinat said, "there is every reason to believe that they will still find happiness with such a moderate fortune."

The Tankerdons and Coverleys and other notables intended to return to America, where they would no longer dispute over the government of a Floating Island.

The same determination was come to by Commodore Simcoe, Colonel Stewart and their officers, the staff of the observatory, and even the superintendent, Calistus Munbar, who had not given up the idea of building a new artificial island.

The King and Queen of Malecarlie made no secret as to their regret for Floating Island, in which they had hoped to peacefully terminate their existence.   Let us hope that these ex-sovereigns found a corner of the earth where they could spend their last days sheltered from political discussions.

And the Quartette Party?

Well, the Quartette Party, whatever Sebastien Zorn might say, had not done so badly, and if they bore any ill-will to Calistus Munbar for having taken them against their will, it would have been sheer ingratitude.

From the 25th of May the preceding year until the 10th of April a little more than eleven months had elapsed, during which our artistes had lived the luxurious life we know. They had received the fourth instalment of their salary, three instalments of which were deposited in the banks of San Francisco and New York, payable to them on demand.

After the marriage ceremony at Auckland, Sebastien Zorn, Yvernès, Frascolin, and Pinchinat went to take leave of their friends, not forgetting Athanase Dorémus. Then they embarked on a steamer bound for San Diego.

Arriving on the 3rd of May in this capital of Lower California, their first care was to apologize through the newspapers for having failed to keep their appointment eleven months before, and to express their sincere regret at what had happened.

"Gentlemen, we would have waited for you for twenty years!"

That was the reply they received from the amiable director of concerts at San Diego.

Nobody could have been more accommodating or more gracious. The only way to acknowledge such courtesy was to give this concert which had been announced for so long.

And before a public as numerous as enthusiastic, the quartette in F major, from Op. 9 of Mozart, was for these virtuosos escaped from the wreck of Floating Island one of the greatest successes of their artistic career.

Such is the end of the story of the ninth wonder of the orld, this incomparable Pearl of the Pacific! All is well that ends well, as people say, but all is bad that ends badly, and was such the case with Floating Island?

Ended, no! It will be rebuilt some day—at least Calistus Munbar says so.

And yet—we cannot repeat it too often—to create an artificial island, an island that moves on the surface of the seas, is it not to overstep the limits assigned to human genius, and is it not forbidden to man, who disposes not of the winds or the waves, to so recklessly usurp the functions of the Creator?

THE END.